D0076699

HOUSEHOLDS AND HOUSING

HOUSEHOLDS AND HOUSING

Choice and Outcomes in the Housing Market

WILLIAM A. V. CLARK

FRANS M. DIELEMAN

No Longer the Property of Bluffton University

CENTER FOR URBAN POLICY RESEARCH
Rutgers, The State University of New Jersey
New Brunswick, New Jersey

Bluffton College Library

Copyright © 1996 by Rutgers — The State University of New Jersey
All rights reserved

Published by the CENTER FOR URBAN POLICY RESEARCH
Civic Square • 33 Livingston Avenue
New Brunswick, New Jersey 08901-1982

Printed in the United States of America

Cover Design: Helene Berinsky

Cover Photograph:
Courtesy U.S. Department of Agriculture
Soil Conservation Service
Photographer: Gordon Smith

Library of Congress Cataloging-in-Publication Data

Clark, W. A. V. (William A. V.)
    Households and housing : choice and outcomes in the housing market
/ William A. V. Clark, Frans M. Dieleman.
      p.   cm.
    Includes index.
    ISBN 0-88285-156-X
    1. Housing — United States.   2. Housing — Netherlands.
    3. Households — United States.   4. Households — Netherlands.
    I. Dieleman, Frans M.   II. Title.
    HD7293.C583   1996
    333.33'822'09492 — dc20   95–52803
                                         CIP

About the Authors

William A.V. Clark, professor of geography at the University of California, Los Angeles, has pursued a long-term interest in mobility, migration, and population change. *Households and Housing* is the outcome of a collaborative project on models of migration and choice in the housing market.

Frans M. Dieleman is professor of geography at the University of Utrecht, the Netherlands, and director of the research school, Nethur. He is interested in national variations in housing markets and the process of tenure choice.

Contents

Figures

Chapter 5

Chapter 6

Appendix

Tables

Chapter 4

Preface

This book grew out of the authors' common interest in the way households choose housing and how the process of housing choice is interwoven with other events in the lives of individuals. The book discusses choices as households experience a housing career in conjunction with changes in the household structure and job careers. It does not examine housing supply or the institutional structure and regulation of the housing market. The stock of dwellings and the nature of the local and national housing market are treated as the context within which choices are made. The stock is the framework that facilitates and limits the choice process, which, in turn, influences the outcomes—the way households are distributed across the housing stock. Thus, the book can be viewed as one about behavior in the housing market, which leads to a matching of households and houses.

The book examines the question of matching in two contrasting housing markets—the United States and the Netherlands. Our contention throughout the book is that the process of housing choice in the Western world shows striking regularities across very dissimilar national contexts. The matching of households and houses is strongly correlated with the same microlevel individual circumstances and macrolevel economic fluctuations in different countries. Dissimilarities between the United States and the Netherlands in market size and tenure structure, as well as the role of government intervention, enable an examination of how the matching occurs in different contexts. They also illustrate where the processes are similar and where they differ because of divergent cultural, economic, and policy contexts. In addition, because the book

is about the embedded comparisons of behavior and choice in the
U.S. and Dutch housing markets, it allows us to indicate some of
the important policy aspects of choice and the outcomes in the
two different housing-market contexts. The choice of the United
States and the Netherlands as context for our analysis of the process of housing choice also has a pragmatic basis. The authors know
these housing markets from personal experience. And, it is impossible to ignore the very rich data on housing in the Netherlands,
which is one of the reasons the Dutch market served as a laboratory for our first series of studies of mobility and tenure choice.
At a later stage, when we decided to pursue a longitudinal approach,
the rich data source of the Panel Study of Income Dynamics stimulated our exploration of the choice process in the United States.

We view the approach and findings of this book as complementary to the results of economic studies on housing demand.
The same variables are important—income, wealth, household
composition, and number of wage earners. At the same time, we
go beyond elasticities and demand equations to illustrate the way
households are matched to houses. An important part of this approach is to emphasize the dynamic models of tenure transitions
and the role of life course events in creating these transitions. Thus,
although we occasionally refer to the work in housing economics,
the results of these studies are not examined in any detail; nor do
they form a main part of the text.

Much of the information gathered in this book is based on ten
years of research into housing market choice. We have chosen to
bring this work together for two main reasons. First, the work was
published in a wide variety of journals and is not easily available
to those who are interested in the principal research findings and
the relationship of our research to other housing research by demographers, sociologists, and planners who work in the housing
field. Second, the research papers have extensive sections on the
methodologies and statistical analysis; in this study, we have at-
tempted to focus on the main findings and placed the technical
details in an appendix on techniques. In this way, we think the
book will appeal in general to graduate students and urban scholars who are interested in the new work on life course approaches
to housing choice.

We are grateful to a number of journals for permission to reprint figures, diagrams, and tables. This literature has been published in a wide variety of Dutch, British, and U.S. journals including: *Environment and Planning A, The Netherlands Journal of Housing and the Built Environment, Urban Studies, Housing Studies, Tijdschrift voor Economische Geografie,* and *The Annals of the Association of American Geographers.*

The research undergirding much of this book would have been impossible without our longtime collaborator Rinus Deurloo, who was involved in our early research on cross sectional models of housing tenure choice, and who is still involved in our strategy of setting housing choice within the conceptual structure of the life course. Jeffrey Garfinkle provided programming and analysis assistance and numerous able graduate and postgraduate students, including Suzanne Davies-Withers, Suzanne Staals, Dorien Buckers, and Jetske Klink, have contributed directly or indirectly to the ideas and structure of this book. Our colleague Claartje Mulder read the entire text and made numerous helpful comments. We wish also to acknowledge the creative contribution of Chase Langford who designed the figures and diagrams for the book. The text was completed while William Clark was a Guggenheim Fellow.

The book is organized into six chapters. The first chapter sets the context of the two housing markets and describes the housing market structure in the United States and the Netherlands. This initial chapter is followed by three chapters that progress from the theoretical notions of the life course and housing selection, to the decision making of residential mobility and tenure choice, and to housing choice and housing consumption. Chapter 5 returns more explicitly and in greater detail to the influence of context within which the housing choices are made. A concluding chapter looks at the outcomes of the housing choice process, reiterates the findings, and includes some policy and planning observations. We emphasize throughout the book that the differences in housing market behavior are in the details and at the margins, and that there are striking commonalities in housing market behavior in controlled and less controlled housing markets.

William A.V. Clark
Frans M. Dieleman

1

Housing Choices in the United States and the Netherlands

Introduction

This book is designed to demonstrate the interconnections between the housing stock and households. The focus is on understanding the demand for housing and the way in which the demand is fulfilled as households select housing. This book is concerned with both the decision to move one's residence and the resulting type of housing choice. The housing supply—the stock of dwellings—is the context within which households make choices and acquire housing.

Residential relocation is the household decision that generates housing consumption changes, which ultimately changes the residential mosaic. It is not merely a decision about changing locations; it is also a decision about tenure—about whether to own or to rent. Although relocation can be within the same tenure, the concept that has dominated research into housing markets is the process of changing from renting to owning, as most countries in the Western world have moved from predominantly rental societies to societies of homeowners. Thus, tenure choice will be central to the analysis in this book. It does, however, discuss the residential relocation decision as the impetus for housing choice. In this sense, the aims of the presentation are circumscribed to an effective discussion of how households are distributed within the housing system and what influences their choices.

The process of "matching" households and houses is examined

in this book in two very dissimilar housing markets—the United States and the Netherlands. There are at least two reasons why it is both revealing and useful to view the process of housing choice against the background of two nations with dissimilar housing histories and differing tenure structures. First, it demonstrates that regularities in mobility and tenure choice are present and hold up in both national contexts. This suggests a robustness in models of the matching process of households and housing which is central to the discussion in chapters 3 through 5. Despite differences in social context, in policy intervention and in "housing culture," the generalized choice processes operate similarly. Second, and conversely, there are important differences in the outcomes of the matching process of households and housing in the United States and the Netherlands, as will be illustrated in chapter 6. One can demonstrate that the nature of the Dutch housing system has "cushioned" some of the recent housing problems of homelessness, inner-city decay, and overcrowding, which have reemerged in Western societies.

There are also some pragmatic reasons for comparing the process of housing choice in the United States and the Netherlands, such as the availability of excellent data at the household level in the Netherlands. This data covers substantial periods of housing market fluctuations, and the authors have worked with this material for the last decade. The decision to analyze the mobility process against these two backgrounds, however, also relates to a debate that has emerged in the last few years on the relative roles of both market forces and government regulations in the housing market.

Some scholars, mostly in the United States where government regulation of housing is relatively limited, suggest that market mechanisms can efficiently allocate housing, and that housing markets respond to the effective demand of consumers (Nesslein 1988). Rising real incomes will create an increased supply of good housing, and the cost of new construction is much lower if the government does not hamper the process. As a corollary, Nesslein argues that the welfare state arrangements, which were designed to expand the supply of good shelter for the entire population, may have lowered, rather than increased, the level of housing investment.

Other scholars, mostly from Western Europe where government intervention in housing has flourished during the long period of rising incomes and expectations from 1950 to 1980, hold that the housing commodity cannot be allocated efficiently, and certainly not fairly, without government intervention in the market process. In this view, market forces result in an unattractive rental sector, urban slums, and housing polarization (Ambrose 1992). Kleinman (1995) argues that in France and Britain, where housing policy took an explicit turn toward the market during the late 1970s and 1980s, this has indeed led to a situation in which housing needs are left unmet and housing is in increasingly short supply.

This is not the place to take a position in this debate. This book is not about housing policy and policy outcomes but, rather, about the behavior of people in the housing market. Yet, it is a fact that throughout Western Europe, government regulation exists and influences both construction and demand for housing. In this book, the Netherlands presents an example of the regulated housing markets of Western Europe. Actually, even among the countries of Western Europe, the Netherlands is remarkable for the magnitude of government regulation and its extremely large social (public) rented housing sector. It is, therefore, a good housing market to contrast with the relatively free housing market of the United States.

Chapter 2 presents the theoretical notions about the character of the housing stock, the mobility process over the life course, and the way in which mobility and housing choices are interlinked. The following three chapters elaborate on the way individuals and households, with particular age and income characteristics, relocate within particular housing markets and what influences their choices. We also demonstrate that both national and local social and economic contexts do affect the final form of the outcomes. Chapter 6 examines the aggregation of individual actions into general outcomes in the residential mosaic. Before beginning a discussion of the processes of mobility and housing selection, however, it is very important to have a clear idea of the aggregate context within which the choices are being made, which is the intention of chapter 1.

This first chapter is designed to illustrate the overall structure of the housing markets in the United States and the Netherlands.

It begins with a historical review of the development of homeownership, because the move from rental housing to homeownership is one of the most salient trends in Western societies during this century. Not all societies have moved in this direction at the same pace, however. This is partly owing to housing market regulation, although the rate of increase in real income is also a factor. As will be demonstrated, the United States is among those countries that have rapidly and dramatically become nations of homeowners, while the Netherlands is an example of nations that are still predominantly renter societies.

In addition to tenure, this discussion of the nature of the housing stock within which choices must be made is limited to the type of dwellings, the price and value of housing, and the geographical location of housing within metropolitan areas. The wide range of characteristics of the stock remains intentionally unexamined because, as will be demonstrated—apart from tenure—type, price, and location are the major points households consider when moving from one dwelling to another. They are also the main characteristics considered in the examination of outcomes of housing choice in chapter 6.

The Historical Context of Homeownership

In the majority of Western economies, the role of private rental housing has contracted dramatically (Power 1993). Notwithstanding, during the 1990s there is still considerable variation in ownership rates, and the trajectories in the homeownership rate vary considerably (fig. 1.1). The United States is one extreme of a nation of predominantly homeowning households and has been such for much of the past four decades. But the United States was not always a nation of homeowners (fig. 1.2). The change came after World War II. The ownership rate had hovered in the 45 percent to 47 percent range for most of the first half century but, beginning in 1945 (the Census year is actually 1940 although the real change began after World War II ended), the rate of ownership increased steadily in each decade. It has stabilized in the last ten years at about 64 percent.

Many countries in Western Europe, such as the United King-

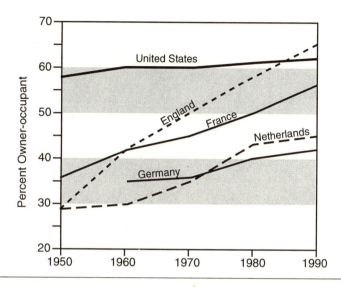

FIGURE 1.1
Development of the homeownership sector in five Western countries
from about 1950 to 1990

Source: Elsinga, 1995. Redrawn by permission of Delft University Press.

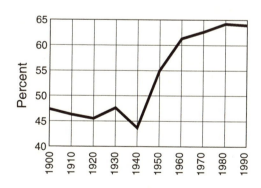

FIGURE 1.2
Owner-occupied units in the United States

Source: U.S. Bureau of the Census, *1990 Census Housing Highlights* CH-S-1–
1, 1991.

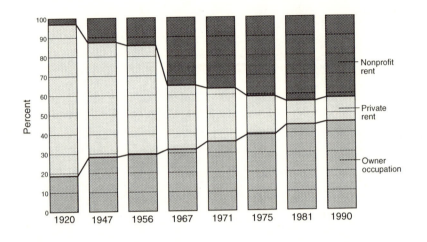

FIGURE 1.3
Development of housing tenures in the Netherlands, 1920–1990

Source: Adapted from Hoekveld et al., 1984.

dom and France, have also had relatively rapid increases in the proportion of homeowners; they are now approaching the United States in the proportion of dwellings that are owned (fig. 1.1). In other countries, such as the Netherlands, Germany, and Switzerland, rental housing is still the largest single part of the stock. It is, however, split differently in various countries between private and nonprofit sectors of the market. In Germany, private rent still remains the largest single tenure (38 percent), while in the Netherlands the role of private rental housing declined after World War II (fig. 1.3). The Dutch government pursued a policy of mass provision of nonprofit rental housing, which, in the 1960s and 1970s, made this the largest tenure in this country (Harloe 1995). Now homeownership is the largest single sector of the market. It is greater than either private rental or public rental but not larger than these two sectors combined. Thus, most Dutch households are still in the rental sector (Dieleman and Everaers 1994). The same situation can be observed in Germany, where 40 percent of households are owners, and the majority rent a private or subsidized housing unit in the public rental sector.

Unlike many European countries, and the Netherlands in par-

TABLE 1.1

Proportion of Public Housing of All Rented Housing
in Selected Cities in the United States (%)

	Baltimore	*Washington*	*Philadelphia*	*New York*
Publicly Owned	7.3	6.2	7.3	10.4
Federal Subsidy	5.7	5.3	3.5	4.0
State/Local Subsidy	1.0	1.0	1.2	3.8
Other	1.0	1.2	0.9	2.7
Total	15.0	13.7	12.9	20.9

Source: U.S. Bureau of the Census, *American Housing Survey* 1991.

ticular, the United States has eschewed any serious commitment to a subsidized housing program. There are, however, almost five million housing units that are publicly owned or that have some form of federal, state, or local subsidy. This constitutes approximately 4 percent of the U.S. housing stock in comparison with 40 percent of the housing stock in the Netherlands. Most subsidized housing is located in the central cities, but more than a million units of subsidized housing are in suburban and nonmetropolitan areas. Although the proportion of publicly owned and subsidized housing is low for the United States as a whole, in some cities the proportion is closer to that of some European countries. Almost 21 percent of the rental stock is publicly owned or subsidized in New York City, and the proportion varies around the mid-teens for Baltimore, Washington, and Philadelphia (table 1.1). Of course, the rental stock is only approximately half of the total housing stock and is, therefore, considerably less as a proportion of all housing.

The emergence of a strong private ownership sector in the housing market in countries such as the United States and the United Kingdom in particular has generated a view of owner occupation as the preferred tenure, and preferred over alternative renter forms. According to this view, owner occupation is a positive economic and social good and, in turn, generates "positive" social relations. A number of housing economists and sociologists have argued that people do not seek to own houses for financial reasons;

people buy for many reasons, including freedom, choice, security, mobility, pride, and status (MacLennan et al. 1987; Michelson 1977; Saunders 1990).

The process of a shift from a predominantly renter to a predominantly owner society, which happened in many Western societies, did not occur in a vacuum. The massive shift in the United States to a society of owners was facilitated by vigorous government policies that emphasized homeownership. The process included advantageous financing instruments that favored single-family construction at the expense of multifamily rental housing (Sternlieb and Hughes 1980). The combination of forced savings during World War II, changing tastes and preferences, and a new concept of suburban housing created a different way of thinking about housing and tenure. In particular, the intersection of changing tastes in a context of an expanding economy generated and sustained increases in ownership.

In the Netherlands, in contrast to the United States, the very large housing shortages created by World War II led to extensive state intervention in housing. Rent control was introduced and never abolished, and large state subsidies for new construction, and for nonprofit housing, were introduced to boost housing production. In the 1950s and 1960s housing policy became embedded in a much wider social and economic policy to dampen wage demand and strengthen the safety net of the welfare state (Dieleman 1994). Moderate rent increases by the national parliament and support for nonprofit housing became prerequisites for agreements on low wage demands in the private sector, which in turn led to low rates of inflation. Under this political regime, nonprofit housing developed into a well-organized housing sector, providing attractive and relatively cheap housing, much of it in the form of single-family row housing, which could compete with owner-occupation for the median-income consumer. This situation has changed in the last decade under the pressure of cuts in government spending and the switch to more market-oriented policies (Priemus 1995).

Type and Value of the Housing Stock

At least in recent history, during the past fifty years or so, housing has assumed a special role in the economy as well as in people's desires and perceptions. There is an extensive literature on the role and implications of the various housing modes in the developed Western nations. Most pronounced is the notion that single-family housing in owner occupation, often suburban, is the apogee for all families as they progress through their housing career (Michelson 1977; Saunders 1990).

The transformation of the housing market must be set within the context of changing tastes and the relationship of housing costs and incomes. After World War II, the expansion of the single-family housing stock in the United States, made famous by Levitt and other mass production builders, created a "stripped down" 800-square-foot average house with one or one and a half baths. By the mid 1950s, it was an 1,100-square-foot house and two baths; in the 1970s, it was a 2,000-square-foot house and two and a half baths (Sternlieb and Hughes 1980). It is not surprising that the United States should have become a nation of homeowners when the opportunities for ownership include such gains in housing quality.

The components of the increase in housing and housing quality included relatively cheap land, inexpensive loan money, and the decision not to front load many of the community infrastructure costs. The cost of land was about 12 percent of the final selling price versus about 25 percent currently, and mortgages were available for a rate as low as 4 percent and 5 percent, and in the 1970s, still 7 percent. Even more critical perhaps was the fact that the building industry did not have to create the infrastructure of the residential development (Sternlieb and Hughes 1980).

The stock that is on allocation—the stock available to U.S. households in 1990—was largely composed of one-family homes, about 64 percent of the stock. In addition, in the last decade, the largest numerical increase in housing units was of single-family homes (fig. 1.4). Two- to four-unit structures constituted just under 10 percent of all units. Interestingly, mobile homes had the largest percentage increase in the last decade.

About 40 percent of all U.S. housing is in central cities, and

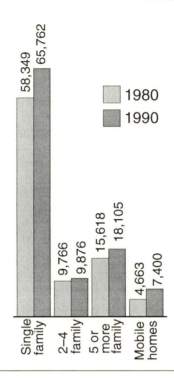

FIGURE 1.4
Housing stock distributions in the United States, 1980, 1990 (000s of units)

Source: U.S. Bureau of the Census, *1990 Census Housing Highlights* CH-S-1–1, 1991.

60 percent is in the suburbs. Within the central city/suburban breakdown, there are major differences in ownership rates. The suburbs are almost 71 percent in ownership, and that figure has declined from the highest peak in the late 1960s and early 1970s when almost all the suburban housing was in the ownership sector.

In the Netherlands, as in the United States, the housing stock is mainly single-family housing (fig. 1.5). But a much larger part of this stock, most commonly in row housing, is in the subsidized rental sector. And, proportionally, the Netherlands has more multifamily housing than the United States, largely in the rental-housing sector, both in the private and public parts of that sector. Thus, both couples and families who prefer single-family homes over

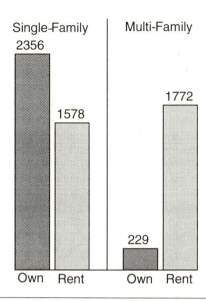

FIGURE 1.5
Tenure, structure, and type of dwelling—the Netherlands, 1990
(thousands of units)

Source: Netherlands Central Bureau of Statistics (CBS).

multifamily dwellings can also find such stock in the rental sector in the Netherlands. Consequently, they are less obliged to buy if they want to live in single-family housing than their counterparts in the United States.

Because the Dutch government promoted the construction of fairly small, but well-equipped, dwellings at moderate prices, the stock is for the most part now four-room housing, and most of the dwellings outside the cities are in planned row house developments. This is quite different from what one observes in other European countries, where new construction is mostly geared to the top end of the market. The Dutch government encouraged housing standardization, whereby many parts of the building are pre-fabricated off the building sites and then assembled on site. This system created a large stock of relatively good-quality and moderately priced housing. At the same time, this approach created a stock of considerable uniformity across the country. Thus, a high proportion

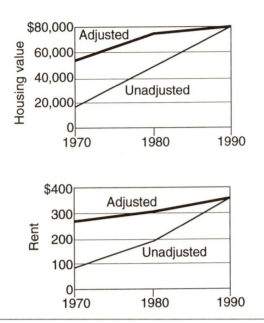

FIGURE 1.6
Median housing value and median contract rent in the United States,
1970–1990

Source: U.S. Bureau of the Census, *1990 Census Housing Highlights* CH-S-
1–1, 1991.

of dwellings, both in the rental and in the owner-occupied stock,
are quite comparable in size, equipment, and appearance.

In addition to tenure and type of dwelling, the price of owner
housing and rents for rental housing figure prominently in the housing choice process of individuals and households. Housing values
and prices tend to fluctuate substantially, sometimes over relatively
short periods and, consequently, either enhance or limit the opportunities for those households who want to adjust their housing
consumption to changed preferences and circumstances. In dollar
terms, in the United States, the median value of owner-occupied
dwellings increased sharply from just under twenty thousand dollars in 1970 to more than eighty thousand dollars in 1990 (fig. 1.6).
For many households, the purchase of a house was a good investment and a hedge against inflation even when the rise in price is

adjusted for the consumer price index. The increase in adjusted prices was somewhat greater than that for rental housing, but renters do not gain the increases in housing equity; therefore, in periods of relatively high inflation with rising housing costs, there is an impetus for households to shift from renting to owning.

If one considers the distributions of housing values and rents, in both instances the majority of the housing stock is in the lower values and rents. In the relatively small rental sector in the United States, however, the availability of affordable rental housing is clearly more limited than in its relatively large counterpart in the Netherlands (fig. 1.7).

The price for a large part of the housing stock in the Netherlands, both in owner occupation and in rental occupation, is still relatively moderate despite the rapid increases and significant fluctuations in the value of owner-occupied houses (figs. 1.8 and 1.9). In terms of government policy, households with median incomes can afford rents up to approximately 650 guilders (about $375) and can enter the owner market up to a price of roughly 175,000 guilders (about $100,000). In the 1970s, the Dutch government heavily subsidized rental housing, both in terms of subsidies for new construction and housing allowances to rental households. During this period, the buying price for owner-occupied houses soared and generated windfall equity profits for those already in the ownership sector but consequently made entry into homeownership much more difficult. In the 1980s, the situation reversed. Government gradually limited financial support for public rental housing and, under the government-sponsored system of rent control, rents actually increased above the levels of inflation and increases in consumer prices. There was a simultaneous severe drop in the prices for owner-occupied houses. More recently prices increased again but were in 1990 still below earlier levels. Obviously this affected housing choices and is reflected in the models of tenure and housing type choice in later chapters.

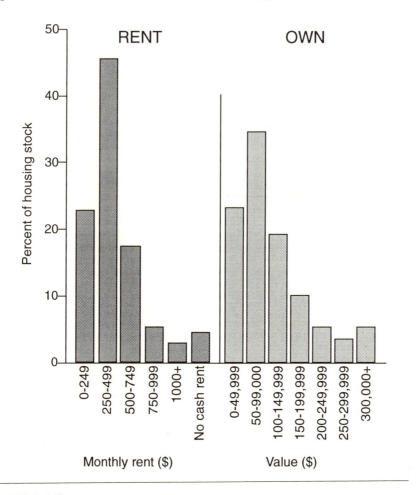

FIGURE 1.7
Rent and price of the U.S. housing stock, 1990

Source: U.S. Bureau of the Census, *Census of Population and Housing*, 1990.

The Spatial and Temporal Expression of the Housing Stock

Because it is also of interest to provide a locational perspective on housing allocation and consumption, we have included the spatial dimensions of the housing market and the way the spatial component of housing influences the choices and decisions that occur within it. Indeed, the location of housing and the eventual incre-

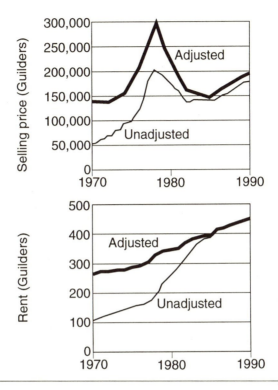

FIGURE 1.8
Average selling price and average rent for the Netherlands, 1970–1990

Source: Elsinga, 1995 and Netherlands Central Bureau of Statistics. Redrawn by permission of Delft University Press.

ments to the stock are useful in defining a spatial pattern of housing.

Housing is physically expressed as residential land use and, as such, is the single largest component of land use in the city. In geographic terms, approximately 35 percent to 45 percent of the land area of most cities is absorbed by residential land use. If one recognizes that the transportation system for most cities absorbs another 30 percent, one appreciates the importance of housing and the transportation system that binds the city together. More than two-thirds of the built environment is composed of housing and the network that links housing to the workplace.

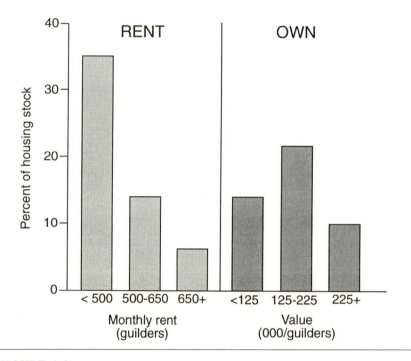

FIGURE 1.9
Rent and price of housing stock, the Netherlands, 1990

Source: Redrawn from Ministry of Housing, Physical Planning and the Environment (MVROM), 1992.

Housing is not produced and added to the current stock in regular increments. In fact, additions to the housing stock, so-called housing starts, vary considerably with economic upturns and downturns. Consequently, graphs of additions to the housing stock also fluctuate (fig. 1.10). Of course, the additions show a general upward trajectory in response to increasing population, but it is far from a regular or steady increase in new housing. The increase in subsidized housing and public-sector housing in Holland and the emergence of mobile homes in the United States have created a greatly diversified housing stock.

A glance at the diagrams of dwelling-unit construction makes clear the cyclical nature of additions to the housing stock. Overall, the housing stock has been expanding, but there are three- to five-year lows and highs in the production of housing as well as

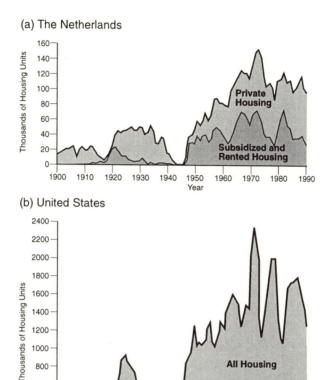

FIGURE 1.10
Dwelling unit construction in (a) the Netherlands and (b) the United
States, 1900–1990

Sources: Netherlands Central Bureau of Statistics and U.S. Census of Population and Housing.

very large downturns in housing production during the two world
wars and smaller downturns in the economic recessions of the
1970s and 1980s.

The temporal variation in building construction is played out
in the spatial creation of the residential mosaic. When the cycles
of building activity are expressed as roughly concentric additions

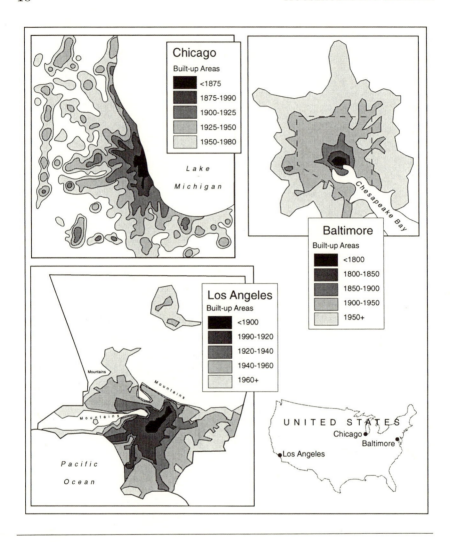

FIGURE 1.11
Examples of growth patterns in Baltimore, Chicago, and Los Angeles

Source: Adapted and redrawn from *Contemporary Metropolitan America,*
1976, by permission.

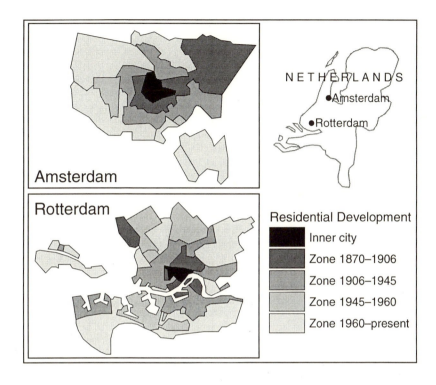

FIGURE 1.12
Growth patterns of the largest cities in the Netherlands

Source: Redrawn from Dieleman and Musterd, 1992, by permission of Kluwer Academic Publishers.

to the city, one finds zones of building that are broadly related to the timing of development. Thus, maps of the age of residential development encapsulate the graphical presentation of varying rates of building, and as most new construction is at the edge of the current city, the patterns are ones of accretion at the edges of the existing city. Of course, spatial infill and redevelopment are also parts of the spatial expression of the residential fabric. The housing patterns (figs. 1.11 and 1.12) for the United States and the Netherlands have been linked to the various eras of city growth. The initial building formed a high-density urban core—the period

of the "walking city"—common in Europe and in some cities on
the East Coast of the United States. Now, the walking city takes
up only a fraction of modern U.S. cities that have been restructured by innovations in urban transportation and especially by the
widespread use of the automobile. The intersection of the extensive growth in the urban transportation system and the rapid increase in the housing supply over the last three decades has pro-
foundly transformed American and European cities. The enormous
number of additions to the housing stock in the 1960s and 1970s
created a spatially extensive city that differed greatly from that of
the past. The size of each of these rings is directly related to the
demand for housing, as the population of the cities grew and sup-
pliers were able to build housing to meet these increasing demands.
Simultaneously, the eventual accretion of housing set in motion
the process of creating neighborhoods and social areas within the
city. The patterns of housing created by the particular way in which
housing developed in metropolitan areas constitute neighborhoods
and communities and thus provide a context for understanding
consumer choices in the housing market. Thus, maps of housing
in metropolitan areas as widely divergent as Chicago and Amsterdam have embedded within them the classic pattern of decline in
density from the center of the city and, of course, differentiation
by age and housing type.

Because the age of housing is relatively easily documented, and
usually newer housing is built at the expanding edge of the city,
an approach that considers the city in terms of the age of housing
is a useful way of presenting various descriptive data on housing
in the city. At the same time, the aging of the housing stock is one
of the fundamental forces in the housing market. One might be
inclined to think of housing as having a very long life; indeed housing in some cities has been in place for more than a century. The
fact is, however, that housing has a finite life span, which depends
on the quality of the construction and subsequent maintenance and
repair. Whereas housing in Europe frequently has an economic life
close to 100 years, in the United States, the life of housing is often much shorter. In any event, housing does age, and new housing is built mainly on the edge of the existing stock. These two
facts provide a means of describing the changing pattern of housing in urban areas.

In both U.S. and European cities, tenure, housing type, and value have structured the urban mosaic within which households make their choices. This chapter presented various data on tenure, type, and value, which describe the structure of the two housing markets central to this study. The geographic content of the housing markets has been described, though mainly in terms of the temporal additions to the housing stock. The presentation included data of different forms of government intervention and a discussion of their implications for the creation of the housing stock. Overall, the variables that were used to describe the housing stock are the central variables that will reappear in the discussions of tenure choice and outcomes in the housing market, and are the same that will occur throughout this examination of the United States and Dutch housing markets.

2

Housing and the Life Course

Theoretically, the presentation and thesis of the present study is structured around the concept of the life course as an organizing principle for studies of choice in the housing market. The life course paradigm views the life course of an individual, or of a family, as a series of interrelated events that are bound up with larger social forces and geographical contexts. The life events—leaving home, getting married, having children, changing jobs—occur in the life of most individuals and families. These events usually affect decisions about moving from one house to another and from one locale to another. The life course paradigm also emphasizes the continual process of choice that occurs in certain periods and places.

The life course concept is a powerful organizing approach for examining decisions in the housing market. It specifically recognizes that moving from one dwelling to another is embedded in the sequence of marital and fertility events which occur in the household and in the continuous process of income change over the occupation career. Housing market circumstances, however, such as composition of the local housing stock, mortgage rates, and prices of various types of housing also influence residential mobility and housing choice. Thus, the life course involves not only individual life events but also social forces and structures. This intersection is a central element of understanding housing choice because it involves structure (the housing stock), social forces (changing societal and economic contexts which, in turn, influence the housing stock), and individual life events.

The central methodological approach of this book employs

models of choice and the concepts of event history. The former models include logit formulations, the analysis of tables (ANOTA), and chi square automatic interaction detection as tools for evaluating the choices and outcomes of household decisions. These categorical techniques provide a rich source of information about which households end up in what housing. The event history techniques enable us to evaluate particular events or triggers in creating and determining choices, as well as to set the course of events within the broader contexts of metropolitan and regional variation in housing markets. The event history analysis provides information about the way in which households choose housing and what internal (to the household) and external events influence those choices.

Research on housing choice has evolved into two completely separate domains (Grigsby 1978). One of these is especially concerned with housing prices and understanding the way in which various aspects of dwellings contribute to the housing price. This view of the housing market has been pursued mainly by economists. A second approach focuses more specifically on the choices made by individual households and the changing patterns of housing distribution across the population. This view is reflected primarily in the work of planners, geographers, and sociologists. These individual views of the housing process can be described in another way to emphasize the philosophical differences in approaches to housing.

First, as examined by economists, the process of housing and tenure choice has emphasized choice as a competitive process in a market with a large number of buyers and sellers. Within the housing market, households are considered to maximize utilities subject to a contemporaneous budget constraint (Arnott 1987, 974). Households choose unit size and quality and landlords and builders, through reconstruction, demolition, rehabilitation, and maintenance, choose structural density and quality of their housing over time (Arnott 1987, 980). Since housing is a composite good (in economic terminology), a dwelling can be described by various characteristics, each of which contributes to the value associated with a complete dwelling. One cannot buy an aspect of the dwelling separately, however; a dwelling is a bundle of housing services, the value of which is really related to a combination of characteristics. Economists use the hedonic price function to estimate the utility, or, in less rigorous terms, the value of particular aspects of a dwelling, such as number of rooms and age of the dwelling. Estimating what individuals are willing to pay for elements of housing is a central component of the hedonic model.

In the second approach, housing production, distribution, and consumption are intertwined with the basic dynamics of the society within which housing is produced. In these studies, the structure of housing tenure has a particular social compact as well as definite political and ideological implications (Gray 1976). Housing tenure is placed at the center of debate about the sources and maintenance of social class divisions and inequalities. These authors emphasize the importance of housing consumption and issues of access of various types of households to the different parts of the housing stock (Power 1993).

Although issues of social inequality or social class divisions are not addressed, the argument in this book is more closely associated with the second approach to the housing market because the emphasis is on the process of residential mobility and its outcomes. This discussion, however, is not so much concerned with class and inequality as with choice and the context of choice. Demographic characteristics of households and the economic and spatial contexts within which the choices are made are central to this discussion throughout the book. Much of the housing choice literature uses demographic characteristics only in passing, but here specific characteristics of the household—age, marital status, size and composition—are central. Finally, choices are not made in a vacuum. They vary by region and housing market and with eventual changes in both the economy and the housing inventory. An analysis is provided that incorporates these changes in the choice process.

The Nature of Housing and Housing Services

Access to housing, along with access to work, health care, and education, is a central element of the operation of modern urban societies. Issues of housing provision, therefore, have been, directly or indirectly, a mainstay of local and federal programs in developed economies for the past century. Understanding the matching of households to housing is a fundamental element of understanding our present society and has been at the heart of research by economists, geographers, and planners. The centrality of "matching" is reflected in the struggle over large-scale publicly subsidized housing in many European countries and the United States in the simultaneous conflict between homelessness and inner-city decay and housing abandonment.

At the most basic level, housing is often referred to as shelter, because it fulfills this basic human need. At the same time, it is the single most important item of consumption. Households spend from 20 percent to 30 percent of their income to buy or rent a dwelling. Housing cost now ranks with food as one of the most important fixed household expenditures. As a result, a significant focus within housing studies is on who consumes what. Because a fundamental division in the housing market is related to tenure, a natural focus is on who owns, who rents, and what type of housing is owned or rented.

Housing as shelter is a relatively simple concept, but when we consider its range and diversity, the way in which it can confer status and access within the metropolitan area, and how much our lives are bound up with our houses, we recognize the complexity of this concept. Considering its intricate interaction with societal and political concerns and policies, we are faced with a many-faceted, incredibly complex concept. The following analysis is an attempt to provide some understanding of housing in modern urban society. Before turning to the sorting process whereby households end up in particular niches in the housing market, however, it is useful to review some of the notions and concepts that have developed around housing.

First, housing is expensive to build, it is modified only with difficulty, and it is one of the most lasting of consumer durables. The housing market is, therefore, dominated by the supply of the existing stock of dwellings. The yearly additions to the stock through new construction and modification of buildings are relatively small. The supply of dwellings, in terms of numbers and quality, is inflexible in the short term, which easily creates shortages in periods of rapid growth of urban populations as well as considerable fluctuations in rents and prices.

Housing derives added importance from its location. When a household rents or purchases a home, it acquires not only the physical unit, but because of its particular location, a neighborhood and a set of public services or lack thereof. Since almost all housing is fixed in location, the result is the structure of the city. The city grows by increments of housing and since these are usually added to the margin of the city, the consequence is a geographic zonation of the city by housing type, age of the structures, and variations in density around the central core of the city (chapter 1). Even cities like Los Angeles, which have a tendency toward a multinodal structure, still have an observable zonation or pattern in the distribution of housing.

Various imperfections in the housing market, related to location and available supply, together with the argument that shelter is a basic human need, have led governments to intervene in providing housing. This was especially the case in Western Europe during the postwar period when the welfare states introduced extensive housing legislation, including rent control, subsidies for production and consumers, and stimuli for the growth of a substantial nonprofit or social rental housing stock. Housing developed into an important sector of regulation of society by the nation-state and became part of the political process.

Housing is often defined and we know it most simply as a physical facility—a housing unit that provides shelter, occupies land, and requires various infrastructure services, most notably energy power, water, and waste disposal. At a secondary level, however, housing also provides access to local education (schools), jobs, amenities (parks), and neighbors (the social environment). Third, housing is an economic good, a consumer durable that can be traded or exchanged in the housing market. Housing is property, an asset whose value will often increase and which can be used as a security for a loan. Buyers of a dwelling can borrow money against this asset in the form of a mortgage to be repaid in a regular flow of small sums. Fourth, housing is a sector of the economy, just as are numerous other industrial and service activities. Finally, housing is part of the political process and is often affected by changes in government regulations and political philosophies, when political power passes from one party to another. It is the intersection of these definitions that creates some of the complexity in discussions about housing and housing markets.

The present discussion of housing should also note that housing provides housing services, ranging from the internal structure of the unit, the space and amenities of the house itself, to the services that derive from the location in absolute as well as relative terms. The location of the house provides a series of environmental and social services. The flow of these services, sometimes referred to as the bundle of services associated with a particular dwelling, is what is consumed by the homeowner or renter. The flow of housing services is usually gauged by single measures of prices or rents. The previously mentioned hedonic method used by economists is one technique to attach implicit prices to the various components of the housing bundle.

The Life Course and Housing Choice

There is a broad body of research generated from cross-sectional analyses of mobility, tenure choice, and housing selection that began with the basic life cycle analysis of residential mobility. The initial work on the family life cycle concept suggested a series of stages in the life cycle, stages that coincided with a particular structure and organization of the family. These analyses of family structure categorized families by type of family organization (Rossi 1955). The stages were largely defined by the expansion and contraction of families in the course of the child-rearing years. As used initially by sociologists, such as Glick (1957) and Sorokin and associates (1931), the stages were demographic categories defined by the size of the family unit, the ages of the head (heads) of the household, and the presence of children.

Categorization of families was enlarged by Lansing and Morgan (1955) who suggested that households pass through a series of "stages" of the life cycle. Indeed, they defined a series of categories from young and single, passing through various marital status categories with and without children, to an older, and again single, status. The emphasis in these categorizations was on a linear progression along an imagined traditional life cycle (fig. 2.1).

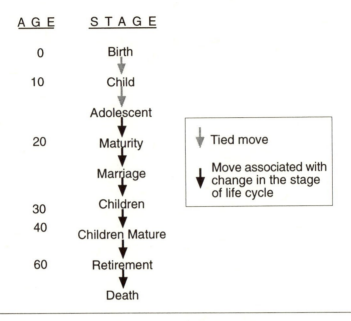

FIGURE 2.1
A linear approach to the life cycle and mobility/migration

Each stage in the cycle is characterized by a different size and composition of the family. A move from one stage of the life cycle to another provides the impetus for relocating and housing change. In this conceptualization, a change in the life cycle is associated with greater probabilities of moving and housing change. The housing needs of the young household in particular are most likely to be out of balance with the actual housing, and during this time one is far more likely to move and change housing consumption.

The life cycle is, thus, paralleled by changes in the housing career. At each stage of the life cycle, the individual or household is in a housing unit (fig. 2.2). Children leave the parental home and usually rent small apartments before marriage or cohabitation; then over time, they move into a succession of housing types of increasing space and in concert with the changed residential space needs of the household. The stylized diagram is designed to reflect these changing needs and responses over the life cycle and aging process.

A great deal of research has examined the life cycle and the

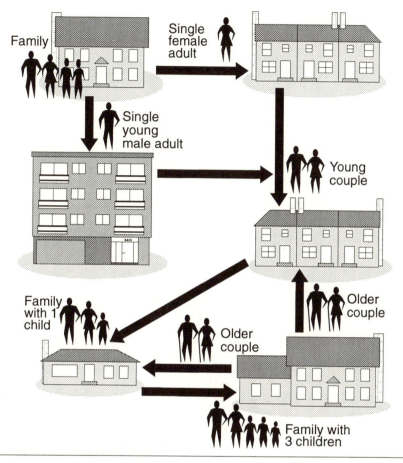

FIGURE 2.2
The intersection of life cycles and housing careers

categorization of household structure. There is little agreement, however, on the structure of the categories of the life cycle or which classification is best. Nor is there much agreement on either the variables to define the classifications or the impact of increasing numbers of nonfamily and alternative family compositions (Quigley and Weinberg 1977). Indeed, during the past two decades, all Western societies have undergone substantial and far-reaching changes in household composition generally and within the family specifically. The very large increase in individual households, single-

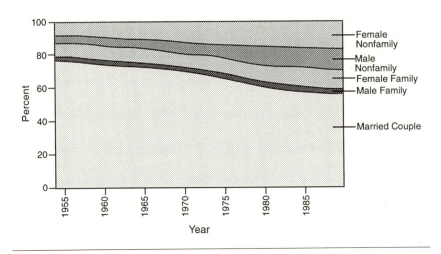

FIGURE 2.3

Changing household composition over time in the United States

Source: U.S. Bureau of the Census, *Current Population Reports*, Series P–20, No. 441, 1989.

parent families, and two-income households, often without children, means that one can no longer speak of a normative family structure. Households and families are different than they were thirty years ago. Married-couple households in the United States have declined from almost 80 percent of households in the 1950s to slightly more than 60 percent in 1989 (fig. 2.3). Data for the Netherlands show very similar processes, despite the cultural differences (fig. 2.4). There has been a dramatic decline in the number of large households. By 1985, one- and two-person households constituted more than 50 percent of all households in the Netherlands. The processes that have influenced the changing family structure include delaying marriage, voluntary childlessness, and increasing divorce rates.

An alternate approach that incorporates notions of the life cycle but is more responsive to the nature of change is both a theoretical advance and a practical alternative. The life course is both a richer conceptualization of change in family and household structure and allows other changes to be incorporated within the notion of life course trajectories. The life course paradigm is an out-

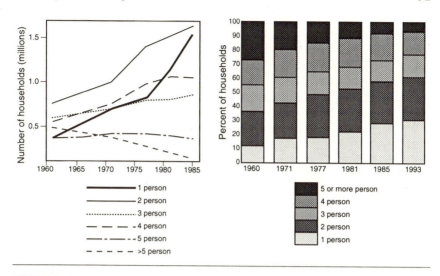

FIGURE 2.4
Household composition in the Netherlands by absolute numbers and percentages, 1960–1993

Source: Ministry of Housing, Physical Planning and the Environment (MVROM), 1989, and Netherlands Central Bureau of Statistics.

growth of a general concern with the problem of modeling space–time processes (Mayer and Tuma 1990). The models are designed to allow the analysis of more than one process so that changes in family composition, housing, and jobs can be linked together. The models that have been used in these cases (often called hazard models or event-history models) are related to examining particular events that occur periodically, such as marriage, the birth of children, and, of course, residential mobility and housing relocation. They are all part of understanding the way in which families change over time. The emergence of these models and the concept of the life course have provided an interdisciplinary approach to time-dependent changes. The life course can be used to link economic, sociological, and geographical variables and to incorporate the individuals and the various events affecting them as they proceed from birth to death.

The notion of the life course emphasizes that the process of an individual through life can be viewed as a sequence of events.

The events obviously include a wide range of occurrences from those related to family formation, to education and career decisions, and not least to housing and shelter decisions, which are then interrelated with the decisions about family and career. People complete their education, enter the labor force, get married (move), buy a house (move), have children, and eventually retire. Within the research on the life course, there has been a concern to utilize the life course as an overarching conceptual structure to examine changes in family composition. Just as these models can be used to examine changes (transitions) in families, or individuals, they can also be used to consider other transitions in the housing market (housing careers), in occupational careers, and so on.

The research in life course analysis has focused on the individual life span and the way in which that individual life span is shaped and organized, not merely by the decisions of individual actors but also by the cultural beliefs of the individual and the context, both social and spatial, in which the individual is situated. The aim of life course analysis is to look at individual life events and the patterns of life trajectories in the context of the social processes that generate these events and trajectories. In diagrammatic form, we can envisage the parallel streams of events in household changes, in housing changes, and in job/occupation changes. Residential relocations cut across these trajectories and interrelate the trajectories. One can consider the links as time dependencies between one event and another.

The stylized presentation (fig. 2.5) depicts the three paths related to household structure, job/occupational changes, and housing career intersections. Events occur in any of these "trajectories," and the residential move—relocation behavior—clearly intersects with the other changes. Considering that one can visualize a household proceeding through a series of changes related to occupational careers, housing transitions, and other events during the passage of time, all influenced, in turn, by the evolving structure of society, some model format is required within which to analyze and measure these changes and their correlates. Event history analysis is such a methodology. The core of the event history methodology is the ability to examine sequences of events and to model the intervals between the events (the spells), the number of events, and the probability of their occurrence (the risks or hazards of oc-

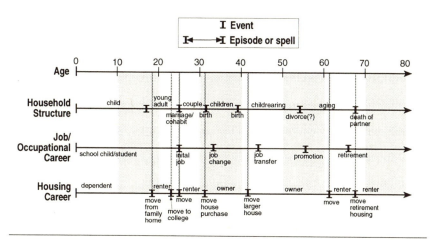

FIGURE 2.5
The life course and household/housing trajectories

currence), in relationship to independent variables. Event history data is the raw material from which to construct or examine life courses. Event history data provide information on the time at which an event occurs, such as when a member of a sample changes from one state to another (getting married, having children, changing residence). For every member in the sample, in a longitudinal data set, there are data on the sequence and timing of events, the states occupied, and the duration in each of the states. Event history analysis refers to the set of methods that can be used to examine the events, their timing, and the intervals between them (Allison 1984). Event history *data* (data in the process of changing from one state to another) is the raw material from which to construct or examine life courses. Event history *analysis* is one important way of examining these events (Mayer and Tuma 1990; Allison 1982 and 1984).

Event history data is collected from panel surveys which were relatively rare until the 1970s; only since the early 1980s, when the number of panels increased and when new techniques to process such data became more widely available, has longitudinal panel data analysis assumed a central role in social science research. Its popularity stems in part from its presumed ability to allow and control for various "individual effects." It also permits characterization of individual decisions and action processes operating over time. This is contrary to more traditional models (cross-sectional) that enforce a single time unit within which agents make their decisions and take their action.

There is an essential difference between life cycle conceptualizations and life course paradigms. The former focuses on stable stages, while the latter focuses on age-specific transitions between stages. It is useful to think of life cycle categories as the predefined stages through which households pass in a normative manner. The life course, by contrast, emphasizes the trajectories of individuals as they pass through life from birth to death. To reiterate, the life course emphasizes the linkage between age and interaction, with the larger societal changes within which aging occurs the "socially patterned trajectories of individuals" (Mayer and Tuma 1990, 6).

Although the life course conceptualization sets up an organizing approach to the analysis of housing change, one also requires measures of the outcomes of housing choices. The categorical models, which analyze the intersection of household composition variables and variables that measure the characteristics of housing, provide this part of the presentation. The life course focuses on triggers and events; the categorical model deals with the outcomes of the temporal choices of households interacting with the housing market.

Housing Contexts and Housing Comparisons

It is clear from the discussion thus far that mobility behavior and tenure choice are influenced by household type, including age, size of the household, and income. These are the forces at the microlevel—at the level of the individual and the household—that help to explain mobility and housing choice. The same type of household, however, will likely be confronted with different choice situations because it is either in a very different housing market or it is making choices in an expanding or contracting economy. Thus housing market choices do not occur in a vacuum; they are set within the changing economy, they vary from region to region, and they are affected by government policy. Therefore, conditions

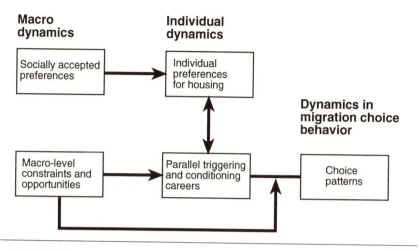

FIGURE 2.6

The context of housing and tenure choice

Source: Mulder, 1993.

at the macrolevel also influence the outcomes of the movements of households through the housing stock. This complex process in which general goals, household and individual preferences, and macrolevel constraints and opportunities interact leads to a set of observed choice patterns (fig. 2.6). The observed patterns of mobility and housing and tenure choice are usually referred to as "revealed" choice behavior.

Choice is also related to individual and household preferences. These preferences can be conceptualized as concrete transformations of more general goals of people (Mulder 1993). General goals are assumed to be universal; preferences are not. Preferences will vary from one individual to another and during the life course of a particular individual. Preferences for housing and tenure are, thus, influenced and constrained by parallel careers (family formation and dissolution, and job and income change) over the life course. At the same time, choice patterns also reflect macrolevel constraints and opportunities (fig. 2.6). Opportunities at the aggregate level are created exogenously to the individual, in the form of available housing vacancies. The way in which the individual or household interprets the choice set available for individual selections also depends on individual preferences and resource levels themselves. Constraints at the macrolevel are, in a sense, the negative counterpart of opportunities. Shortages in the housing market or unfavorable economic circumstances are examples of exogenous constraints on individual or household choice (Mulder 1993).

The analysis of contextual influences on housing choice in chapter 5 focuses on three important aspects of contexts: how choice occurs within the opportunities and constraints of a particular housing stock; how it is influenced by changes in the national economic context; and how it varies with the level of government regulation of the housing market.

As noted earlier, the stock of dwellings is not constant but is changed by additions and deletions—the latter at the center and the former in the suburbs. Both processes change the context within which choices occur. During the last three decades, the housing supply in the United States and Europe has expanded rapidly, particularly in owner-occupancy dwellings. Even in Holland, where much of the housing stock is subsidized, substantial increments to both the public and private housing stock have taken place.

Then, housing choice is impacted by larger economic events and circumstances which vary by time and region. The increase in income and assets among large numbers of the population of Western countries over the last two decades has increased the demand for both owner-occupied housing and larger and better equipped dwellings. But short-time fluctuations in income prospects, mortgage rates, price of owner-occupation and rent, and levels of new construction also affect the level of mobility and choice for one type of housing or another.

The third context for understanding the process of housing choice is the level of government regulation of the housing process. Clearly, there are similarities between the behavior of households in European cities and North American cities. But to what extent do the same variables provide an understanding of behavior in the housing market? To answer this question, it is necessary to explore mobility behavior and tenure choice in two different sociopolitical settings—the relatively free housing market of the

United States and the highly controlled Dutch housing market. In the Netherlands, a national system of rent control as well as planning of the level and location of new dwelling construction has spawned mass production of nonprofit rental housing, which now accounts for 40 percent of the stock generally and 50 percent in cities such as Amsterdam and Rotterdam. Naturally this influences choice patterns. The comparative focus emphasizes the institutional and political content within which housing choices are made. The working hypothesis of this study with respect to the last question is that housing choice will be more clearly dominated by economic factors in the United States than in the Netherlands, where government regulation of the housing market is strongly developed.

Summary

This chapter introduced the nature and complexity of housing and reviewed some of the basic concepts that are used to organize the analysis of housing choices in this book. It introduced housing as a context within which it is possible to focus on housing choices and consumption. The central and critical focus of the chapter, however, was on the life course paradigm and how it can be used to analyze and understand choice across housing market contexts. To reiterate, the goal is to provide an interpretation of how individuals choose housing based on their household composition and income characteristics. The aim is to link households and houses and to create understanding of the choices that households make and how households come to be distributed across the housing stock.

It is obvious from this discussion that housing is a complex good, in both the variety of characteristics that affect the housing choice process of individuals and households and its spatial fixity. Size, age, tenure, and location of the dwelling are important in the considerations of housing when a family moves. One cannot acquire only one aspect of a dwelling separate from others, however; therefore, housing is also referred to as a bundle of housing services. The quality of housing varies considerably among neighborhoods; therefore, housing location plays an important role in consumer choice. The neighborhood in which the dwelling is located provides access to local education (schools), jobs, amenities (parks), and to particular neighbors (social environment) of the community.

Mobility behavior and tenure choice are clearly interrelated. Before the tenure choice is specifically examined, however, it is necessary to consider some aspects of residential mobility because it is the process that intersects with the macrolevel context and initiates the changes in the housing market.

3

Residential Mobility and the Consumption of Housing Space

Residential mobility—moving from one location in the city to another—is the process that creates change in the housing market. Together with new construction of housing, it is one of the prime stimuli for the changes in the housing market and, in turn, influences housing demand and housing consumption. In the end, mobility is interesting because it is the behavior whereby individuals and households match their household needs for residential space to the available housing stock. In the normal operation of the housing market, the mismatch of housing and households is the critical driver in creating mobility and housing selection. Of course, this is an imperfect mechanism, and there is considerable regional and national variation in the ability of the mobility process to accomplish the matching of households and housing. Preferences of mobile households cannot always be satisfied, because of lack of opportunities in the housing stock on the one hand and income constraints which limit choice on the other. At the same time, the mobility process, even as modified by government intervention and the varying composition of the housing market, is the mechanism that brings the matching into focus.

Residential change occurs as a result of short-distance local moves within one city—or even one part of a city—as well as from longer-distance migrations from one region of a country to another. In the United States, about 60 percent of all moves are local moves within a metropolitan area, and the rest are combinations of regional moves and new immigrants entering the country. Although

TABLE 3.1

Distribution of Movers within Localities, between Localities, and
from outside the Country in Six Countries, about 1981

	Percentage of Movers		
	Within Localities	Between Localities	From Outside the Country
Belgium	57.4	27.9	4.2
Great Britain	71.9	23.7	5.3
Ireland	52.5	35.1	12.4
Japan	71.9	27.7	0.4
New Zealand	73.1	18.7	8.2
United States	60.5	26.1	3.4

Note: 'Localities' refers to communes in Belgium, counties in Great Britain,
Ireland, and the United States, ken (prefectures) in Japan, and statistical areas
in New Zealand.

Source: L. Long. 1992a. Reprinted from *Population Studies,* vol. 46, by permission of Population Investigation Committee, London.

there is some variation across countries in the proportion of movers who stay within a particular locality, most movers are local
(table 3.1). For a limited set of countries, local moves vary from a
low of about 53 percent, in Ireland, to a high of 73 percent, in New
Zealand. Moves between localities are in the range of 25 percent
to 35 percent. About half of the interlocality moves constitute
longer-distance migrations between states. Thus the intralocality
and shorter distance between locality moves constitute a very high
proportion of all moves. This is important, because these are what
can be called adjustment moves *within* the housing market.

It is useful to conceptualize movers as partial or total displacement movers as this conceptualization emphasizes the sociospatial
context within which housing choices and relocations occur. When
a move occurs nearby and does not break the web of contacts with
friends and work, it can be viewed as a partial displacement
(Roseman 1971). Many of the old interactions with friends, family, and even work will not change (fig. 3.1). When the move in-

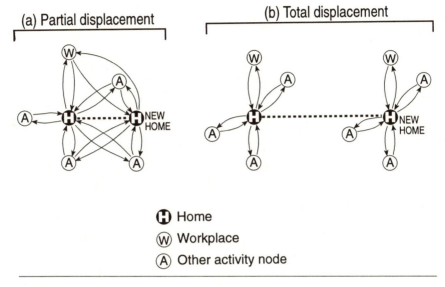

FIGURE 3.1

A schematic of partial and total displacement moves

Source: Adapted from Roseman, 1971.

volves a greater separation between the old house and the new house, and there are no, or limited, ties, then the migration is a total displacement migration. Moves which occur within one housing market are partial displacement moves. Moves of this type are mostly referred to as residential mobility, because the main reason for the move is to match household needs to housing characteristics. The emphasis in this book is on these moves because the process of matching of households and houses is the main theme of the presentation.

The Correlates of Migration and Mobility

The extensive research on residential mobility has documented the interconnection between migration and mobility and age, socio-economic status, space, and tenure. One of the earliest and still relevant findings from studies of migration and mobility is the role

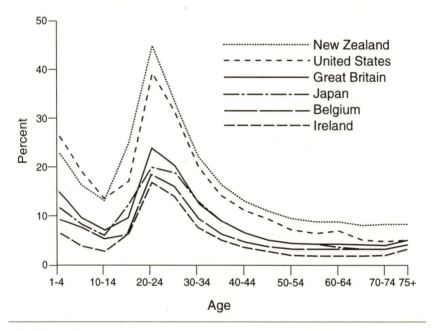

FIGURE 3.2
Percentage of population that changed residence in one year

Source: Adapted from Long, 1992a, by permission of *Population Studies*, vol. 46, and Population Investigation Committee, London.

of age in distinguishing the likelihood of migration and mobility. Young adults between the ages of twenty and thirty-five are the most migratory segments of the population. This is true for different cultural contexts and across all spatial scales (fig. 3.2). Of course, the actual proportions of those who move are higher in some countries than others. For example, Long (1992a) documents that the United States is one of the countries with very high rates of mobility (though, in fact, New Zealand has the highest rates); Western Europe and Japan have much lower rates of moving from place to place. In the age range of thirty to thirty-four, the rate of migration and mobility drops considerably. In the United States in 1990, about 18 percent of the total population had moved during the past year, and 32 percent of the population between ages twenty-five and twenty-nine. The graph of mobility/migration by

TABLE 3.2

Migration by Tenure in the United States, 1989–1990

	Percent Moved in the Past Year
Owner Occupied	8.3
Renter Occupied	32.4
In Central Cities	
Owner Occupied	10.3
Renter Occupied	30.0
In Suburbs	
Owner Occupied	7.8
Renter Occupied	34.9

Source: U.S. Bureau of the Census, *American Housing Survey* 1991, General Housing Characteristics.

age, which is replicable for various countries, shows the classic peak of mobility in the young adult years. The reason is that during this period in the life cycle many changes typically occur that generate mobility, such as household formation and expansion and career and income changes. The high mobility of younger children is generated by family-related moves. In some graphs, there is a slightly higher rate of mobility associated with the very oldest age cohorts. This increase in the mobility rate has been related to retirement moves and to moves prompted by the loss of a spouse.

It is a fact that people who rent are much more likely to migrate than people who own their homes (table 3.2). Renters are three to four times more likely to move than owners. In the Netherlands, renters are less mobile, in particular in the large social rented sector (publicly subsidized housing), but the mobility ratio of renters is still twice as high as that for owners (Everaers and Davies 1993). The explanation is directly related to their involvement in the housing market. Those individuals and households who are interested in owning a house and who have invested the search costs in locating the house are more likely to be making a long-term locational commitment. There is also the "sunk costs" of broker and bank fees associated with the move to ownership. Of

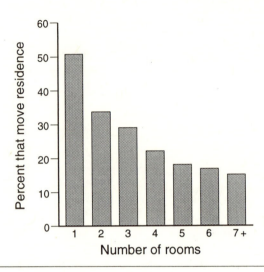

FIGURE 3.3
Mobility by size of dwelling, the Netherlands

Source: Everaers, 1990. Redrawn by permission of the Netherlands Central Bureau of Statistics.

course, many renters are single, have a smaller stake in the apartment, and find it easier to relocate.

Mobility is also linked to space and "room" consumption. The amount of space available to a household and the "fit" of the household to the house are important measures of disequilibrium and of the stimulus to change houses. People and households living in small houses are prone to move as soon as larger dwellings can be found (fig. 3.3). Once larger houses are occupied, the propensity to move decreases. This also occurs because these larger dwellings are frequently single-family homes and owner-occupied houses. One must also recognize, however, that many one- and two-room dwelling units are occupied by younger renters who have a higher propensity to move. Thus, age and size of unit are confounded to some extent.

Educational level and income (socioeconomic status) also seem to be related to the rates of mobility. The higher the level of education of an individual or in a household, the greater the chance of moving at all age levels. In the United States, a clear trend ex-

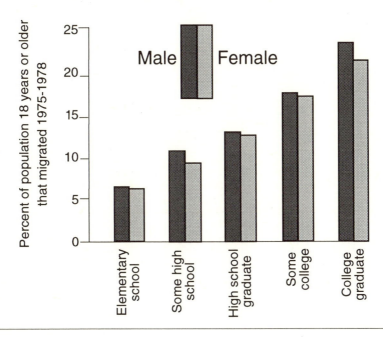

FIGURE 3.4

Migration by level of education, the United States, 1975–1978

Source: U.S. Census of Population, 1978.

ists in the percentage of the population that moved (fig. 3.4). A college graduate is three times as likely to move as a person with a basic elementary education. Mobility is also related to income. In the Netherlands, two-earner families and couples are one-third more likely to move than one-earner families, showing the increased scope for adjustment of housing with growing income (fig. 3.5). The relationship of mobility and income is somewhat complicated, however, because income is also related to age and type of household.

Finally, a family's residence history has an effect on the likelihood of mobility. The initial simplistic notion of cumulative inertia, that the longer individuals or households stay in a residence, the longer they will continue to stay, has been refined to reflect a more subtle appreciation of how the probability of staying is related to duration. When data on migrants are disaggregated by age and tenure, much of the cumulative inertia is explained away as

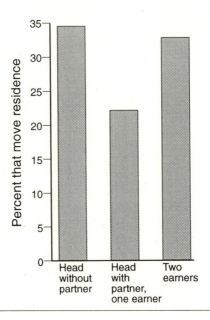

FIGURE 3.5
Mobility for single heads of household and one- and two-income
households, the Netherlands

Source: Everaers, 1990. Redrawn by permission of the Netherlands Central
Bureau of Statistics.

an artifact of aggregated data. Thus, owners have a much greater
likelihood of "staying" after a move than renters.

There is a debate, however, whether duration-of-stay effects
have an independent meaning. As Mulder (1993) suggests, one
could postulate the existence of a "learning-by-doing" scenario in
which households that have moved more frequently develop a taste
for "restlessness" and pay less attention to the location-specific
capital that accrues with longer residence. Thus, "movers" as opposed to "stayers" came into existence. But, like Mulder (1993),
one can take the view that duration is one among a plethora of
factors that influence mobility. It is now clear that one can separate the duration of residence effects owing to cumulative inertia
from those effects that are artifacts of aggregating subpopulations
with differing intrinsic rates of mobility (Clark and Huff 1977) and,
in fact, cumulative inertia has little if any observable effect on the

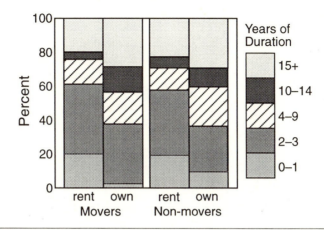

FIGURE 3.6
Duration of stay by tenure, end of 1989, the Netherlands

Source: Redrawn by permission of the Netherlands Central Bureau of Statistics, 1993, and Delft University Press.

mobility rate. At the same time, there are effects of the particular pattern of previous moves and the duration between them. Increasing lengths of stay do not necessarily mean decreasing likelihoods of moving. That is only one of three possibilities. Mobility likelihoods can decrease, increase, or remain constant as a function of increasing lengths of stay. By incorporating events and the intervals between them, duration can be incorporated in the decision-making process. It is not only the duration since the last move that is critical, but both the total number of moves and the order of occurrence that *can* have an impact on the subsequent probability of moving. At the same time, measures of duration do distinguish between owners and renters and increase with age (fig. 3.6).

Age, marital status, the presence of children, income, tenure, space disequilibrium, and the previous history of moves, all intersect to define the likelihood of moving and influence the amount of housing consumed. For the United States and Western Europe, one can conclude that internal migration is closely linked with the change from single to family status, which is associated with age and, in turn, with educational attainment and tenure position.

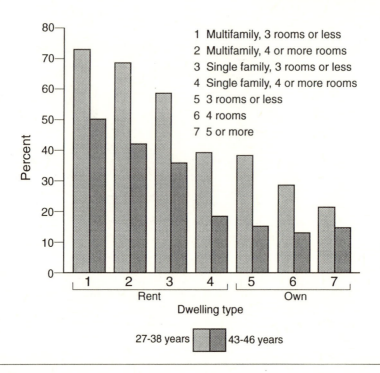

FIGURE 3.7
Propensity to move in the next two years by age of head, tenure, and
size of unit, the Netherlands

Source: Adapted by permission from Hooimeijer and Linde, 1988.

Models of Mobility

The effect of the intersection of the head of household's age and
space and size of the dwelling on the propensity to move is clearly
illustrated in figure 3.7. Mobility decreases from small rental flats
to large single-family, owner-occupied dwelling units. Across all
eight dwelling types, the propensity to move is consistently higher
in the younger age category than for householders in their forties.

In the literature on residential mobility, these complex relationships between mobility and characteristics of households and
dwellings are usually unraveled with multivariate models. Using this
approach, an analysis was undertaken of the dependent variable
of move/no move and eight independent explanatory variables that

TABLE 3.3

Factors Mostly Related to Mobility for Owners and
Private Renters in the Netherlands (PRU analysis)

Step	Added variables	Explained variation (PRU)	G^2
Owners			
1	Age: < 35, 35–44, ≥ 45 Years	0.022	323.11
2	Number of Rooms: 1–2, 3, 4, 5, ≥ 6	0.030	432.11
3	Income*: < 20, 20–29, 30–42, ≥ 42 (x 1000 g)	0.054	426.30
Renters			
1	Age: < 35, 35–44, 45–54, ≥ 55 Years	0.086	723.92
2	Size of Household: 1, 2–4, ≥ 5 Persons	0.107	906.18
3	Rent*: ≤ 149, 150–249, 250–549, ≥ 550 (g)	0.130	1004.64

* without missing values. g = guilders.

Source: Clark et al., 1986. Reprinted from *Environment and Planning A,* vol.
18, by permission.

measure age, number of rooms (space), size of household, price
and type of house, income, ratios of rooms to size of household,
and price of house to income. In this data set, tenure was controlled
by dividing the data set into owners and private renters. The proportional reduction of uncertainty coefficient (PRU) was used to
select variables from a subset of the eight variables that seemed
most related to the propensity to move (see appendix for technical details on PRU). Consistent with the arguments of age, space,
and cost, the model selected age, number of rooms, and income
as the prime explanations of the variation in the decision to move
or not to move (table 3.3). Simply stated, the PRU technique se-
lects variables (and combines categories of the independent variables) in a stepwise fashion so that they are hierarchical explanations of the move/no move decision (fig. 3.8). Clearly, age is a prime
explanatory variable for the moves of owners. Note how the proportion moving decreases across the age categories. The addition
to the size of the previous dwelling (available space) adds both to
our explanation and to the understanding of the probability of moving for owners. The addition of a second variable shows that even
though age is the critical variable, there are large differences in

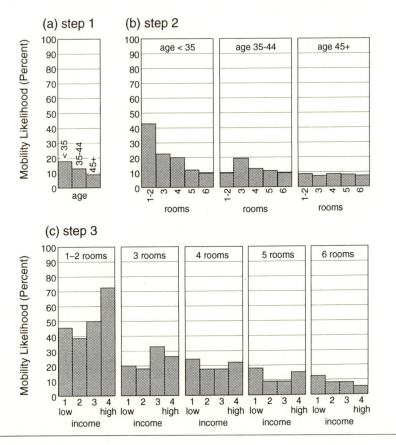

FIGURE 3.8
Mobility likelihoods for Dutch owners by (a) age, (b) number of rooms, and (c) income

Source: Clark et al., 1986. Redrawn from *Environment and Planning A*, vol. 18, by permission of Pion Limited, London.

the mobility rates of households living in smaller versus larger dwelling units. There is a decrease in mobility by age *and* across dwelling unit sizes. The figure also illustrates that there are interaction effects between age and number of rooms. Finally, income modifies the relationship between age and available space. Income effects are more pronounced for younger movers (both under thirty-five years of age and for thirty-five to forty-four age groups) where higher incomes and smaller units generate greater mobility. For larger units, income is less influential. For older age groups, income is only really important for smaller units. Clearly, income is the enabling or constraining variable in the mobility process.

A very similar structure is created for the mobility of private renters in the Dutch housing market. The most important explanatory variables are age, size of household (which we can think of as the mirror image of number of rooms), and rent (a parallel to income for owners). The composite diagram (fig. 3.9) shows decreasing mobility by age (down the scale) and increasing mobility from small households to larger households. There is a general tendency for households with higher rents to be more mobile, but there is also evidence of a U-shaped structure to mobility by rental cost. These results almost certainly reflect the impetus for low-rent households to try to seek better quality housing, and higher rents imply both greater flexibility and moves out of the rental sector to ownership. Overall, results from both the owner-occupier and private rental sector (the sector closest to the U.S. rental market) emphasize the role of age, space (rooms or household size), and costs in creating differences in mobility rates.

Another approach to integrating age, space, and tenure in a model to explain the likelihood of moving is to use some form of regression model to estimate the strength of the relationships (table 3.4). The outcomes of this analysis of the U.S. data confirm the direction and size of the effects of these variables on the likelihood of moving. Measures of age (defined as age of head of household under forty years) and age squared (the quadratic form reflects the peak in residential mobility in the twenty- to thirty-year-old age bracket and then the steep decline after about age thirty-four years) are negative and positive as expected. Younger households are more mobile than older households. Tenure (owner versus renter) is negative; owners are less likely to move than renters. Finally, a measure of space consumption is also significant and negative. The measure of room stress (actual consumption/required consumption -1) has a U-shaped function with either high negative values of room stress or high positive values of room stress. Both high and low stress values lead to mobility. Values near zero suggest relative equilibrium. The results are similar for all households and for households that have the same head over an eighteen-year period.

One-person household

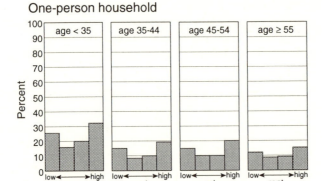

Two- to four-person household

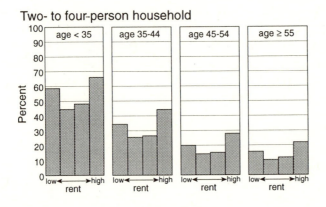

FIGURE 3.9
Mobility for Dutch renters by age, household size, and rent

Source: Clark et al., 1986. Redrawn from *Environment and Planning A*, vol. 18, by permission of Pion Limited, London.

However, the room stress variable is larger for all families, including families with changes in the head of household. Clearly, it is a reflection of the impact of family composition changes being translated into space stress.

TABLE 3.4

Factors Related to the Mobility of Families with Same Head and All
Families in the United States, 1978–1987

Variable	β	Standard error	χ^2	p
Same Head				
Room Stress	−0.060	0.038	2.44	0.118
Room Stress Squared	0.025	0.012	4.45	0.035
Age of Head	−5.663	0.157	1297.57	0.000
Age of Head Squared	8.644	0.700	152.65	0.000
Tenure (Owner)	−1.223	0.039	976.32	0.000
All Families				
Room Stress	−0.076	0.037	4.20	0.040
Room Stress Squared	0.028	0.012	5.34	0.021
Age of Head	−6.411	0.142	2033.44	0.000
Age of Head Squared	11.061	0.629	308.84	0.000
Tenure (Owner)	−1.235	0.036	1154.09	0.000

Note: Pooled cross-sectional data

Source: Clark, 1992. Reprinted from *Environment and Planning A,* vol. 24,
by permission.

Life Cycles and Housing Careers

The relationship between age and mobility has been integrated into
the sociological concept of the life cycle. As noted in the introduc-
tory chapter, within the life-cycle perspective, migration is a part
of the adjustment process in which individuals and families bring
their housing consumption into equilibrium with their changing
needs. At very young ages, individuals move as part of the larger
household. Later, the individual establishes a separate residence
and moves "away from home." These initial moves may also in-
volve changes in occupation and other changes related to family
composition—changes including marriage and the addition of children. Later, divorce and separation affect the chance of moving.
Thus, passage through a series of changing familial status positions
leads to associated moves through the housing market. The initial
conceptualization of the life cycle mentioned in chapter 1 was of

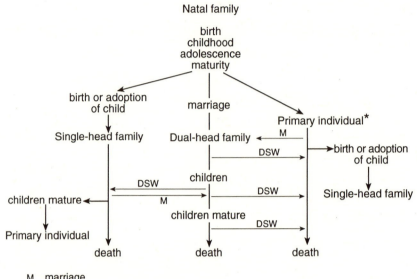

FIGURE 3.10
An expanded life cycle with varying household compositions

Source: Stapleton, 1980, fig. 2m. Redrawn from *Environment and Planning A*, vol. 12, by permission of Pion Limited, London.

a linear progression from leaving home to "nest leaving," as young children, in turn, left the parents' home. Now, it is clear that the progress is far from linear, and various conceptualizations suggest a structure much more like a tree or bush with numerous alternate paths and outcomes (fig. 3.10). Divorce, separation, and widowhood, and single-parent families have restructured household compositions. Even if the sequence of changes in the life cycle from pre-marriage to widowhood is far from linear, however, the large majority of households still go through the various obvious stages of marriage or cohabitation, rearing and launching children, and the empty nest and widowhood stages (fig. 3.11). The relationship of these stages with age is still quite clear, although the age at which households enter and leave the various stages varies considerably. Childbearing and childrearing dominate the years from twenty-five

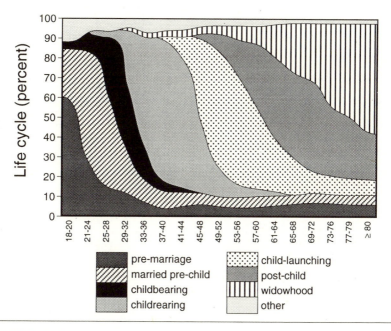

FIGURE 3.11

The intersection of the life cycle and the age of the head of the household, the Netherlands

Source: Hooimeijer et al., 1986. Redrawn with permission from *Housing Studies*, vol. 1, Carfax Publishing Co., Oxfordshire, England.

to fifty. Child-launching begins in the forties and is largely completed by age sixty. Thus, the well-known stages in the life cycle still capture the majority of households, with obvious implications for the housing market.

Much of the work on life cycles was classificatory in emphasis and focused on age and family status, while many decisions in the housing market are enhanced or limited by household income. As Kendig (1990) points out, homeownership rates vary widely by occupational groups and other social categories at all stages of the life cycle. And, in his examples, homeownership rates vary from 55 percent to 85 percent for lower versus higher income households (Kendig 1990). The classification, however, is necessarily static and does not capture the dynamics of moving through the

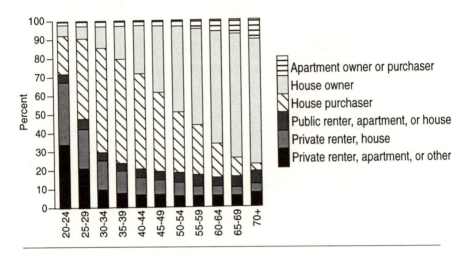

FIGURE 3.12
Distribution of dwelling tenure, household type, and age of the
household head

Source: Kendig, 1990. Redrawn by permission of University of Wisconsin Press,
Madison, Wisconsin.

housing market as the household ages and changes its composition and income level.

The concept of the housing career is an attempt to draw a relationship between the life cycle, exemplified in figure 3.10, and
housing-market behavior. The housing career employs the same
metaphor as the occupational career. The metaphor suggests a
number of steps as households seek to improve their housing over
their life course (fig. 3.12). The figure is a reflection in housing
terms of the stage of the household and its composition. The housing career recognizes explicitly that households are going through
a process that involves a series of dwellings that are closer and
closer to their long-term needs and preferences (fig. 3.12). This is
one of the explanations why households in multifamily rental dwellings move more than those in single-family or owner-occupied
dwellings. Less desirable houses are, therefore, more readily available than the preferred status of owner-occupation (table 3.5). Of
course, toward the end of the life course, one would expect changes
to "downsize" the housing consumption, although the process ap-

TABLE 3.5

Percentage of Households that Moved in the Period 1978–1981,
by Rental Sector, Age of Household, Previous Housing Type,
and Housing Market Type in the Netherlands

Previous Housing Sector	Age, Head of Household	Housing Type	North and Southwest	Randstad
Private Rental	<35	Single-Family	50	33
		Multi-Family	61	35
	35–45	Single-Family	36	20
		Multi-Family	44	30
	>45	Single-Family	15	12
		Multi-Family	20	13
Public Rental	<35	Single-Family	26	34
		Multi-Family	57	41
	35–45	Single-Family	23	13
		Multi-Family	50	29
	>45	Single-Family	10	8
		Multi-Family	15	12

Source: Deurloo et al., 1986. Reprinted from *Stedebouw en Volkshuisvesting*, vol. 67, by permission.

pears to be less clear in the later stages of the housing career. The progression is discontinuous, and breakpoints are formed as a household moves from one dwelling to another. Obviously, households select from a series of "relatively" discrete housing submarkets, which constitute a hierarchy of choices from rental multifamily housing to owner-occupied housing (table 3.5). The focus on the link between life course and the move between housing types reemphasizes the role of changes in household structure and the resulting disequilibrium, which, in turn, again raises the centrality of space and unit size and the nature of housing consumption.

The Consumption of Residential Space

The discussion of the mobility process has demonstrated the critical role of physical space in the mobility process. The notion that demand for increased space creates residential mobility is a basic premise that has guided much of the research on residential relocation. The research findings of the past two or three decades have consistently reflected the importance of space in the residential mobility process. Following the work of Rossi (1955), the research findings of numerous mobility studies have given primacy to the link between housing adjustment and residential mobility, and especially the demands for additional space. This issue will be considered further in the discussion of the role of triggers in the mobility process. Although it has been established that space needs can be generated by changes other than those associated with changes in the life cycle, the link between the life cycle, housing adjustment, and the changing needs of space is still a major component of understanding residential change in the city.

When the mobility process was conceptualized as one in which households moved in response to life cycle changes that generated differing needs for housing, the central link was between *household* characteristics and *housing* characteristics, a relationship that has remained at the center of studies of housing and mobility. The way in which households are distributed across the housing stock has been a central element of studies of upward mobility (Myers 1983; Pitkin and Masnick 1986), of changes in the demand for housing (Sternlieb and Hughes 1986), of suburban/central city differences in housing/household links (Gober 1986), and of the link between the life cycle and tenure shifts (Morrow-Jones 1988).

Analyses of changing housing consumption and mobility processes in both European and U.S. contexts document the fact that, in general, the number of rooms and the amount of space are greater after a move than before the move. In a study of one metropolitan area in the Netherlands, the number of rooms and actual room space increase for all but older smaller households (table 3.6). Of course, much of this is related to the actual relocation process—the movement into ownership is clearly related to increasing space for each person. The same data also document the distinct relationship between age, family size, and housing size. Larger

TABLE 3.6

Change in Housing Consumption by Household, Life Cycle,
and Size of Unit in Tilburg, the Netherlands

	Average Number of Rooms		Average sq. meters per Person		
	Pre-Move	Post-Move	Pre-Move	Post-Move	Number of Households
Single-Person Household					
15–29 years	3.1	3.5	88.4	97.3	58
30–50 years	2.8	3.5	79.3	100.0	130
50+ years	3.7	2.5	97.5	75.7	549
Two-Person Families					
15–29 years	1.4	1.8	38.5	51.3	704
30–50 years	1.5	1.9	42.7	55.6	520
50+ years	1.8	1.5	47.5	43.0	1,161
Three-Person Families					
15–29 years	1.2	1.6	32.7	42.6	491
30–50 years	1.2	1.4	32.6	40.4	705
50+ years	1.3	1.3	34.9	37.6	271
Four-Person + Families					
15–29 years	1.0	1.2	28.7	30.0	408
30–50 years	1.0	1.1	27.4	33.1	1,985
50+ years	0.9	0.9	25.4	29.1	223

Source: Clark et al., 1984. Reprinted from *Annals,* vol. 74, by permission of Association of American Geographers.

families consume much less space for each person than smaller families (table 3.6).

Data from the American Housing Survey show that, overall, 72 percent of the movers increased their space when they moved, and 28 percent decreased their space (fig. 3.13). For all movers, the average increase in rooms per person was about 0.17, or about one-fifth of a room. When one further decomposes the mobility process and the link to physical space one finds that, as expected, those who move within the ownership category *increase* their space, but the increase is quite small. Those who move from rent-to-own increase their space much more significantly, as do those who move within the rental sector. Again, as expected, those

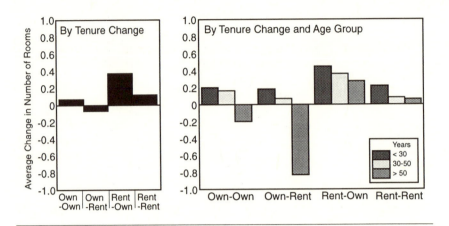

FIGURE 3.13

Average change in space consumption, the United States

Source: U.S. Bureau of the Census, *American Housing Survey,* 1989.

moving out of the ownership sector are the ones who decrease their space.

A further decomposition by age adds to the understanding of the mobility/physical space relationship (fig. 3.13). There is a dramatic difference between households under fifty years and older households (with the exception of one-person households). Although younger households always increase their space with a move, the households over fifty decrease their space in both own-to-own moves and, of course, in the "downsizing" own-to-rent moves. This discussion illustrates again how the need for extra space and the wish to downsize space consumption, both closely associated with stages in the life cycle, act as triggers for residential mobility.

Triggers and Timing of Moves

Although the relationship of age and family composition was employed as a useful marker in the mobility process, the dynamics are more concerned with changes over the life course, changes that are, in fact, the triggers that generate disequilibrium and the resulting move. Myers (1985) has established the link between two-income families and the increased number of women in the work force to "divisions" in the housing market. He provided specific evidence that first-time buyers increasingly delayed childbearing and continued full-time employment in an effort to enter the owner market. The issue, also discussed by Rudel (1987), highlights the notion of the way in which the decision making by households is embedded in family composition changes. Mulder and Manting (1994) show how people and households go through a "coordinating process" in which they organize and synchronize activities in parallel careers. In sum, the paths of individual households through the housing stock are influenced by life transitions and local housing markets.

Moving Out and Increasing Family Size

Leaving the parental home is the first independent move. Whether the trigger is the desire for independence, the formation of an initial household, or enrollment in higher education, it is one of the major triggers in the mobility decision. Since World War II, children have left their parents' home at ever younger ages. As Goldscheider and Le Bourdais (1986) point out, finding children older than the very early twenties living with their parents has gone from a commonplace occurrence to a distinct rarity in the United States. This seems to be a common trend in all Western societies. In the Netherlands, women leave their parents' home at an average age of twenty-one and men at twenty-three.

At least in Europe, and now increasingly in the United States, there is a gap between the "leaving-home" stage and marriage. Later age at marriage means a period in which unmarried young people live apart from their parents. Even so, both in the United States and the Netherlands about 30 percent of all young people leaving home do so to get married (Goldscheider and Da Vanzo 1989). Another quarter of the nest leavers in the Netherlands start to cohabit without marriage.

A large number of moves from the parental home in both countries are related to college attendance (37 percent in the Netherlands). As many as one-third of the moves are made to what has

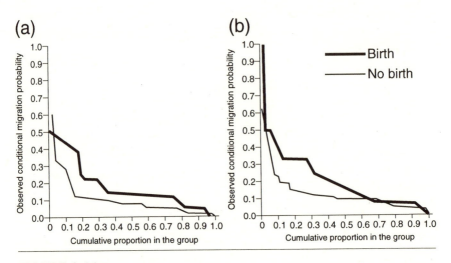

FIGURE 3.14
Observed conditional migration probabilities for (a) the private rental
sector, and (b) renters in subsidized rental housing for households with
and without births, Tilburg, the Netherlands

Source: Clark et al., 1984. Redrawn from the *Annals*, vol. 74, by permission
of Association of American Geographers.

been described as semiautonomous housing market entrance (dormitories, residential rooms, and so forth) rather than through an
independent entrance into the housing market. Forty-six percent
of those in the Netherlands who leave the parental home live alone.
Although marriage is still one of the important independent triggers for mobility in the housing market, and for the first move out
of the parental home, over time marriage has decreased in importance as a trigger.

Clearly, the anticipated or actual birth of a child can bring
about the need for more space. There is unquestionable evidence
of the impact of the birth of a child on the local mobility process.
For households in the private rental sector or in the subsidized
rental housing market, there are clearly higher probabilities of
moving with the addition of a child (fig. 3.14). The figures com-
pare the conditional probabilities of moving of analogous families
with and without the addition of a child. In both cases a birth has
a "triggering" effect on the likelihood of moving. In the cases of

both private renters and households in the public sector, the households that have an addition to the family are consistently more likely to relocate.

Timing

An important additional component in understanding the mobility process and the links to the housing market is the timing of the move. It extends the discussion of the nature of triggers in the section above.

The reason for examining the timing of moves is that changes in residential location are often associated with other transitions in the lives of the households that move. Major transitions in the lives of individuals, such as job changes or changes in household structure, tend to make them reevaluate previous locational decisions and examine the extent to which they are in equilibrium with their new circumstances. Thus, a natural question is the timing between a change in marital status and a move, if only because the timing of marriage is very likely to be associated with the timing of a residential relocation of at least one of the partners.

The links between the timing of marriage and the time to migrate can be demonstrated by comparing the survivor functions, assuming no relationship of marriage and moving (independence) and assuming a relationship between marriage and moving (fig. 3.15[a]). The likelihood of relocation is much higher during the period immediately following marriage. Note that the observed survivor function is considerably "lower" than the function under independence. Even this analysis may understate the connection as individuals were examined for moves *following* marriage and some may have moved in anticipation of it. A graph of the unordered relationship—that is, whether move or marriage occurred first— makes the case for a conditional relationship even stronger (fig. 3.15[b]). The difference between the two functions is larger for the unordered than for the ordered relationships.

The issue of timing also relates to a transition in family status from a couple to a family with children. The event of becoming a couple or a family and the event of a move from renting to owning occur mostly within very brief intervals (Clark et al. 1994). For

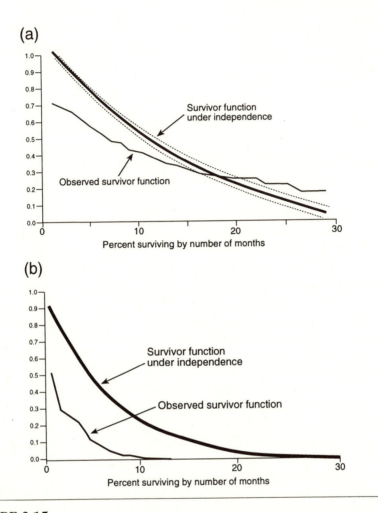

FIGURE 3.15
Graphs of the survivor function of "staying," that is, not moving, (a)
following marriage and (b) without regard to whether the move occurred
before or after marriage

Source: Odland and Shumway 1993. Redrawn from the *Journal of the Regional
Science Association* 72, figs. 7 and 8, by permission.

TABLE 3.7

Length of Time in the Episode before the Move
from Renting to Owning in the United States, 1970–1987

Length in Years	Percentage of Episodes with Known Start Year and a Move	
	Couple	Family
< 1	43.9	37.9
< 2	22.1	21.6
< 3	13.7	11.4
< 4	8.1	11.4
< 5	5.3	5.8
< 6	2.3	3.7
< 7	2.0	2.8
< 8	1.0	2.5
< 9	0.8	0.7
<10	0.5	0.9
<11	0.0	0.4
<12	0.0	0.4
<13	0.3	0.3
<14	0.0	0.1
No. of Episodes	394	708

Source: Clark et al., 1994. Reprinted from *Urban Studies*, vol. 31, by permission.

couples and families that make this move, it is likely to happen within three years after the couple or family status began (table 3.7). Almost 80 percent of the couples made this move within three years after becoming a couple, while approximately 71 percent of the family households made this transition within three years after starting their family.

The close link between moving, buying a house, and household expansion is further substantiated by analysis of the age period in which the move from renting to ownership is made (table 3.8). More than 50 percent of the moves occur between ages twenty-five and thirty-five; overall, approximately 80 percent of the shifts to ownership occur when the head of household is under thirty-five years of age. Of course, this is also the segment of the

TABLE 3.8

Episodes by Age Category for Couples and Family Households that
Moved from Renting to Owning in the United States, 1970–1987

		Proportion by Age Category at Time of Move				
	N	<25	25–34	35–44	45–54	55+
Couple	443	31.2	51.2	6.3	4.5	6.8
Family	924	20.6	56.1	18.6	3.8	1.0

Source: Clark et al., 1994. Reprinted from Urban Studies, vol. 31, by
permission.

life course when decisions are made about marriage and when to
have children.

The other side of the story is told by looking back from families who moved and became owners before they had children. Thus,
it is possible to examine the episodes of family households that
were couples previously for the timing of their eventual move to
owning a house. To reiterate, the distinction between the groups
is, of course, whether or not the household makes a move to ownership as a couple and later becomes a family unit, or whether the
couple transitions to family status from being a couple while renting and eventually moves into ownership in the family stage of the
life course. In this way, one is examining the interrelationship of
move and family status transition.

About 21 percent of couples in the Panel Study of Income Dynamics sample moved from renting to owning while they were
couples. Significantly, of the couples, 38.7 percent became family
households within two years of the move to ownership and over
60 percent within three years (fig. 3.16). One could suggest that
for those couples who moved and entered ownership, it appears
to be a previewing of the decision to have children. The decisions
to form a stable relationship as a couple and/or family and to move
into owner-occupation seem to be closely related. Probably both
are elements of one longer-term strategy of establishing stability
in the partnership, the housing situation, and the employment situation at that particular stage in the life course.

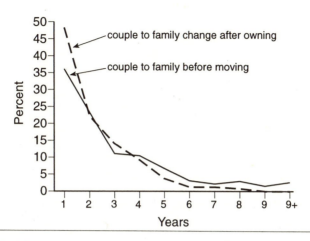

FIGURE 3.16
Timing of conditional moves to ownership, the United States

Source: Clark et al., 1994. Reprinted from *Urban Studies*, vol. 31, by permission.

Constraints on Moving

Thus far, there has been an examination of the mobility process and the changes and timing of the event in relationship to other life course events. There are, however, clear constraints on who can move, how frequently, and where they can move. Such constraints are determined by the family and income status of the household itself. As has been illustrated in this chapter, once a family has been established and a move into owner-occupation has been made, the propensity to move decreases. This situation exists at least partly because constraints on moving arise from the activity patterns of other members of the household and because so much income and resources are tied up in the house. Socio-economic position of the household can also act as a constraint on mobility. Employees can change jobs more readily than the self-employed; therefore, their residential mobility is also higher.

But constraints on moving also arise from more general economic circumstances and from opportunities or lack thereof in the local housing market. When economic and income prospects are low, mobility also tends to decrease. A slump in the market for owner-occupation and high interest rates for mortgages have been seen to discourage people from moving (Dieleman and Everaers 1994). A shortage of housing can also reduce mobility considerably. In the urbanized western part of the Netherlands (the Randstad), a shortage of housing has persisted for decades, while in the south and north of the country, the supply of housing has been relatively ample. This has dampened mobility in the Randstad as compared to elsewhere in the country. When the most important variables related to the frequency of moving are controlled for, large regional differences in the level of mobility become apparent in the rental sector. Lack of opportunities clearly limits choice, and, in chapters 4 and 5, this theme of discrepancies between preferences and opportunities will reemerge.

Summary

This chapter has focused on residential mobility—the process of moving from one location to another. At its heart is the assessment of the propensity to move, the likelihood that an individual or household will relocate at some point in the life course. Most individuals and households move short distances—within one city or even one part of a city—and this residential mobility is the process whereby people bring their needs and preferences into adjustment with their housing consumption. It is the mismatch of housing needs and the current characteristics of the housing, the amount of space, the number of rooms, and the disequilibrium between household size and space that is the driving force behind residential mobility.

Much residential mobility occurs between age twenty and thirty-five, when many other events in the life course, such as family formation and movement up the career ladder, take place. Mobility is more frequent for people with higher incomes and levels of education, and, of course, renters are far more likely to move than owners. Owners have much more tied capital, but they are also more likely to be older than renters.

The relationship between age and mobility has been integrated into the concept of the life cycle. As people move through various stages of the life cycle, from "nest leaving" to widowhood, they adjust their housing situation to their life-cycle stage. Thus, changes in the life cycle act as triggers for residential mobility. The initial move from the family home, and the formation of a new household, either in marriage or cohabitation, can be achieved only by making a residential move. The timing of a move from one dwelling to another is often synchronized with changes in the stage in the family life cycle, such as starting a family. At the same time, income levels, general economic circumstances such as a recession and poor job opportunities, and high interest rates or a shortage of housing units, restrain and/or discourage people from making a residential move.

4

Housing Choice and Housing Consumption

In the previous chapters, considerable effort was made to develop and explain the notion of the life course and the link between stages and events in the life cycle and *mobility* in the housing market. The discussion in chapter 2 made clear that it is not only the probability of moving that is related to the trajectory of the life course, but the types of housing choices are also linked to the progression of individuals and households through life. This link between the life course concept and behavior in the housing market is used as an organizing principle for this chapter on housing choice. Housing choice, like mobility in chapter 3, is mainly treated as actual behavior, or "revealed preference." In chapter 5, the emphasis will be on how housing preferences and revealed choice patterns are influenced by the economic and political context within which housing choices are made.

To link the concept of the life course to patterns of housing choice, it is necessary to introduce the notions of the housing career and the hierarchy of housing submarkets. The housing career employs the same metaphor as the occupational career. The metaphor suggests several steps as households seek to improve their housing over the life course. Utilizing the notions of the housing career, movement through the housing market can be seen as a progression from the parents' home to relatively simple, small, and inexpensive independent housing, which is followed in turn, when resources increase and family composition changes, by moves to larger and more expensive dwellings. The most critical step in this process is the move from renting to buying.

TABLE 4.1

Hierarchy of Nine Submarkets for the Netherlands

Submarkets (g = guilders)	Number of units (×1,000)
Rent, multifamily, < 3 rooms	622.6
Rent, multifamily, 4+ rooms	591.7
Rent, single family,< 3 rooms	197.5
Rent, single family, 4 rooms	645.6
Rent, single family, 5+ rooms	495.4
Own, ≤ 4 rooms, –g150,000	504.2
Own, ≤ 4 rooms, +g150,000	173.6
Own, 5+ rooms, –g150,000	362.3
Own, 5+ rooms, +g150,000	429.6
Total	4,022.5

Source: Hooimeijer et al., 1986. Reprinted from *Housing Studies*, vol. 1, by permission of Carfax Publishing Company, Oxfordshire, England.

In a sense, a housing hierarchy is being postulated—a series of "relatively" discrete housing submarkets. These submarkets are constructed on the basis of the most important aspects of housing choice, such as tenure, size, type, and price of dwellings. For instance, in the Netherlands, a hierarchy of nine submarkets—from multifamily rental to private ownership—was developed (table 4.1). The rate of turnover lends some credibility to the notion of the hierarchy of housing submarkets. Small, multifamily rental dwellings have high rates of turnover, because they are low on the continuum of household preferences. They are most often the initial "starter" unit for new households. At the upper end of the hierarchy, turnover is much lower, because these dwellings are closer to the long-term preferences and needs of households.

The housing career is clearly linked to the life course of households and the expansion and later reduction in household size (fig. 4.1). Households in the expansion stage (married, pre-childrearing) are increasing their space and the cost and size of the dwelling. An upward move in the figure is defined as a move up the hierarchy of dwelling types. A lateral move is a move within the same

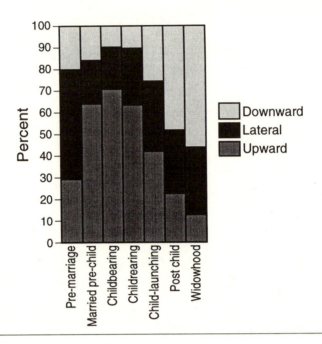

FIGURE 4.1
The relationship of filtering (moving through the housing stock) and the stage in the life cycle in the Netherlands

Source: Hooimeijer et al., 1986. Redrawn from *Housing Studies*, vol. 1, by permission of Carfax Publishing Co., Oxfordshire, England.

type of housing, and a downward move is down this hierarchy of dwellings. From the child-launching stage on, many households start to downsize their housing consumption in terms of housing costs and space, although mobility is low in these stages of the life cycle. In a sense, households move up the hierarchy of submarkets more quickly than they reduce their housing consumption.

The focus on the link between the life course and the move between housing types extends the discussion of the role of changes in household structure in creating mobility responses and actual housing choices. Although the relationship between the life cycle and the patterns of housing choice is far from direct, it can serve as a general and overarching structure for the discussion of housing choice in this chapter. Housing choice, from the initial move from the parental home, until the last departure from the housing market, will be discussed in a sequence that parallels the way in which the housing career develops over the life course.

Tenure change is among the most important events in the life course of individuals. Although it is an individual or household decision, it has ramifications well beyond the household itself. For the household, the move is related to greater stability and lower probabilities of moving after the move; it also has implications for the probability of increases in assets and about location within the metropolitan area. Numerous studies across fairly divergent national and cultural contexts point out that homeownership, which involves greater security, not to mention possible capital gains and subsidies, is the eventual goal in the United States, Australia, the Netherlands, and other European nations. For society, the shift to owning has implications for political participation and political affiliation and, consequently, for the way in which society as a whole changes over time.

To reiterate, this substantive chapter has been organized to parallel the actions that occur in the housing market (fig. 4.2). It proceeds from a discussion of initial entry into the housing market to correlates and patterns of housing choice for those already in the housing market. This is followed by a discussion of the process of tenure change, which is the move from renting to owning and the major focus of most economic analyses. Renters and owners of housing are treated consistently as separate groups of households making housing choice decisions, and entry into homeownership and moving from owning to renting are treated as separate processes that are related to quite different events in the life course. The last two major sections of the chapter examine reversing the process, the moves from owning to renting, and the nature of moves "down the hierarchy."

Initial Housing Market Entry

The first contact with the housing market comes when young adults leave home. This move is a major step in the transition to adulthood, and the move into the housing market is often associated with setting up a household and the creation of an independent

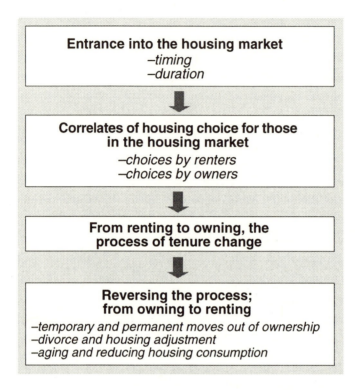

FIGURE 4.2
The housing choice sequence

lifestyle (Goldscheider and Da Vanzo 1985). The majority of nest leavers do so either to get married or to live with a partner (co-habit) without marriage, while another large group of movers who leave the parental home do so to pursue higher education. It is a critical moment in the life of children who depart from the paren-tal home. It involves changes for both the individual leaving home and for the family being left behind (Lelievre and Bonvalet 1994). When the last child leaves the parental home, the parents enter the empty-nest stage, a period of extremely low mobility for the aging parents.

As Lelievre and Bonvalet (1994) emphasize, leaving home is often a process rather than a clear-cut event. Leaving the parental home does not necessarily correspond with settling into an independent dwelling. Children are prone to return "home" for longer or shorter periods, and sometimes for several years, following a job loss or marital disruption. The length of this process is also influenced by the financial independence of the young adults. It is further affected by the housing market circumstances at the time when they enter, or attempt to enter, the market, which, in turn, influences the ease or difficulty of establishing independent living arrangements in the housing market.

Young adults who move into independent living arrangements for the first time, "starters" in housing market terminology, are an important element of the total mobility process. For the Netherlands, in the period 1978 to 1989, they accounted for more than 42 percent of all moves in that year (Everaers and Davies 1993). The contribution of starter mobility to all moves is often overlooked in the mobility and housing choice literature, which focuses primarily on households that are "in" the housing market. Of course, the importance of starters in the mobility process varies with the country and region, and is quite dependent on the age structure of the population and patterns of migration between housing markets for the young adult population.

The importance of the process of leaving the parental home as a general contributor to overall mobility rates is even greater, if one includes those moves that have been described as semiautonomous housing market entrance: moves to dormitories, residential rooms, and so forth (table 4.2). Nearly one-third of all the nest leavers in the Netherlands move into such semiautonomous housing, and almost half (46 percent) of those that leave the parental home to live alone also move to semiautonomous housing. For those who move into their own dwelling, the rental sector is by far the most common choice, and usually at the lowest end of the market (Linde, Dieleman, and Clark 1986).

The housing choice of starters, however, varies with age, household position, and the presence or absence of a job and the associated income. Of those who leave the parental home to get married, a large group buy houses (table 4.2) and, if there are two income earners, this percentage increases to over 50 percent. This finding alone indicates the importance of analyzing choice patterns in more detail and connecting those choices back to the life course trajectory, the housing career, and the housing hierarchy. The

TABLE 4.2

Initial Household Position and Initial Tenure of Nest-Leavers
(cohort 1985), the Netherlands

	Initial Tenure (%)					
Initial Position	Rent	Own	Other	>1 Move	Total	%
Alone	39.6	8.0	46.5	6.0	536	6.3
Married	47.5	43.7	7.9	—	313	7.3
Cohabit	63.4	19.0	15.4	2.3	306	6.4
Total	48.0	20.6	27.7	3.6	1,155	100

Source: Mulder and Manting, 1994. Reprinted from *European Sociological Review*, vol. 10, by permission of Oxford University Press.

relationships are considerably more complicated than suggested by an initial glance at figure 4.1.

As noted earlier, the initial entrance into the housing market is a process rather than an event. First exits begin at about age seventeen in the United States and are driven by the very large attendance at two- and four-year colleges. The "exit rate" rises rapidly to almost 0.5 by age eighteen and declines thereafter, with a secondary peak at about age twenty-two (fig. 4.3a). The earliest leavers enter the semiautonomous housing market: relatives, group housing (college dormitories), and living with housemates (Goldscheider et al. 1993). In the United States, more than one-third live in group quarters when they make their first move and, in combination with living with housemates, the proportion rises to over 50 percent of all first moves. As the time away from the parental home increases, the choice of group quarters and housemates reverses with the latter becoming the larger proportion. Almost 60 percent of those with some experience living away from home were living with housemates, either in marriage or cohabitation.

The nest-leaving process and the entry into the housing market is complicated by the "interactive" nature of the nest-leaving process. Some leave for very short periods before returning home. About 20 percent of all young adults under twenty-three in the United States reported that their period away from home was less

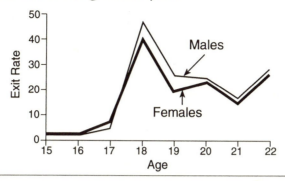

FIGURE 4.3a
Age and gender rates of exit from the parental home per 1,000 for those
staying away more than four months

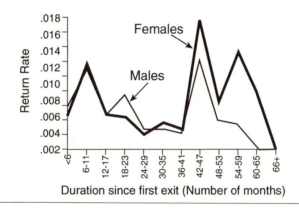

FIGURE 4.3b
Rate of returning home by duration away (four or more months) and
gender

Source: Goldscheider et al., 1993. Redrawn from *Demography*, vol. 30, by permission.

than four months (fig. 4.3b). The largest return spike is after the
four years of college. However, this return is generally followed relatively rapidly by a second exit, often within the first year, and 75
percent within two years. Thus, by the mid-to-late twenties, most
young adults are in the housing market. The timing and rates of
return are related to both changing economic conditions and to
the changing patterns of age at marriage and family formation.

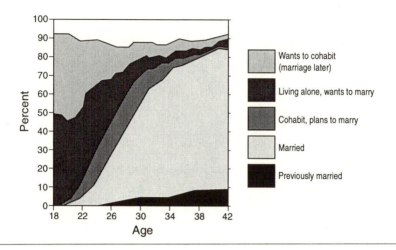

FIGURE 4.4
Plans for future living arrangements of men, the Netherlands

Source: Latten and Cuypers, 1994. Adapted from *DEMOS*, vol. 10, by permission of Netherlands Interdisciplinary Demographic Institute.

Once again, the life course assumes a critical role in mobility and housing market interaction, as can be seen in figure 4.4. There are dramatic changes in the choices of starter households. By age thirty, couples entering the housing market in the Netherlands are either married or cohabiting.

Patterns and Correlates of Housing Choice

Subsequent moves within the housing market of those who have already made the initial entry are clearly related to income, but there are important additional variables that influence the rapidity and succession of movements in the housing career. Age, size of household, marital status, and presence of children are all important variables. In addition, characteristics of the previous dwelling play a role. The rent or value of the previous dwelling is a context within which choices will be made, as are the size and the physical space of the previous dwelling. These factors influence the bundle of housing attributes the household will seek in a new dwelling: whether it will choose, indeed can choose, to rent or own, and for how much space it will settle. They also determine the decision of whether to choose multifamily or single-family housing and, to a lesser extent, the location of the housing. Thus, one can define dwelling choice categories by rental cost, house value, size of the structures in which the units are located, and the number of rooms in the units.

The extensive literature on tenure choice and housing consumption contains several hundred references. However, as noted in chapter 1, this literature is quite divided between the research contributions of urban and housing economists, who have emphasized the consumption aspects of tenure and housing choice, and the contributions of demographers, geographers, and urban planners, who emphasize the demographic context of housing and tenure choices. Generally, these two literatures do not cross-reference each other, although the models, the concepts, the variables, and even the ideas are often very similar.

Findings on Housing Consumption and Investment

Housing economists have stressed the importance of ownership, not merely as a consumption decision by households as they progress through different household stages, but also as an investment decision. As examined by economists, the process of housing and tenure choice has emphasized choice as part of a competitive process in which imperfections in the housing market are ignored, and the housing market acts as a competitive market because it has a large number of buyers and sellers. This approach gives income a central role in housing choice and, specifically, in house purchase. Dynarski (1985, 1986) and Plaut (1987) report that older (wealthier) families in disequilibrium are consuming more housing than their counterparts in equilibrium, that young movers consume less housing than young nonmovers and have higher income elasticities than nonmovers. Haurin and Gill (1987) report that uncertainty about income reduces demand for ownership. In a theoretical paper, Plaut (1987) focuses not only on the consumption issue but also on the timing of tenure changes. He concludes that the timing of changes will reflect both consumption and financial (investment) considerations. Major contributions by Henderson and Ioannides (1983, 1985, 1987, 1989) set out a series of important findings on housing and tenure choice. They confirm that, as wealth increases, the probability of homeownership increases. Whereas age increases the likelihood of owning, and asset values are important with respect to consumption, they do not influence the tenure choice directly but via their general influence on consumption. Economists, however, are not unaware of the potential benefit from considering both demographic and economic variables in the housing consumption decision. Henderson and Ioannides (1983) suggest a model that outlines a way for evaluating the dual role of housing as a consumption and an investment good, and follow this with behavioral models that integrate family characteristics, wealth, price, and expenditure measures in their equations to explain tenure decisions (Henderson and Ioannides 1987). They show that consumption rises with age, education, race (white), and family size (for renters).

A common way of measuring the demand for housing is by means of the concept of elasticities of demand. Income elasticity of the demand for housing, for example, measures the change in demand for housing with a unit change in the level of real income. The income elasticity of demand ranges in various studies from 0.89 to 1.46, which suggests that income elasticity for housing is at least unity and may even be slightly higher (Glennon 1989). This means that households are willing to devote a relatively large portion of extra income to buy more housing, and/or more quality of housing. From their structural and reduced form equations, they conclude that, for both renters and owners, the demand for housing is quite wealth inelastic (the demand is there whatever the income level). These results confirm other cross-sectional results that housing demand is income inelastic and price inelastic, and that younger people with lower education and lower current income face an increased probability of being denied a mortgage (Henderson and Ioannides 1987).

Findings from Demographic Analyses of Housing and Tenure Choice

While economists have emphasized the role of economic variables in housing choice and in the shift from renting to owning, it has been an article of faith among geographers, demographers, planners, and sociologists that the step from renting to owning is much more than a simple decision of investment or consumption, and that it is directly linked to positions and change in the family life cycle—the stage at which the household is in the aging–having children continuum. Demographers, planners, and geographers have been concerned with teasing out the complexity of the inter-relationship of housing and tenure choices and family composition. Morrow-Jones (1988) emphasizes the strong effects of the life cycle to the extent of arguing that affordability may not be so critical. Indeed, she reports that the desire to own is not diminished by the high cost of housing, and she reiterates an oft-cited finding that housing has shelter as well as investment roles to play in society. Davies and Pickles (1991) have suggested a competing risk model of household transitions through the housing career. They conclude that households (in a British study) do not appear to move to maximize capital gains, but such gains as are made are incidental to the moving process.

Two other important findings emerge from the demographic studies of tenure. First, Myers (1985) has established the link between two-income families and the increased number of women in the work force to divisions in the housing market. His specific evidence on first-time buyers shows increasingly delayed childbearing and continued full-time employment in order to enter the owner market. Second, Rudel (1987) shows there are links between income, inflation and rising interest rates, and homeownership—wealthy young couples without children were more likely to own than less wealthy couples with children. These findings highlight the notion of the way in which the decision making by households is embedded in both family composition and societal changes. The paths of individual households through the housing stock are influenced by broader social changes as well as life transitions and local housing markets.

Housing Choices

The next two sections will illustrate how actual choices by households that are already in the market as independent actors are linked to household characteristics as well as their previous housing situation before they decided to move. This presentation generates a more detailed picture of the "behavioral" choices of individual households, and the interplay between household composition on the one hand and housing type on the other, than would be possible by measuring elasticities alone. This is accomplished by exploring the way in which the interrelationships between income constraints and demographic variables affect tenure and housing type choices. This approach appears to be complementary to economic models of housing demand and is an approach that provides a more nuanced picture of choices and outcomes in the housing market.

Consumer choice is still the selection of a single dwelling from "a large number of alternatives indexed by their characteristics and prices" (Quigley 1983, 125). Thus, the choice is usually defined as the selection of one housing type from among the alternatives in a defined set, and a large part of the detailed presentation will examine the joint choice of tenure and housing type.

The structure of this analysis and presentation is built around a series of research methods that link households and housing consumption. First, a statistical technique is used to identify the important variables in the choice process for different households. It is a step-by-step procedure, chi-squared automatic interaction detection (CHAID), in which the most important characteristics of households are selected in order and related to their choice patterns. Then, a technique called ANOTA (the analysis of tables), somewhat akin to regression analysis, is used to develop a simple model of the combined effects of household characteristics and previous housing situation on dwelling choice. These techniques are explained formally in the appendix.

This study is concerned with tenure and housing-type choice given that a move occurs. It is not concerned with tenure choice per se, but rather with a choice of a housing bundle that includes tenure. It is logical in such a situation to argue that present income, present marital status, and so on might be expected to influence the choice among alternatives. It is to be expected that income will play a major role in determining housing choice for both renters and owners. There are, however, also distinct differences in the groups and their housing market position, which suggests that it is better to treat the groups separately. In the first place, many households in the rental sector, before they move to another house, are one- or two-person households, while owners are predominantly two-person households and families. Second, many owners have built up equity in their house, which will have an effect on their choice patterns for subsequent dwellings. And, third, in both the United States and the Netherlands, the previous tenure position largely determines the tenure of the next dwelling. The large majority of renters remain renters, and owners remain owners. Thus, although there are important transitions between rentership and ownership, the markets also have a very separate structure and composition.

Choices by Renters

Overall, more than 80 percent of all renters in the U.S. market remain in the rental sector. The proportion is lower among Dutch public renters (those in the subsidized sector of the rental market) and private renters who stay in the rental market. About 70 percent move in the rental sector, and about 30 percent make the shift to ownership. The destination choices for renters are designed to reflect the fact that considerably more moves occur within the rental sector than from rent to own. Other important elements of the "bundle of housing attributes" for renters in the choice set are type of housing, price, and size of unit. For the Netherlands, more rental units are constructed as single-family row houses than in the United States, and because there are more moves to ownership in the United States, two choices in the ownership category are introduced into the U.S. choice set.

Income is selected as the most critical variable. It is the variable that accounts for the greatest variation in choices across the six types of housing in the choice set. Even more significant is the fact that income is the most important variable in explaining the distribution of housing choices of both U.S. and Dutch renters (figs. 4.5, 4.6, 4.7). Lower-income households move within the rental

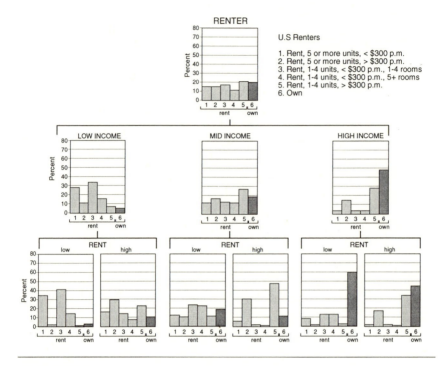

FIGURE 4.5

Choices by renters in the U.S. housing market

Source: Constructed from data in Clark et al., 1990.

housing sector, and the lower the income the greater the probability that the move will be to a lower-rent unit, and into a multiunit structure in the Dutch case. All but 5 percent of the low-income households move within the rental stock. Of households with incomes in the middle range, the proportion of those moving from rental to owner housing increases to almost 20 percent in any one move. For the highest-income households, the proportion of those moving into the owner sector increases to almost 50 percent in any one move. In this presentation not all the details of the actual table have been reproduced in graphic form. The intent is to demonstrate the fundamental differences in the choices of low-, middle-, and high-income groups. The technique actually produces greater richness in the income effects breakdown that is shown in an example in the appendix.

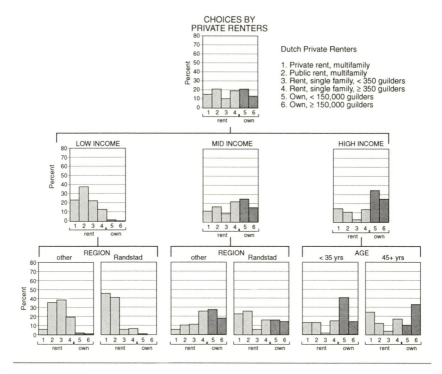

FIGURE 4.6

Choices by private renters in the Dutch housing market

Source: Constructed from data in Deurloo et al., 1987.

For renters in the Dutch housing market, the results are not quite comparable, although again income plays the principal role. In the Dutch housing context, renters are divided into those in the private market and those in the social subsidized sector of the market (actually the larger group). Even so, the pattern of higher income households moving from renting to owning is consistent in the Dutch housing market as it is in the U.S. market (fig. 4.7). The private renters are closest to the rental market in the United States. For private and public renters, a great many of the higher-income households purchase a house, and the low-income households, by contrast, move within the rental sector. The choice patterns from low income to high income are especially clear in the Dutch private renter sector. The higher the income, the greater the movement to expensive, owned units.

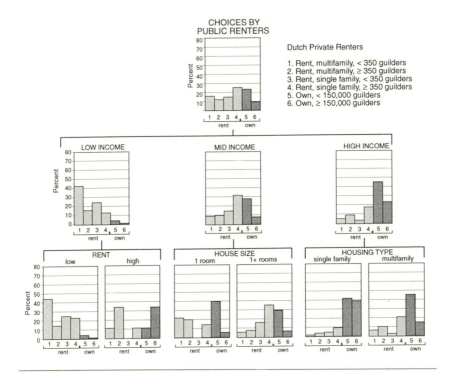

FIGURE 4.7
Choices by public housing renters in the Dutch housing market

Source: Constructed fom data in Deurloo et al., 1987.

The second-level variables differ considerably, especially for public renters, across markets and by type of renter. The second-level variables, which distinguish among the six choice classes, are the attributes of households and previous dwelling. Note, however, that the distinctions are between the choice sets within each of the three income categories. For U.S. renters, following income, the rent of the previous dwelling is the most important second variable. The contrast is between those who are already paying higher rents against those with low rents. Even for low-income households, those already paying higher rents are likely to move up to ownership, and this tendency increases with income level. For Dutch private renters, the distinction at the second level is whether or not the renting household is in the Randstad (Amsterdam, Utrecht,

Rotterdam, and The Hague). For private renters in the lowest income group, there are large differences between the Randstad and the rest of the country. In the Randstad, the greatest proportion of moves is toward a multifamily rented house (87 percent for private renters, 82 percent for public renters). Outside the Randstad, a sizable group can obtain a low-rent, single-family house, especially families that are eligible for such houses in the public sector. Thus, metropolitan, rather than peripheral, location is the defining variable for the choice of renting or owning for two of the income groups. The reason is that the rental housing stock in the metropolitan part of the country is so different from the rest of the Netherlands. Therefore, the geographical context in which the choices are made is central to a complete understanding of the choice decisions which will be discussed in chapter 5.

The movement from the rental sector to the owner-occupied sector is much larger for the next income group, especially for families with a young head of household; older households are more likely to stay in the rental sector. In addition, there is a significant proportion of moves toward more expensive, rented, single-family housing. Households moving from the private-rental sector in the Randstad, however, are less able to "trade up" and they often remain in the less-desired multifamily housing. High-income movers from the rental sector, not unexpectedly, prefer to shift into the ownership sector, especially if they leave single-family housing in the public-rented sector. Age is clearly another important factor, however. Older households are much more likely to remain in the rental sector. Regional differences in the structure of the housing market do not appreciably influence the choices of this income group. For the highest income group, age is the defining variable for choices of type of rent and entry into homeownership. For public renters, rent, age, space, and type of house all play a role—and differentially for varying income groups.

This study does not illustrate a third-level variable selection, but the technique does utilize additional variables to further distinguish the choices within renting and owning. Where a third-level variable emerges to distinguish groups, it is age and space in the case of private renters, and region, household size, and type of house for public renters. The additional variables indicate that public renters, younger households, and smaller households move up to ownership but older households do not (the age effect). House-holds in the Randstad are more constrained in their moves to own-ership (the regional effect). Clearly, at the third level, the variabil-ity of individual circumstances intersecting with the housing market is beginning to play an important role.

In sum, income is the critical enabling/constraining variable for all renter households that move, both in the United States and in the Netherlands, although the housing markets are structured quite differently. The pervasiveness of income effects is repeated in both the public and private rented markets in the Netherlands. The life-cycle variables, such as age and household size (and the related variable, number of rooms), enrich our understanding of the choice patterns. The choices of one-person households and older heads of households are quite different from the choices of larger and younger families. In the public-rental sector in the Neth-erlands, the patterns of choice are influenced by various govern-ment rules governing entry into, and movement within, the pub-lic-rental sector, which are certainly a factor in these more diffuse patterns.

Thus far, choices have been examined variable by variable, and the results indicate how income and life cycle variables play out their role in choices. It is now time to consider the effects of a com-bination of the variables on the choices within the choice set. How does the combination of attributes of a household and its current housing situation influence its selection of housing types when moving? In this sense, the study parallels the structure of chapter 2 where it first examined correlates (of mobility) and then the com-bined effect of the correlates via a regression model.

At this stage, the study introduces its second technical ele-ment—the categorical technique, ANOTA (appendix)—which per-mits examination of the links between "bundles of household at-tributes" and bundles of housing attributes. Coefficients from the ANOTA analysis demonstrate the relative role of a particular cat-egory of a household's attributes to the selection of a particular choice category. The coefficients can be interpreted as partial re-gression coefficients, showing the "effect" of membership in a par-ticular category on the likelihood of a particular choice. As coeffi-cients are corrected for possible interactions of other household attributes they can, literally, be added together to show the com-

TABLE 4.3

Coefficients for Dwelling Choices of (Previous) Renters in the United States (ANOTA Analysis)

Destination	Average	*Income (×1,000)*				
		< $5	*$5–14*	*$15–19*	*$20–29*	*≥$30*
1	15.6	10.8	4.1	–3.2	–6.8	–8.1
2	15.1	–2.0	1.4	1.9	2.1	–4.6
3	17.5	9.8	4.6	–3.0	–6.5	–8.6
4	11.5	2.3	3.6	0.1	–2.5	–6.6
5	20.7	–5.3	–1.3	5.4	4.0	–1.1
6	19.6	–15.5	–12.4	–1.2	9.8	29.0

Destination	Average	*Rent Previous Dwelling*			
		<$200	*$200– $299*	*$300– $399*	*≥$400*
1	15.6	0.3	5.0	–1.8	–6.6
2	15.1	–11.5	–4.2	7.4	12.9
3	17.5	15.5	–0.0	–7.1	–11.2
4	11.5	7.6	2.5	–5.5	–8.0
5	20.7	–14.9	–2.1	8.5	16.9
6	19.6	3.0	–1.2	–1.6	–4.0

Destination	Average	*Size of Household*			
		1 person	*2 person*	*3 person*	*4 or more person*
1	15.6	13.1	–1.6	–4.2	–8.0
2	15.1	7.0	3.3	–3.3	–8.7
3	17.5	2.5	2.8	0.7	–6.8
4	11.5	–8.2	–2.0	2.5	9.0
5	20.7	–10.7	–2.4	3.3	11.3
6	19.6	–3.6	–0.1	0.9	3.1

Destination
1. Rent, 5 or more Units, <$300
2. Rent, 5 or more Units, >$300
3. Rent, 1–4 Units, <$300, 1–4 Rooms
4. Rent, 1–4 Units, <$300, 5 or more Rooms
5. Rent, 1–4 Units, >$300
6. Own

Source: Dieleman et al., 1989. Reprinted from *Urban Studies*, vol. 26, by permission.

bined influence of attributes of a household on choice. For example, in table 4.3, households with an income of less than five thousand dollars have an estimated chance of selecting multifamily rental of 10.8 percent above the mean. Thus, 15.6 plus 10.8, or 24.4 percent of such households will select low-income rental housing. If they are also a one-person household, the percentage is increased by 13.1 percent to 37.5 percent, and, if they lived in inexpensive rental housing before moving, it increases to 42.5 percent. In probability terms, they have almost a one in two chance of choosing this household type. The estimated probability that such households will choose ownership is close to zero (all the signs for such households for the category ownership are negative).

It is possible to generalize the rich detail of table 4.3 into a graph of housing choices by households (fig. 4.8). In the graphs, contrasting households and their choices are portrayed. They show likely choices for different groups of households and, by implication, of unlikely choices for these same households. The patterns are striking in their contrasts. The lowest-income groups already in the low-end rental stock have a very high propensity to remain in low-end rental housing (choices 1, 2, and 3). These households are highly unlikely to move up on the housing career ladder. Middle- and high-income households, however, do improve their housing situation when they relocate. The likelihood that they remain in the low-rent segment is negligible. Often such households are already in higher-priced, better-quality rental or ownership dwellings and are able to translate this into further advances up the housing career ladder. The rental sector in the United States is clearly segmented between lower- and high-priced units and sectors. When households move, they tend to remain in the high-priced segment, or are unable to escape the lower-priced choices. There is also a very clear tendency for larger households to move into more spacious dwellings—a finding that is consistent with our findings on mobility in chapter 3.

For the Netherlands, the patterns of choice for renters in the public sector is much more diffuse (table 4.4) Even so, the results are still consistent with our theoretical expectations and offer additional detail to what is already known about the determinants of housing choice. Income is still the dominant explanatory factor. Region and type of house play a much less important role. A

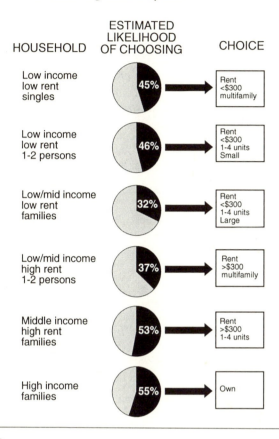

FIGURE 4.8
The relationship of renter choices and household types in the U.S. housing market

significant number of households in the highest income category move to ownership. The probability of doing so for this group increases by as much as 32.9 percent (the sum of categories 5 and 6 in table 4.4). The lowest-income households often move to multifamily, private rental units. Older (≥ 45 years) public-rental householders avoid the owner-occupier sector and usually move to multifamily, private renting. Younger householders, by contrast, enter the owner-occupier sector, mainly the less expensive sector of the ownership sector. This reflects the life-cycle changes of households in the early middle years (additions of children and increasing

TABLE 4.4

Coefficients for Choices from ANOTA Analysis of Public Renters
in the Netherlands

Choice Category	Average	Income (000s guilders)				Region	
		<20	20–29	30–41	≥42	Suburbs	Randstad
1	16.4	22.4	4.9	–7.5	–10.8	–3.1	7.3
2	11.0	1.6	1.6	–0.8	–2.6	–1.8	4.3
3	15.9	6.1	5.3	–0.2	–11.3	2.6	–6.2
4	25.0	–11.4	4.2	7.0	–8.3	1.0	–2.4
5	22.0	–11.5	–8.7	4.5	20.9	2.1	–5.0
6	9.7	–7.1	–7.2	–3.0	12.0	–0.8	1.9

Choice Category	Age			Type of House	
	<35 yrs.	35–44 yrs.	≥45	Single-family	Multifamily
1	–3.3	–3.6	7.7	–5.0	3.0
2	–2.5	–2.1	–5.3	–3.3	2.0
3	–2.6	0.4	3.6	3.3	–2.0
4	0.0	1.4	–1.2	–2.9	1.8
5	7.4	0.7	–11.6	1.7	–1.1
6	0.9	3.2	–3.8	6.1	–3.7

Choice categories:
1. Rent, multifamily, < 350 guilders
2. Rent, multifamily, ≥ 350 guilders
3. Rent, single family, < 350 guilders
4. Rent, single family, ≥ 350 guilders
5. Own, < 150,000 guilders
6. Own, ≥ 150,000 guilders

Source: Deurloo et al., 1987. Reprinted from *Environment and Planning A*,
vol. 19, by permission.

income). The type of the former house is influential in the sense
that those households that leave a single-family dwelling more often buy another house, whereas households that leave a flat/apart-
ment more often enter another flat/apartment (private rental). The
regional variable indicates that within the Randstad, destinations

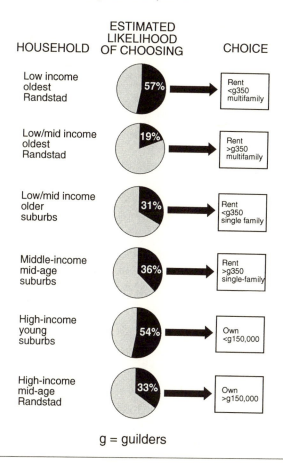

ESTIMATED
LIKELIHOOD
HOUSEHOLD OF CHOOSING

CHOICE

Low income
oldest
Randstad

57%

Rent
<g350
multifamily

Low/mid income
oldest
Randstad

19%

Rent
>g350
multifamily

Low/mid income
older
suburbs

31%

Rent
<g350
single family

Middle-income
mid-age
suburbs

36%

Rent
>g350
single-family

High-income
young
suburbs

54%

Own
<g150,000

High-income
mid-age
Randstad

33%

Own
>g150,000

g = guilders

FIGURE 4.9
The relationship of public-renter choices and household types in the
Dutch housing market

are often to multifamily (private) rental units, as opposed to single-
family destinations outside the Randstad. Moves from the public-
rental sector to multifamily private renting—moves that can be
considered to be downgrading moves—occur for an average of 16.4
percent of the households with incomes less than twenty thousand
Dutch guilders (about twelve thousand dollars in 1990) and who
are over forty-five years of age.

The generalization of the specific results (fig. 4.9) shows that
low-income households move within the inexpensive multifamily

housing sector (choice 1), especially if they are older. Middle- and higher-income families avoid this type of housing. At the same time, the more expensive rental housing and less expensive single-family housing (choices 2 and 3) have a much more mixed pattern of selection. More expensive rental single-family homes in the public sector are the domain of middle-income groups. Low-income groups cannot afford these dwellings and high-income groups have other alternatives available to them. In addition, the allocation rules for housing constrain the choices in the Dutch rental housing market. Proportionally, there is actually a greater movement from the rental to the owner sector in the Netherlands than in the United States, although it is the higher-income groups that make this move. The large public rental stock, 40 percent of all houses, serves a wide range of Dutch households. Both allocation rules—which determine which households can select particular kinds of housing—and housing subsidies for lower-income households affect the choice processes.

Choices by Owners

Owners move relatively infrequently (chapter 3), and only about half of all owners in the United States who do so move within the homeownership sector (fig. 4.10). That this proportion should not be any greater is interesting. In fact, about the same percentage of owners move to renting and, not infrequently, to the less expensive segments of the ownership stock (fig. 4.10). Significantly, a larger proportion of owners move within the ownership sector in the Netherlands than in the United States. Over 60 percent of all moves by owners in the Dutch housing market are ownership to ownership moves. Additionally, in the public and private rental sectors, approximately 30 percent of the moves are up the scale to ownership. In the Netherlands, more moves in the rental sector and in ownership seem to be upward moves, while in the United States moves in the rental sector are more frequently lateral, and in ownership they are frequently moves down the housing hierarchy. There is little doubt that ownership is an attractive destination both for those already in ownership and those who attain upward mobility in Western societies. However, that somewhere

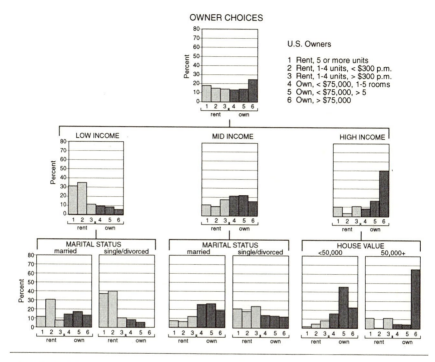

FIGURE 4.10

Choices by owners in the U.S. housing market

Source: Constructed from data in Clark et al., 1990.

between 40 percent and 50 percent of movers do not access, or are unable to access, ownership, is notable in developed economies where ownership is such a central element of the process of upward mobility. It is this finding that emphasizes the importance of decomposing the choice process of owners.

For owners, as for renters, income is the most critical variable in distinguishing among the six housing choice categories (fig. 4.10). The differences between low-, middle-, and high-income owners (defined in this analysis as incomes < twenty thousand dollars, twenty thousand to thirty thousand dollars, and thirty thousand dollars and above) reveal the constraining/enabling effect of different incomes. The majority of low-income owners move "down" the market into inexpensive rental housing. The majority of the group between twenty thousand dollars and thirty thousand

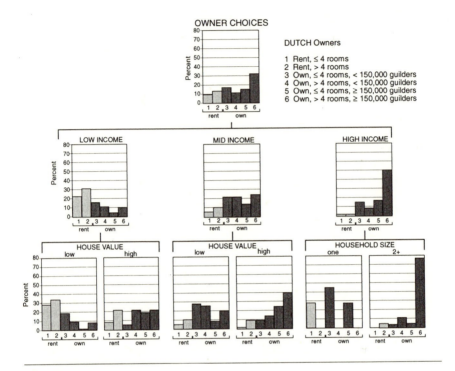

FIGURE 4.11
Choices by owners in the Dutch housing market

Source: Constructed from data in Deurloo et al., 1987.

dollars remain in the owner-occupation sector but move into less expensive owner housing or more expensive rental housing. Higher-income earners usually move into more expensive and larger owner units. Similarly for Dutch owners, a very high percentage of the lowest income owner-occupiers who do move, change from the owner-occupier sector to a rental house (fig. 4.11). In fact, 56 percent move "down" market, whereas the mean for all movers is 22 percent. Only middle-income households and high-income households can afford to stay in the homeowner market. In addition, those who have been able to build up capital and now have a valuable house are able to stay in the owner sector, as will become evident at the second level of analysis.

The second-level variables are marital status, size of household, and value of the previous dwelling. Clearly, these are just the variables which one would expect to play a defining role in the choices of households and owners in particular. Marital status is important for low-income and middle-income owners, and "value of previous dwelling" for higher-income owners in the United States (fig. 4.10). There is a big difference across marital status for owners in the U.S. data, where single persons are more likely to leave the owner market. For many mobile owners in the lower- to middle-income ranges, the reason to move seems to be related to household events, which, in turn, create the need to return to rental housing. For high incomes, the critical variable, actually another variant of the income constraint, is the value of the previous dwelling. More expensive previous homes dramatically increase the probability of staying in the owner market and making an upward move. Price of the previous dwelling is a defining variable for low- and middle-income households in the Dutch data as well (fig. 4.11). It is household size, however, that determines the likelihood of staying in the ownership sector for single-person, high-income households.

The value of this stepped or nested approach to household choice is contained in the important outcome that different variables play roles at different levels. As expected, income is clearly the dominant attribute of the household choice process in the housing market. Within the various income groups, however, other, frequently different, variables play an important role in the choices that households make. This is often lost in simple regression models that deal with a linear set of variables, where the independent variables are evaluated equally for their effects on outcomes of staying in the homeowner market, and that do not always focus on the relative strengths of the variables at different levels. The approach thus far enriches the way in which different variables act for different levels of income.

As for renters, it is useful to consider in greater detail how the bundles of household attributes are related to the housing choices of owners who move (tables 4.5, 4.6). The specific coefficients are aggregated to provide a generalized picture of who is choosing which kind of housing (figs. 4.12, 4.13). The results are clear, concise, and straightforward. It could almost be said that they do not require elaboration. Owner households in the United States behave in a manner completely consistent with a significant income con-

TABLE 4.5

Coefficients for Dwelling Choices of (Previous)
Owners in the United States (ANOTA Analysis)

| Destination | Average | Income (×1,000) | | |
		< $20	$20–29	≥$30
1	18.4	6.9	–4.8	–5.1
2	15.9	10.9	–6.4	–8.7
3	13.6	0.3	4.6	–2.9
4	12.8	0.6	7.8	–5.0
5	14.4	–5.2	5.8	2.6
6	24.9	–13.7	–7.0	19.1

| Destination | Average | Value previous dwelling (×1,000) | |
		< $50	≥$50
1	18.4	–7.0	2.2
2	15.9	5.0	–6.5
3	13.6	–5.4	3.3
4	12.8	7.5	–3.9
5	14.4	13.0	–6.8
6	24.9	–13.0	11.5

| Destination | Average | Size of household | |
		1 person	2 or more persons
1	18.4	21.7	–6.7
2	15.9	2.5	–0.8
3	13.6	–3.5	1.1
4	12.8	–2.1	0.7
5	14.4	–6.1	1.9
6	24.9	–12.4	3.9

| Destination | Average | Marital status | |
		married	not married
1	18.4	–8.9	12.9
2	15.9	–2.8	4.0
3	13.6	–1.8	2.7
4	12.8	3.2	–4.6
5	14.4	4.6	–6.7
6	24.9	5.7	–8.3

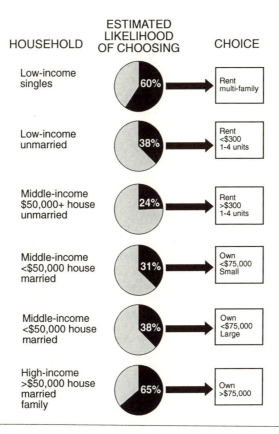

FIGURE 4.12
The relationship of U.S. owner choices and household types in the U.S. housing market

---

TABLE 4.5 (notes)

Destination
1. Rent, 5 or more units
2. Rent, 1–4 units, <$300
3. Rent, 1–4 units, >$300
4. Own, < $75,000, 1–5 rooms
5. Own, < $75,000, 6+ rooms
6. Own, > $75,000

Source: Dieleman et al., 1989. Reprinted from *Urban Studies*, vol. 26, by permission.

TABLE 4.6

Coefficients for Dwelling Choices of (Previous) Owners
in the Netherlands (ANOTA Analysis)

Destination	Average	Income (000s guilders)			
		< 20	20–29	30–42	42+
1	9.2	8.9	3.9	–2.5	–3.8
2	13.2	18.1	9.6	–1.6	–8.3
3	17.5	–5.0	8.7	4.0	0.3
4	11.7	1.9	–0.7	9.3	–2.7
5	15.0	–10.1	–4.2	–1.3	1.5
6	33.3	–13.8	17.4	–7.9	13.1

Destination	Average	House price	
		< 150,000 g.	≥ 150,000 g.
1	9.2	1.2	–3.8
2	13.2	–0.4	–3.6
3	17.5	5.3	–8.4
4	11.7	3.3	–5.1
5	15.0	–1.5	4.9
6	33.3	–7.9	16.0

Destination	Average	Household size (persons)		
		1	2–4	5+
1	9.2	18.9	–1.7	–3.4
2	13.2	1.6	–0.9	2.9
3	17.5	10.9	1.5	–12.6
4	11.7	–7.4	0.1	3.9
5	15.0	0.2	2.5	–10.8
6	33.3	–24.2	–1.5	20.0

Destination
  1. Rent, ≤ 4 rooms
  2. Rent, > 4 rooms
  3. Own, ≤ 4 rooms, < 150,000 guilders
  4. Own, > 4 rooms, < 150,000 guilders
  5. Own, ≤ 4 rooms, ≥ 150,000 guilders
  6. Own, > 4 rooms, ≥ 150,000 guilders

Source: Deurloo et al., 1987. Reprinted from *Environment and Planning A*,
vol. 19, by permission.

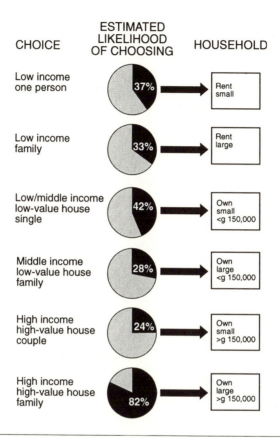

FIGURE 4.13
The relationship of Dutch owner choices and household types in the
Dutch housing market (g=Dutch guilders)

straint on their housing choice (fig. 4.12). Low-income households
choose inexpensive rental units and leave the owner-occupation
sector; households with incomes between twenty thousand and
thirty thousand dollars choose more expensive rental dwellings or
inexpensive ownership; and households in the highest income categories choose more expensive ownership housing. The price of
the previous dwelling is particularly important for the choice between expensive or less expensive ownership. This finding reiterates the importance of entering the homeowner market early and
the possibility of riding up the housing-wealth escalator. The size

of the household is particularly important for the choice of rental units, where single-person households more often choose multi-family units. Together with income and value of the previous house, marital status is important in creating the patterns of choice. In fact, there is a very clear separation between renting or owning and whether or not the relationship involves marriage. Later this chapter will return to the theme of marital status and housing choice.

The choices Dutch owners make are equally well-structured (table 4.6 and fig. 4.13). High-income households with larger families who are already in expensive ownership dwellings, have a combined probability of over 80 percent of moving within the ownership sector. The middle-income households remain in less expensive parts of the owner market, while lower-income households often move back to the rental sector, even if they are families. Household size is an important factor with respect to the choice of a larger or smaller dwelling unit and appears repeatedly in the analysis.

The previous sections on patterns of housing choice by renters and owners who have previously entered the housing market and then move again present convincing patterns of housing selection based on income, value of previous dwelling, and size of household or marital status. The patterns of choice make intuitive sense. Economic variables—income (for owners and renters) and value of the previous house (owners)—dominate choice patterns. Income has a significant and clear impact on the decision to own or rent for households that move. Low-income households move from owning to renting or they stay in the rental sector. Higher-income households have a high probability of buying a house. But the demographic variables, size of household and marital status, also have an impact on tenure and housing choice. Smaller households go to, or stay, in the rental sector more often than larger households, and families have a relatively high preference for buying a larger house.

A comparison of the results for the seemingly dissimilar housing markets in the United States and the Netherlands reveals that the choices for owners are strikingly analogous. For renters there are also broad parallels in the choices for the United States and the Netherlands—income and size of the household play an equally dominant role. In the Dutch market, the role of size of the household is likely the result of policy controls on the access to the large public housing sector, a subject that will be examined in the impacts of context on mobility and tenure choice. Size of household is an important criterion for access to this sector and also influences the type and dwelling size that households can obtain. Since the extensive public rental in the Netherlands consists of predominantly good quality, single-family dwellings, it fulfills an important role in meeting the needs of middle-income households, while the same type of household in the United States is more often in the ownership sector.

The Process of Tenure Change

The discussion of housing choice thus far has focused on patterns of housing choice and attributes of households that determine the choices from a set of alternative dwelling types. This discussion also alluded to the role and importance of tenure in the choice process and will now address the process of tenure change to parallel the patterns of housing choice.

The change in status from renter to owner is one of the most critical events in the life course of individuals and households, with various ramifications. It has already been noted that, for the household, the move is related to greater stability and lower probabilities of mobility afterward. To reiterate an earlier statement, the household decision to buy a house also has implications beyond the nature and level of housing consumption. It has implications for the probability of increases in assets and for location in the metropolitan area. It has often been seen as part of the process of political stabilization and the creation of a particular group of advantaged voters as in the privatization of the council housing in Britain (Saunders 1990). During the 1970s and early 1980s, the homeowner market was viewed as a path to wealth acquisition for middle-class households and a concomitant of economic success and increasing affluence.

The earlier chapters also established that housing choice, particularly tenure change, is a complex event in the sense that it is linked to many other events in, and characteristics of, the household. The timing of the change in tenure status is influenced by changes in household characteristics such as family type, income position, and number of earners in the household. The discussion of tenure change in the next sections will emphasize the *process* nature of tenure change.

It is often overlooked that the reverse process, the move from owning to renting, is also an important event in the life course of individuals and households, as well as a process of significance in the housing market. Substantial numbers of families, single persons, and low-income groups, who are homeowners, make this "downward" step in the housing hierarchy, even to the cheaper parts of the rental stock. Like the process of moving into home-ownership, this shift back to the rental sector seems embedded in, and induced by, a set of other events in the household situation, such as divorce, job loss, aging, or the death of a spouse or partner.

This section of the book will examine the two processes of tenure change in some detail. The findings will be contrasted with the economists' findings from hedonic models of housing demand.

Context and Background

The extensive body of research on tenure choice begins with the general concept that most households want to be owners; certainly, the survey evidence supports this position for U.S. urban populations (Heskin 1983). Only recently has ownership assumed such important dimensions in the urban property markets. The proportion of homeowners was much smaller in the first decades of this century in the United States as well as in Europe. However, during the 1950s and 1960s, which was a period of economic boom and expanding population in the United States, ownership became the norm, and the proportion of homeowners increased dramatically to its present level of more than 65 percent nationwide (Sternlieb and Hughes 1980). Even so, it bears reiterating that in particular locations, including the central cities of large metropolitan areas, and for particular groups such as blacks and Hispanics, the rent-own ratio is much closer to fifty-fifty, and in some situations renters predominate.

The price increases of owner-occupied housing of the 1970s suggested a wealth escalator in which prices would continue to rise, and the property market would provide universal wealth accumulation (Badcock 1989; Hamnett 1992). However, recent experiences emphasize that this scenario has ended and attention is increasingly focused on the cyclical nature of the housing market—a market in which substantial declines in property values may occur. Thus, the market is not an automatic road to wealth, and the declines of house values have put pressure on those who moved most recently to the homeowner market (Dieleman and Everaers 1994; Hamnett 1994).

An appropriate way in which to examine the process nature of moves from renting to owning is to focus on the time, or the duration, spent in one state (renting) before the change to a new state (owning) is made. Using what is essentially a variant of regression modeling, one can link variation in a set of independent variables representing household composition and housing situation to the variation in the duration before changing tenure status. The following chapter will add economic and regional contexts to the explanatory variables.

A Longitudinal Model of Mobility and Tenure Choice

To examine the event of moving from renting to owning, the proportional hazards model, which can also be thought of as a likelihood model, has real advantages. This model can be written as:

$$\log h_i(t) = h_0(t) + \beta Z_i$$

where,

$h_i(t)$ = the hazard function of the survival time of each household,

$h_0(t)$ = any function of time (baseline hazard),

Z_i = a vector of measured explanatory variables for the ith household,

and,

β = the vector of unknown regression parameters associated with the explanatory variables (Z).

The model is easy to interpret. The hazard itself corresponds to the notion of risk (hence likelihood). If two households have hazards of 0.5 and 1.5, it is possible to say that the second household's risk of an event is three time greater, or that the expected length of time until the event occurs will be one-third of the first household's length of time. The coefficients can be interpreted analogously to unstandardized regression coefficients in the linear regression model. An addition of one unit in the independent variable reduces (negative coefficient) or increases (positive coefficient) the log of the hazard by the value of the coefficient, controlling for other variables. (See the appendix for a more complete discussion of the longitudinal modeling approach.) One piece of terminology is important. The analysis of the likelihood of moving to ownership is designed around episodes. Episodes are the time before a change. For example, much of our concern is with the episode or spell when a household was a couple and renting a house or apartment before changing to ownership.

Models of Tenure Choice for Couples and Families

The event of moving from renting to owning as a process that occurs over time is examined in the following paragraphs with data from the Panel Study of Income Dynamics (PSID), a large panel study initiated in 1968 in the United States (Hills 1992).

The data from the sample show that, in effect, only couples and families make the transition to the owner market in the United States (table 4.7). The rates are somewhat higher when calculated from Dutch repeated cross-sectional data, which can also be used to study the move into homeownership (fig. 4.14). The general conclusion that only stable couples and families make the tenure transition to ownership still holds. Interestingly, the estimated number of years to move to ownership is 30 percent to 80 percent longer for family households.

The dependent variable in our proportional hazards model of tenure choice is the episode (or spell) in which the head of the household was either part of a couple or in a family and in the rental sector. The interval from the start of the episode as a renter until the change to ownership is the length of the spell. Figure 4.15

TABLE 4.7

Household Episodes by Family Type and Mobility Rates
in the United States, 1970–1987

Family Type	No. of Episodes	No. Moved to Own	Percent Moved to Own	Estimated Mean No. of Years until Move to Own
Single	4,260	170	4.0	14.3
Couple	2,514	443	17.6	8.9
Single Parent	2,228	98	4.4	14.7
Family	3,594	924	25.7	10.6
Other	5,005	143	2.9	14.8

Source: Clark et al., 1994. Reprinted from *Urban Studies*, vol. 31, by permission.

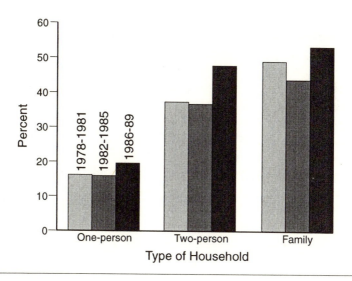

FIGURE 4.14
Renters from 20–59 years of age who move to ownership by type of household, 1978–1989, in the Netherlands

Source: Dieleman and Everaers 1994. Redrawn from *Housing Studies*, vol. 9, by permission of Carfax Publishing Co., Oxfordshire, England.

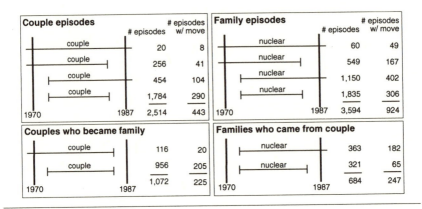

FIGURE 4.15
Episodes for couples and families that were initially renters, 1970–1987, in the United States

Source: Clark et al., 1992. Redrawn from *Urban Studies,* vol. 31, by permission.

illustrates the various types of episodes that were observed and used in the analyses. There were twenty couple episodes that were a couple during the first year of observation (1970) and were still in this household type during the last year of observation (1987). During the period of observation from 1970 to 1987, 1,784 couple episodes were observed from the beginning to the end of their couple status. For the following paragraphs, the reader is referred to figure 4.15 for confirmation of the group of episodes used in the various analyses.

The event history (hazard) model was computed for the 2,238 couple episodes for which the year they began as a couple was known, and the same for 2,985 family episodes (again refer to fig. 4.15). The dependent variable is the time from the start of the episode until the change in tenure status from rent to own (spell length). For the episodes, the independent variables were age of head, whether the head was employed, number of earners in the household, and the household income in each year of observation, variables that have been identified as critical in the tenure change literature. A positive parameter for an independent variable indicates an accelerating effect on the move to ownership, or, alternatively, a decrease in the likelihood of staying in rental status.

TABLE 4.8

Proportional Hazards Regression Model for Move to Own
for Couple Episodes, the United States, 1970–1987

Variable	Coefficient	Risk change per unit of variable (%)
Age at Start of Episode (years)	–0.013	–1.3
Race (black vs non-black)	1.357*	288.5
Hh. Income ($1000, adj.) (t**)	0.019*	2.0
Empl. Status Head (no/yes) (t)	0.116	12.3
No. of Earners (0,1,2) (t)	0.477*	61.1
Rent of Last Unit ($100, adj.)	0.013*	1.3
No. of Rooms of Last Rental Unit	–0.157*	–14.6

* significant   ** time varying

Note: This is only the part of the full table relevant for the argument in this part of the text.

Source: Clark et al., 1994. Reprinted from *Urban Studies*, vol. 31, by permission.

In most instances, the coefficients for the *couple* episodes are consistent with the earlier cross-sectional analysis of housing-choice decision making (table 4.8). Household characteristics have a marked effect on the propensity to move from renting to owning. Age has nearly no influence, which is, of course, the effect of dividing the sample into couples and families and limiting the analysis to couples and families under forty-five years of age. In fact, the number of moves to ownership after forty-five are quite small. This particular categorization reemphasizes that age is more of a step function than a linear relationship of the probability of changing tenure. Being non-black increases the risk of a move by 288.5 percent as compared with being black. As expected, income and employment increase the probability of making the rent-to-own move. The number of earners considerably increases the likelihood of moving. An additional earner in the household increases the "risk" to move to ownership by 61.1 percent. A dual income may be critical to making the change to ownership and, at the same time, makes these households less susceptible to price fluctuations

TABLE 4.9

Proportional Hazards Regression Model for Move to Own
for Family Episodes in the United States, 1970–1987

Variable	Coefficient	Risk Change per Unit of Variable (%)
Age at Start of Episode (years)	–0.000	0.0
Race (black vs non-black)	0.778*	117.7
hh. Income ($1000, adj.) (t**)	0.017*	1.7
Empl. Status head (no/yes) (t)	0.934*	154.4
No. of Earners (0,1,2) (t)	0.067	6.9
Rent of Last Unit ($100, adj.)	0.005*	.5
No. of Rooms of Last Rental Unit	–0.241*	–21.4

* significant   ** time varying

Note: This is only the part of the full table relevant for the argument in this part of the text.

Source: Clark et al., 1994. Reprinted from *Urban Studies*, vol. 31, by permission.

as will be seen later. The rent and size of the rental unit also influence the propensity to move to ownership. Larger amounts of space in the rental dwelling decreases the propensity to buy a house. This further emphasizes the consumption basis of many of the rental moves to homeownership.

The results for families are not very different (table 4.9). The measures of household characteristics and previous unit have the expected signs and are the same as for couples. Again, age is not significant. Notably, the employment of the head is significant and, for a working head, the likelihood of changing tenure is more than one and one-half times as great as compared to a nonworking head. In contrast to couples, the number of earners is not significant. For families, the fact that the head has a job is more important than the number of earners in the family.

Thus, the move into homeownership occurs under very well-defined circumstances, including relative stability of the family relationship—couples and families rather than single parents. Clearly, the former can more logically undertake the commitment of a long-term mortgage and long-term monthly payments. In addition, a household needs a certain cushion of financial resources before entering the homeowner market. Again, of the couple and family households who do buy into the homeowner market, it is those in the higher-income deciles who most frequently make the transition. Finally, the number of earners increases a household's financial resources and financial stability. Thus, the move from renting to homeownership is inextricably bound up with the characteristics of the household—age, race, income, and family size. In this sense, the move from renting to owning can be treated as an event that is closely linked to other events in the life course of a person, such as marriage and income change, which will now be examined as "triggers" in the tenure process.

Triggers and Outcomes

Until now, the discussion has been about the moves of couples and families separately, but obviously the underlying argument is that a change in family status, from couple to family or otherwise, should have an effect on the likelihood of moving, and so it is. If one treats the two groups as one and measures the actual trigger effect of a *change* from couple to family status on the change in tenure, it is possible to illustrate the power of a trigger on the tenure process.

To return to figure 2.5, one can visualize a household proceeding through a series of changes related to occupational careers, family composition changes, income trajectories, and other events such as the decision to rent or own a dwelling. Thus the move from renting to owning in this perspective relates to three other changes that might "trigger" the move: (a) change from couple to family; (b) change from a one- to a two-earner household; and (c) a significant positive income change in the year preceding the move from renting to owning. Figure 4.16 shows the propensity to move from renting to owning by year broken down by these three changes. These simple graphs make clear that the move from renting to owning is consistently related to other changes. First, more of the households that changed from a couple household to a family moved to owning in the next year than those that did not change family status. Second, a larger number of those who had a posi-

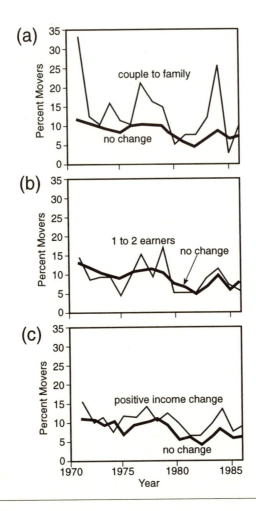

FIGURE 4.16
The propensity to become an owner by (a) change in family status from couples to families, (b) change from one-earner to two-earner status, and (c) for those with a positive income change, in the United States

Source: Deurloo et al., 1994. Redrawn from *Environment and Planning A*, vol. 26, by permission.

TABLE 4.10

Hazards Model for the Total Group of Household Episodes Starting at
Age of less than 45 Years in the United States, 1970–1987

Variable	Coefficient	Risk Ratio
Age (t**)	–0.01	0.99
Race	0.76*	2.13
Income (t)	0.01*	1.01
Empl. Status Head (t)	0.67*	1.96
No. of Earners (t)	0.24*	1.27
Couple of Family Status		
Change Couple to Family in Previous Year (t)	0.38*	1.46
Change 1 to 2 Earners in Previous Year (t)	–0.19	0.83
Positive Income Change in Previous Year (t)	0.18	1.20
Rent (t)	0.01*	1.01
Size of Rental House (t)	–0.10*	0.91

* significant   ** time varying

Note: This is only the part of the full table relevant for the argument in this part of the text.

Source: Deurloo et al., 1994. Reprinted from *Environment and Planning A*, vol. 26, by permission.

tive income change in a year moved to owning in the next year. However, the third change, from a one-earner to a two-earner household in a year, seems less clearly related to the eventual shift to owning in the next year (fig. 4.16).

Again, the hazard model relates the groups of variables, *characteristics* of households, *changes in characteristics* of households, and *characteristics* of the previous rental dwelling to the propensity or the likelihood of *moving from renting to owning* (table 4.10). With respect to characteristics of the household, the results show that white households, higher-income households, being employed, and additional earners, all significantly increase the likelihood of buying a house. For example, the risk ratio for employment status is 1.96, implying that the likelihood of buying a house for employed heads is 1.96 times the likelihood for unemployed heads (not a surprising function, of course). Couples have a higher propensity to make the transition to ownership than families.

The powerful corollary effect of age (of head of household) is present in this analysis. Effectively, the great majority of the movers are less than thirty-five years old. Income and number of earners also have the predicted relationships. Sixty-two percent of the movers have incomes in the top two quartiles, and almost 65 percent of those moving from renting to owning have two earners. These relationships of household type, stage in the family life cycle, income, and job participation with the decision to rent or own a house seem to be present at all times and in all circumstances in Western societies.

Two *changes* in household characteristics have "trigger" effects on the move to ownership. Changing from a couple to a family in the year before the move has a significant and strong effect, and having an *increased* income shortly before the move is also positively related to moving to ownership, although the coefficient is not significant. The change from one to two earners in the previous year is not clearly related to moving to ownership, as was already evident in figure 4.16.

Alternative Specifications of the Tenure Choice Process

The results presented in the previous paragraphs are consistent with the extensive work on the pricing of the "bundle" of housing services and how demand for housing varies with income and other household characteristics and with the price of housing (MacLennan et al. 1987; Henderson and Ioannides 1987; Glennon 1989; Rouwendal 1992). This section lists only brief examples of the results of these approaches to illustrate how the economic viewpoint in these studies differs from the approach in the present study. At the same time, where the variables are the same, the results are quite comparable.

As has been stressed repeatedly, housing is a composite good. A dwelling has a series of characteristics that contribute to the value attached to the whole building, but the various aspects of

TABLE 4.11

Estimation of the Hedonic Price Function, the Netherlands

Variable	Coefficient	Significance
Constant	12.42	(2.1)
Detached	3.99	(7.3)
Corner	–0.38	(–0.7)
Apartment	–5.29	(–5.8)
Age	–0.14	(–13.9)
Rooms	–1.55	(–6.7)
Improvement	–1.50	(–2.7)
N/SW	–1.22	(–1.6)
Randstad	–0.62	(–1.0)
South	4.02	(7.2)
Inhabitants	0.10	(16.7)

Number of observations: 575 R^2: 0.40

Source: Rouwendal, 1992. Reprinted from *Netherlands Journal of Housing and the Built Environment*, vol. 7, by permission.

this consumer good cannot be purchased separately. Therefore, hedonic price equations can be constructed to estimate the implicit price of each characteristic as it contributes to the total value of a dwelling (table 4.11). The type of housing, detached (single-family on an individual lot in U.S. terminology) or apartment, naturally influences the hedonic equation. Detached housing is more expensive than other single-family dwellings, and apartments are less expensive than either of these types of dwellings. A larger number of rooms increases the value (and although the coefficient is negative in its simple form, when squared, it is related to an increase in value). Older houses, even if renovated, are less expensive than newer dwellings. In the hedonic price functions, characteristics of location and neighborhood also show up as important components of hedonic models, as in the example for the Netherlands.

Although this approach to the quality and price of housing is, of course, different from the definition of a hierarchy of dwelling types as introduced earlier, the same attributes of housing occur

TABLE 4.12

Housing Consumption as a Function of Economic Variables

Variable	Owners		Renters	
	Coefficient	Significance	Coefficient	Significance
Wealth	0.0012	(2.48)	0.0010	(1.99)
Price	0.434	(3.53)	0.652	(3.85)
α_i (Tilt)	−0.2803	(1.71)	−0.4062	(2.05)
Financial Assets	−0.019	(2.15)	0.0395	(3.99)
Housing Equity	0.0441	(3.74)	−0.0237	(2.08)
Transitory Income	0.0352	(2.06)	0.0052	(0.28)
Age of Household Head	−0.0010	(1.02)	0.0005	(0.97)
Family Size	0.003	(0.75)	0.004	(1.24)
Education of Household Head	0.003	(0.91)	0.007	(3.38)
Race of Household Head	0.021	(0.88)	0.022	(1.48)
Inflation Rate	−0.388	(1.68)	0.5610	(3.15)
Mill's Ratio	0.049	(1.31)	0.0764	(2.64)
Constant	0.031	(0.37)	−0.148	(2.31)
N	288.000		369.000	
Adjusted R^2	0.2431		0.3267	

Source: Henderson and Ioannides, 1987. Reprinted from *Journal of Urban Economics,* vol. 21, by permission of Academic Press.

in this approach as important indicators: tenure, size, type, and age of dwelling.

Price elasticity of housing deals with the way in which the demand for housing services decreases with increases in the price of housing. In the short run, Glennon (1989) estimates that the price elasticity of demand for housing is −0.6, meaning that, with a unit increase of house prices, the demand decreases by 0.6. Table 4.12 gives an example of the elasticity of demand for owners and renters for various attributes of households, and for other circumstances. Age of household head decreases the likelihood of owning; larger families and a higher socioeconomic status increase housing consumption. Greater equity in the house influences the elasticity for housing consumption by homeowners, as does transitory income. Comparable factors emerged in the analysis of the matching of households and housing in the earlier sections of the chapter. Inflation and other economic circumstances that influence housing and tenure choice will be introduced in chapter 5 on context. Thus, although the approach economists use in their analysis of housing choice and consumption is quite different from the one outlined here, the attributes are replicable. The advantage of the matching and longitudinal analysis is twofold. First, the results reemphasize the importance of the demographic components of housing choice—components that are often only implicit in the hedonic models. Second, the focus on changes in household structure—the "triggers"—are accorded primacy in the process, a primacy that is not present in economic models of housing choice.

Reversing the Process: Moving Back to Rent

Most of the research that has taken up the issue of shifts from owning to renting has been set within the contexts of changing family structure, principally divorce (Dieleman and Schouw 1989), or in terms of aging (Murie et al. 1991). The research on divorce and family structure change reveals that divorce leads to moves predominantly to the rental sector (or within the rental sector) and generally is seen as a setback in housing status (Dieleman and Schouw 1989). As McCarthy and Simpson (1991) argue, the benefits and advantages of homeownership far outweigh the negatives, and homeownership is still viewed as not only conferring status but also providing potential profit and financial security (even in the more recent volatile markets). Hence, it is only a specific event—a "trigger" such as divorce—that is likely to cause households to fall out of the homeowner market.

Other research has focused on the tenure behavior of the elderly (Murie et al. 1991). In research on the Netherlands, it has been suggested that the shifts are related to the value of the occupied homes. Only 30 percent of the elderly homeowners in expensive housing moved to rental housing, while 57 percent of *all* elderly homeowners who moved chose rental housing. The explanation for moves out of the homeowner market varies from the costs and expenses of operating large older homes to the "triggering effects" of loss of a spouse (Pitkin 1990).

For those who have gained access to homeownership but

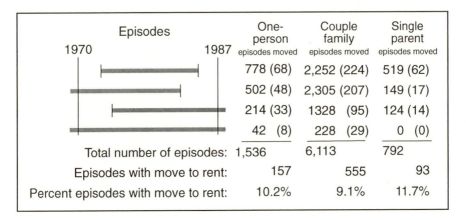

Episodes 1970 — 1987	One-person episodes moved	Couple family episodes moved	Single parent episodes moved
	778 (68)	2,252 (224)	519 (62)
	502 (48)	2,305 (207)	149 (17)
	214 (33)	1328 (95)	124 (14)
	42 (8)	228 (29)	0 (0)
Total number of episodes:	1,536	6,113	792
Episodes with move to rent:	157	555	93
Percent episodes with move to rent:	10.2%	9.1%	11.7%

FIGURE 4.17

Episodes by household type and the number of moves from owning to renting in the United States

Source: Dieleman et al. 1995. Redrawn from *Housing Studies*, vol. 10, by permission of Carfax Publishing Co., Oxfordshire, England.

decide to move back into rental quarters, often one or more of the motives for being in the homeowner market has evaporated. For those who move only temporarily from owning to renting, the same factors for reentry into homeownership apply as for households who make the move from renting to owning for the first time, as will later be seen in this section of the chapter.

Who Moves from Owning to Renting?

Not surprisingly, single-person households and single-parent families are more likely than couple and family households to move from owner-occupied housing to rental housing (fig. 4.17). This is consistent with the literature on tenure choice. Earlier in the chapter, it was shown that couples with a stable partner relationship, a stable employment status, and sufficient income are the dominant household type that will make the transition from renting to owning. It is not surprising, then, that singles, who by definition have only one earner and income, and single-parent families, for whom

TABLE 4.13

Length of Time in the Household Episode Before the Move from Owning
to Renting in the United States, 1970–1987

Spell-length in years	One Person		Couple/Family		Single Parent	
	Percent Moved	Censored	Moved	Censored	Moved	Censored
0–2	44.0	33.6	26.9	19.7	51.9	39.2
2–4	33.6	30.0	37.8	27.8	29.1	34.0
4–6	12.9	15.4	22.3	15.6	13.9	12.4
6–8	4.3	7.3	6.0	10.2	3.8	7.0
8–10	2.6	5.0	4.2	9.2	1.3	4.1
10–12	1.7	3.9	1.4	6.4	0.0	1.4
12–14	0.9	2.2	1.4	4.8	0.0	1.0
14–16	0.0	1.5	0.0	3.8	0.0	0.8
16–18	0.0	1.2	0.0	2.5	0.0	0.2
Total	100.0	100.0	100.0	100.0	100.0	100.0
N	116	1,164	431	4,126	79	589

Source: Dieleman et al., 1995. Reprinted from *Housing Studies,* vol. 10, by
permission of Carfax Publishing Company, Oxfordshire, England.

the partnership stability no longer applies, are most prone to leaving homeownership to become renters.

The finding is substantiated when one looks at the number of years households are in the episode of single, couple/family, and single parent, before they move from owning to renting (table 4.13). Many of the singles and single-parent families who move from owning to renting have been in that household type and in ownership for less than two years. Therefore, changes in household situation are clearly related to the decision to move to a rental unit. For couples/families, the reverse is true. Many of these households have been in that household type and owners for a long time—from four to eight years—before the move from owning to renting was made. Evidently this move is not related to family changes but is more likely triggered by other events, such as the move over long distance for job reasons. This will be discussed later in the chapter.

When the moves are further disaggregated by age, it becomes

TABLE 4.14

Household Episodes with a Move from Owning to Renting
in the United States, 1970–1987

Age in Move Year	One Person(%)	Couple/Family (%)	Single Parent (%)
<25	6.4	17.3	4.3
25–34	24.8	46.1	37.6
35–44	9.6	20.4	37.6
45–54	8.3	6.8	17.2
55–64	9.6	5.0	3.2
65–74	15.3	2.3	—
75+	26.1	2.0	
Total	100.0	100.0	100.0
N	157.0	555.0	93.0

Source: Dieleman et al., 1995. Reprinted from *Housing Studies*, vol. 10, by permission of Carfax Publishing Company, Oxfordshire, England.

even clearer which households under what circumstances make the move from owning to renting (table 4.14). Single-parent families move from owning to renting at relatively young ages, when the dissolution of families through divorce is also most likely to occur (Dieleman and Schouw 1989). Of course, the single-person household category also includes a group of persons that has gone through divorce. This is also reflected in table 4.13, which substantiates that many of these individuals have been in the single-person episode for only a relatively short period. Among single-person households, there is also a substantial group of elderly owners who were moving from owning to renting. A quarter of these movers are over seventy-five years old (table 4.14). These are clearly people in the stage of the life course now referred to as the "fourth age" (Warnes 1993). This part of the life course comes with bereavement (especially for women), fewer friends and relatives, and illnesses, all conditions that may necessitate a housing adjustment move.

Couples and families with children exchange homeownership for rent in smaller proportions than singles and single-parent families. Yet, because so many of those living in owner occupation are couples and families in the first place, in sheer numbers, they are

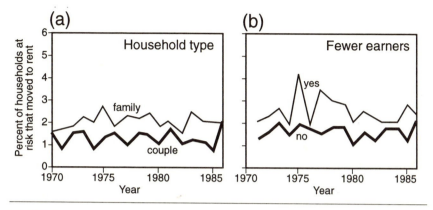

FIGURE 4.18

Rates of moving (a) from owning to renting for couple and family
episodes and (b) from ownership for households who lost an income
earner, the United States

Source: Clark et al., 1994. Redrawn from *Urban Studies*, vol. 31, by permission.

the dominant group of households to make this move. It is, therefore, important to analyze in what situations they make the tenure change. As was suggested above, such a move may be triggered
by long-distance migration and followed by reentry into homeownership later on (as will be discussed subsequently in this chapter).
It may also be related to the birth of children and the decision to
leave a job by one partner of a previous two-earner couple (Clark
et al. 1994). Figure 4.18 confirms this argument. Of the couple and
family households who make the move from owning to renting,
there are consistently more families with children than couples who
make this move, and more households that have lost an earner
shortly before the move than those who have not.

To explain the likelihood of moving out of homeownership into
renting, one can evoke two obvious sets of circumstances that are
used as explanatory variables in the regression models (table 4.15).
The first set of three variables relates to household status, and the
second set of three variables relates to employment income status. All variables in the model are significantly related to the propensity to move from owning to renting, and all parameters have
the expected sign. Couple/family households have a lower propen-

TABLE 4.15

Proportional Hazards Regression Model for Move from Owning to
Renting for All Household Episodes in the United States, 1970–1987

Variable	Coefficient	Risk ratio
Age (≥55 vs. < 55)	–1.13*	0.32
Hh. Type (Couple/Family vs.		
One-Person/Single Parent)	–0.36*	0.70
Children (yes vs. no) (t***)	0.26*	1.29
Empl. Status Head (no/yes) (t)	–0.28**	0.76
Income ($1,000, adj.) (t)	–0.02*	0.98
Earner Loss in Last 2 Years (t)	0.43*	1.53

*= significant at 0.01
= significant at 0.05   * time varying

Source: Dieleman et al., 1995. Reprinted from *Housing Studies*, vol. 10, by
permission of Carfax Publishing Company, Oxfordshire, England.

sity to move to rental housing than singles and single-parent families. When the household has children, there is a greater likelihood
of moving to renting. Households without an employed head also
enter the rental market in greater proportions than households with
an employed head. Loss of an earner in the two years before the
move is significantly related to the propensity to move from owning to renting. The lower the income, the more likely the move to
the rental market. And a move to rent is more often experienced
at a younger stage in the life cycle. Thus, there seem to be three
situations in which the move from owning to renting occurs with
some frequency. The first relates to economic/job-related reasons,
including long-distance migration and job loss for at least one of
the movers. The second two relate to changes in family status, divorce, and aging. The next section considers housing tenure choice
under these circumstances in more detail.

TABLE 4.16

Number of Couple and Family Households that Moved from
Owning to Renting by Short- and Long-Distance Moves;
Reasons Stated for this Move, in the United States, 1970–1987

	Move Distance		
Purpose	*Short*	*Long*	*Total*
Productive Reasons 1970–1974	17	39	56
Productive Reasons 1975+	19	78	97
To Get Nearer to Work 1975+	9	12	21
Consumption Reasons			
1970–1974	31	8	39
Expansion of Housing 1975+	46	8	54
Contraction of Housing 1975+	27	6	33
Other Household Related 1975+	25	7	32
Neighborhood Related 1975+	13	12	25
Response to Outside Events	65	28	93
Ambiguous or Mixed Reasons	50	14	64
Other, not Known	33	8	41
Total	335	220	555

Source: Dieleman et al., 1995. Reprinted from *Housing Studies*, vol. 10, by permission of Carfax Publishing Company, Oxfordshire, England.

"Downward" Moves

For couple and family households, the reasons for moving from owning to renting are listed in table 4.16, broken down for short- and long-distance moves (across a county boundary in the United States). Indeed, the majority of households that made a long-distance move also state that the move from owning to renting was related to employment reasons. Clearly, couple/family households who move to other jobs in a different housing and labor market are unacquainted with the housing market in the new area of work and residence and, therefore, make a choice for renting temporarily instead of buying a house immediately.

Couple/family households who move from owning to renting over a short distance list housing, family, neighborhood, mixed reasons, and "outside events" as the major causes of the tenure

TABLE 4.17

Likelihood of Moving Back to Owning for Couple/Family Households
Who Previously Moved from Owning to Renting, the United States,
1970–1987

Duration of Stay in Renting (Years)	Move Distance		
	Short	Long	Total
< 2	87	57	144
< 3	26	22	48
< 4	16	17	33
< 5	15	9	24
< 6	2	5	7
< 7	1	—	1
< 8	2	3	5
< 9	—	1	1
< 10	—	—	—
< 11	1	1	2
< 12	1	—	1
Moved to Own Again	151	115	266
Censored	184	105	289
Total	335	220	555
Mean Length of Rental Spell (Years)	5.5	4.6	5.1

Source: Dieleman et al., 1995. Reprinted from *Housing Studies*, vol. 10, by permission of Carfax Publishing Company, Oxfordshire, England.

transfer. The desire for a larger or a smaller house, changes in neighborhood structure, and events in household circumstances evidently trigger the move to another dwelling or neighborhood, thereby taking a switch from owning to renting for granted. The reasons given by couples and families to move from owning to renting over short distances also suggest that the stay in renting could be of a temporary nature only. In fact, table 4.17 illustrates that, for many couples and families, a move from owning to renting is only a short break in the status as homeowner. For approximately 50 percent of these households, a move back into ownership is observed. The table also shows that many couples and family households buy another house soon after moving into renting. The ma-

TABLE 4.18

Proportional Hazards Regression Model for the Move into Ownership, for Couple and Family Episodes that Previously Had an Owning to Renting Move, in the United States, 1970–1987

Variable	Coefficient	Risk Ratio
Age (t**)	–0.00	1.00
Couple (vs. Family) (t)	–0.24	0.78
Income ($1,000, adj.) (t)	0.01*	1.01
Number of Earners (0,1,2) (t)	0.35*	1.42
Short-Distance Move (vs. long distance)	–0.11	0.90

*= significant at 0.01   ** time varying

Source: Dieleman et al., 1995. Reprinted from *Housing Studies*, vol. 10, by permission of Carfax Publishing Company, Oxfordshire, England.

jority of the households that return to homeownership status do so within two years. After three years, 75 percent of the short-distance movers and 69 percent of the long-distance movers have returned to owner occupation. So both a long-distance migration for job reasons and a short-distance move for housing and family reasons can trigger a switch from owner to rental status. However, it is frequently only a short intermission in the renting sector between the move from one owner-occupied dwelling to the next.

Not all couple/family households that move from owning to renting return to homeownership. The same factors that influence the decision to remain in rental housing or to buy a dwelling for the first time now also influence the decision to return to owning relatively soon or to remain a renter more permanently (table 4.18). Income and the number of earners are the most critical variables impacting a return to ownership or a prolonged stay in renting. As may be expected, higher income and a larger number of earners stimulate the return to ownership. Although the parameters of the other variables are not significant, they have the expected sign. Families have a higher propensity to return to ownership than couples, and older households have a lower propensity to return to ownership than younger households, which is completely consistent with the fact that in the "fourth age" people leave ownership for good. Couples and families who move over long distances for job reasons and leave owning for renting are more likely to return to owning than those who move locally and enter the rental market for non-job reasons. To reiterate, long-distance movers rent a house at the destination for an interim period because they are unfamiliar with the housing market, have had no opportunity to recognize the market, and may have a temporary loss of an earner. Although this also occurs for short-distance movers, relatively more couples and families in this category remain renters, indicating that the reasons for leaving ownership are more pressing and permanent.

Divorce is obviously one of the critical triggers that changes household composition and, consequently, living arrangements. Because as many as half of all marriages end in divorce in the United States, and 40 percent in Western countries generally, it has now become a major factor in the mobility and housing choice process. By creating new households that are quite different in composition than the original household, the size and (usually) economic changes in the household create a demand for additional and different housing. Divorce can be seen as a process that interrupts the housing career. It is also the primary cause of "slippage" from owner occupation.

The events of divorce and changing residence usually do not occur close together in time but interact over a period of months or years. In most instances, one or more of the partners leaves the initial home long before the divorce is official. Many people find temporary housing before they make a "restart" as an independent unit in the housing market (table 4.19). The first moves may include shifts to the homes of relatives or friends—a common move for those who first exit the marital home. This process alone generates substantial mobility in the housing market. McCarthy and Simpson (1991) report that 20 percent of divorced individuals made more than two moves between the time of the separation and three years after the divorce. Even those who have child custody make frequent moves, and for non-custody fathers, the number of moves ranges between three and eight. As a result, our data on the mobility of the divorced population is much less complete, since official statistics often do not catch the frequency of moves of such individuals. From the few studies that are available, four interrelated factors emerge as determinants of moves after sepa-

TABLE 4.19

Number of Moves between Separation and Three Years
after Divorce: Respondents and their Former Spouses

| | *Fathers* | | | | *Mothers* | | | |
| | *custody* | | *noncustody* | | *custody* | | *noncustody* | |
Number of Moves	N	%	N	%	N	%	N	%
0	54	59	56	12	204	41	4	5
1	23	25	119	26	160	33	21	25
2	10	11	130	29	82	17	31	36
3	4	4	69	15	30	6	19	22
4	1	1	51	11	11	2	5	6
5	0	0	12	3	5	1	3	4
6	0	0	5	1	0	0	1	1
7	0	0	5	1	0	0	0	0
8	0	0	5	1	0	0	0	0
>8	0	0	1	0	0	0	1	1
N	92	100	453	100	492	100	85	100
Mean Number of Moves	0.64		2.13		0.99		2.24	

Source: McCarthy and Simpson, 1991. Reprinted by permission of Avebury,
Aldershot.

ration: gender, occupational/income status, child custody arrangements, and duration of the marriage (McCarthy and Simpson
1991). For the Netherlands, the income consequences of divorce
are particularly severe for married women (fig. 4.19). Many of these
women are left without income from a job (there is lower workforce
participation in the Netherlands as compared with the United
States and, indeed, in comparison with other European countries)
but with custody of the children. Of the men who are divorced,
80 percent have job income, but 35 percent of the women draw
welfare benefits.

Previous sections documented that single-parent families and
single persons have a relatively high propensity to leave owner occupation. Duration of marriage, socioeconomic status, and custodial
arrangements all influence this process (fig. 4.20). If marriages are

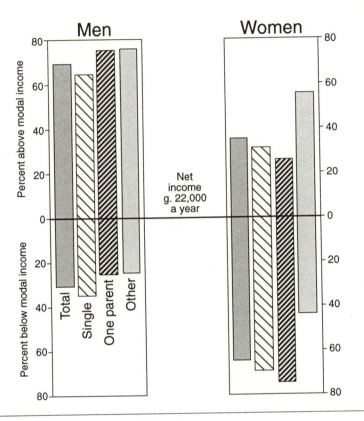

FIGURE 4.19
The relationship of income and divorce by gender and household
composition in the Netherlands (g = guilders)

Source: Dieleman and Schouw, 1989. Redrawn from *European Journal of Population*, vol. 5, by permission of Kluwer Academic Publishers.

of short duration, many who go through divorce are forced to leave
the owner sector because of insufficient equity in the house to
maintain this tenure status. And, those who have lower-paying jobs
and custody of the children are most affected and are forced down
the hierarchy of dwelling choices. Moves from single-family to multifamily dwellings occur frequently, and "downward" moves are
common (table 4.20). Finally, the divorce affects the amount of
space available—especially to the individual who leaves the house
after the family breakup.

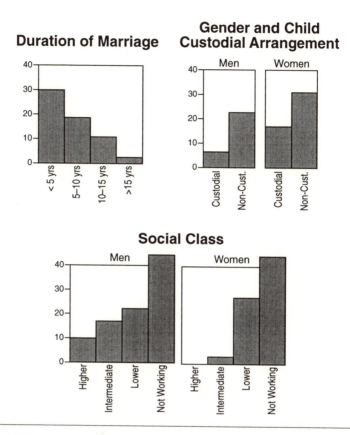

FIGURE 4.20
Percentage of persons slipping out of owner occupation

Source: McCarthy and Simpson, 1991. Redrawn from *Issues in Post Divorce Housing*, by permission of Avebury, Ashgate Publishing Limited, Aldershot, England.

Unlike divorce, which is an interruption in the housing sequence, aging is a much smoother transition but with no less important effects on housing consumption. As households reach the post-child and widowhood stages of the life cycle, rates of residential mobility become quite low, as shown in chapter 3. Many individuals remain in the same dwelling and living environment as long as they can and so "age in place." Entire neighborhoods that housed young families with children in the 1950s are now undergoing a process of aging because the older residents remain where

TABLE 4.20

Housing Choice upon Divorce: Tenure, Type and Size of Dwelling
in the Netherlands

Moved from	%	Moved from	%
Rent to Rent	60	Single- to Single-Family	33
Rent to Own	4	Single- to Multi-Family	43
Own to Rent	26	Multi- to Single-Family	6
Own to Own	10	Multi- to Multi-Family	18
Total	100	Total	100

Present compared to previous number of rooms	%
More	12
Same	20
Less	68
Total	100

Source: Dieleman and Schouw, 1989. Reprinted from *European Journal of Population*, vol. 5, by permission of Kluwer Academic Publishers.

they raised their children and where they were at the peak of their housing careers (fig. 4.21).

Changes in household status and in labor-force participation also act as triggers for mobility and changes in housing consumption as part of the aging process. In 1990 only 24 percent of the males in the age category of sixty-one to sixty-four were still in the labor force (Hooimeijer, Dieleman, and Kuijpers-Linde 1993). Early retirement, good pension facilities, and equity in the owner-occupied housing create opportunities to make a complete change of residential environment for at least some of the older households. The field of retirement migration (Warnes 1993) now examines the effects of longer-distance migration (and across countries) and away from the very large metropolitan areas such as London, Paris, and New York.

At older ages, households reach widowhood (fig. 4.22). Even at that stage, however, many older single persons are well able to care for themselves and prefer to live independently. The main reason for moving from one dwelling to another at older age relates

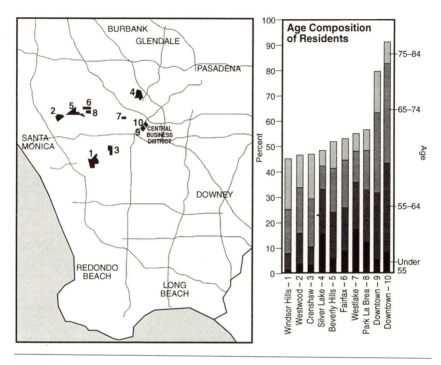

FIGURE 4.21

Distribution of population in selected "oldest communities" in the central Los Angeles area

to health changes. When a move occurs, it is, therefore, not surprising that it is to smaller dwellings and from owning to renting (table 4.21). Moves into the post-child stage are clearly influenced by the value of the dwelling when the household is already an owner. Owner-occupiers with substantial equity in the house remain in that tenure but move to smaller and less costly dwellings, while many households in less-expensive owner occupation move to the rental sector. In the widowhood stages, the predominant moves are to smaller rental dwellings, and sometimes (up to 9 percent of all the elderly in the Netherlands) to housing that is specifically designed for the elderly.

The tenure change literature generally has focused on the shift from renting to owning. It seems that the reverse process, the shift from owning to renting, is no less important, as it occurs for about

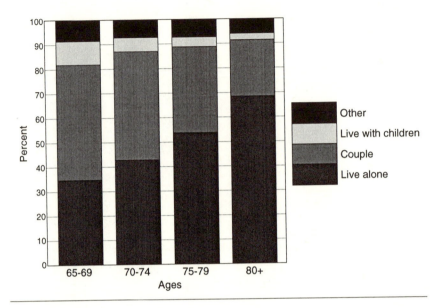

FIGURE 4.22
The relationship of living arrangements and age for older households in
the Netherlands

Source: Relou and Keilman, 1991. Adapted from *Bevolkingsvraagstukken in
Nederland anno 1991*, table 1.27, by permission of Netherlands Interdisciplinary
Demographic Institute.

10 percent of homeowner episodes, and completes the picture of
transitions in the housing market. The discussion can be summa-
rized by distinguishing four groups of households that make this
move. First, there is a group of single-parent families, who have
gone through the process of divorce. Stability in a partnership situation, an important prerequisite for being in homeownership, is
absent, and the possible dual-income situation, often a trigger for
buying a house, no longer exists. A move to rental dwellings is un-
derstandable in this context. And it is unlikely that a move back
into homeownership will occur soon. For a second group of households, older single persons, the move from owning to renting is also
likely to be permanent. These households will mostly have moved
into ownership at an earlier stage of the life cycle, as a couple or
family with children. At an older age, bereavement and decreased

TABLE 4.21

Housing Choice of Movers in the Post-Child Stage, the Netherlands

	Rent				
	Multi-Family		*Single-Family*		
	3+ Rms	*4+ Rms*	*3-Rms*	*4 Rms*	*5+ Rms*
Rent Multi-Family, 3+ Rooms	57	9	17	9	—
Rent Multi-Family, 4+ Rooms	45	20	19	8	—
Rent Single-Family, 3- Rooms	38	8	32	17	—
Rent Single-Family, 4 Rooms	33	10	22	26	6
Rent Single-Family, 5+ Rooms	32	14	15	18	10
Own 4 Rooms, < g150,000	27	9	17	11	—
Own 4 Rooms, ≥ g150,000	9	—	—	5	—
Own 5+ Rooms, < g150,000	22	—	26	8	—
Own 5+ Rooms, ≥ g150,000	—	—	—	—	—
Total	36	11	17	13	4

	Own				
	4 Rooms <g150,000>		*5+ Rooms:* <g150,000>		*Total* %	*Total* × 100
Rent Multi-Family, 3+ Rooms	—	—	—	—	100	136
Rent Multi-Family, 4+ Rooms	—	—	—	—	100	159
Rent Single-Family, 3- Rooms	—	—	—	—	100	53
Rent Single-Family, 4 Rooms	—	—	—	—	100	109
Rent Single-Family, 5+ Rooms	—	—	—	—	100	99
Own 4 Rooms, < g150,000	18	7	5	—	100	·66
Own 4 Rooms, ≥ g150,000	12	47	7	8	100	29
Own 5+ Rooms, < g150,000	8	7	15	12	100	28
Own 5+ Rooms, ≥ g150,000	26	39	4	27	100	48
Total	6	7	2	4	100	726

g = guilders

Source: Hooimeijer et al., 1986. Reprinted from *Housing Studies*, vol. 1, by permission of Carfax Publishing Company, Oxfordshire, England.

physical vigor make homeownership no longer desirable and sometimes impossible.

For a third group, couples and families, renting is only a brief
interlude between moving from one owner-occupied dwelling to
another. This is especially true for the long-distance movers. The
fourth group of households, couples/families moving to rent over
a short distance, is more diffuse. Many reasons cited relate to the
character of the dwelling or neighborhood or to "outside events"
or "ambiguous or mixed" reasons. For many households in this
group, the stay in rental quarters is quite short, and they can be
observed in the homeowner market again. The reasons for drop-
ping out of homeownership thus are short changes in circumstances that quickly disappear again, probably directly related in
part to the process of selling the old and buying the new dwelling.

Summary

Housing choice, the type of dwelling that households select when
they actually move, is the crux of the book. Just as mobility (chapter 3) is related to the life course, so is the decision about the type
of house and tenure—what we have called the housing career—
related to the life course. The metaphor of the housing career suggests a number of steps as households gradually improve their housing over the life course. Movement through the housing market can
be seen as a progression from the parents' home to simple and inexpensive housing, followed by moves to larger and more expensive dwellings, as resources grow and the composition of the family changes. The housing career is, thus, linked to the life course
of households, as they expand and later reach the reduction stage.

It has also been postulated that there is a series of discrete
housing submarkets that form a housing hierarchy. This hierarchy
is based on aspects of dwellings such as tenure, size, type, and price
of houses. Households in the expansion stage of the life course
(married, childrearing) mostly move upward in the hierarchy, and
from the child-launching stage on, some households start to
downsize their housing consumption in terms of housing costs and
space.

These concepts of the life course, housing career, and housing hierarchy are employed in this chapter to follow households from their first entry into the housing market to their departure as independently living units. The first move from the parents' home is a major step in the transition to adulthood. Much of this movement is related to marriage or cohabitation or participation in higher education. These "starters" in the housing market most often move into semiautonomous housing and into the rental sector and form a substantial section of all mobile households—a fact that is often overlooked in the literature. At the same time, leaving the nest is often a process rather than a clear-cut event; many young adults return to their parents' home for a certain period and then move out again at a later stage.

Later housing choices are much more clearly related to income, although other factors such as age, size of household, marital status, and presence of children are also important. In addition, the characteristics of the previous dwelling can have an impact on the type of new housing that is chosen. Size and tenure of the previous house are important determinants of housing choice.

There are real differences in the patterns of choice for renters and owners, although the underlying variables of income, age, and so forth are the same. Economic variables, such as income and equity in the house, dominate the choice patterns. Low-income households are often trapped in the rental sector, and higher-income households ultimately make the transition to ownership, a finding that has been well-documented in previous literature. However, demographic variables, age, and size of household do have an important effect on housing choices.

A comparison of choice patterns in the United States and the Netherlands reveals that the choices of owners, and the factors mostly related to choice patterns, are strikingly analogous. There are also broad parallels for renters—the role of income and size of household is equally dominant in both countries. There are, however, also clear differences for renters because the public rental sector is so large in the Netherlands. A large proportion of the rental sector is of good-quality housing, and a large segment is single-family housing. Thus, it fulfills an important role for both lower- and middle-income households, while in the United States middle-income households are more often homeowners.

The change in status from renter to owner is one of the most important events in the life course of individuals and households and has far-reaching ramifications. It creates the possibility of increases in assets as house prices rise (during the 1970s and early 1980s the homeowner market was viewed as a path to wealth acquisition for middle-class households) and has implications for location in the metropolitan area. It really is only couples and families that make the transition from renting to owning in significant numbers, in both the United States and the Netherlands, and even they do so only when the household relationship is relatively stable and when there is some job security. Three other groups of factors influence the propensity to move from renting to owning. Changes from couple to family, from one earner to two earners, and positive income change "trigger" moves. The size and price of the rental dwelling influence the propensity to buy (smaller housing and higher rents increase this propensity). And, housing market and economic circumstances influence the likelihood to buy.

The reverse process, moving down the hierarchy from owning to renting, is also an important event in the life course of individuals and households. Again, three main circumstances trigger such a move—divorce, widowhood, and long-distance moves for job reasons. Divorce is obviously one of the critical triggers that change household composition and, consequently, living arrangements. Many people move in, temporarily, with family or friends, before they make a "restart" in the housing market as an independent unit.

Aging is a much smoother transition and may lead gradually to less housing consumption. Even when households reach widowhood, however, many older single persons are well able to care for themselves and prefer to live independently. It is health changes that can lead to moves to smaller dwellings and from owning to renting.

5

Economic, Policy, and Geographical Impacts on Housing Choices

---

Individuals choose whether or not to move, and they make choices about whether to own or rent. These housing market choices do not occur in a vacuum; they are set within the changing economy, they differ from region to region in a country, and they are affected by government policy. In chapters 3 and 4, the context within which processes of housing choice and tenure choice occur were put aside, and the emphasis was on "revealed" choice behavior—choice patterns as they actually occurred. Constraints on choice were viewed only in economic terms which, of course, are important influences on the level and quality of housing that people are able to attain. Context effects at the macro level, however, are wider than income effects at the individual level. Socially accepted preferences and constraints and opportunities at the macro level also condition and limit housing choices.

A good example of how individual preferences for housing are not only driven by individual circumstances but are also the result of socially conditioned preferences at the macro level is the way in which individuals and households view the trade-offs of owning versus renting dwelling units. As in most other Western societies, the United States slowly shifted from a predominantly renter to a predominantly owner society during this century. As noted in chapter 1, the shift to a society of owners was facilitated by direct government policies that effectively favored single-family housing construction at the expense of multifamily rental housing. A fortuitous combination of rapidly increasing personal incomes and new concepts of mass producing single-family housing allowed many of the new urban dwellers to indulge their taste for low-density suburban homeownership.

The Netherlands also shifted from a predominantly private rental housing market at the beginning of the century to an ownership-dominated market. Beginning in the 1950s, however, the Dutch government also pursued a policy of massive intervention in the housing market, which would be considered extensive even by Western European standards (Harloe 1995). The public rental sector was heavily subsidized and advertised by the government as the "Dutch Dream" of how society and, in this case, the housing market should be organized (Dieleman 1994). As a result, although owner occupation is important, public housing is an equally important sector of the housing market. Thus, public and private homeownership in combination represent the majority of the housing market in the Netherlands.

Government intervention created a particular preference structure. A significant majority of those who enter the housing market as independent households, or who move within the housing market, express preferences for rental housing (table 5.1). This was still generally true even as recently as the late 1980s, when economic circumstances and housing policies made it very attractive to own rather than rent. To some extent, this is reflected in the preferences expressed in table 5.1, but the strong tradition of renting is still quite clear.

This chapter examines the economic and political context that affects the housing choice of individuals. Again, revealed choice rather than preference will be at the heart of the analysis. There is now a large literature on the development of housing policy (Lundqvist 1992; Harloe 1995; Power 1993; Kleinman 1995). This study, however, will look at only some of the aspects of these policy issues because the emphasis of the book is on the matching of households and housing, not on housing policy per se. As chapter 1 demonstrated, housing has a very clear geographical expression in the urban landscape. This will constitute the third element of the context that influences and shapes housing choice. We will deal with economic context, policy influences, and spatial aspects in sequence.

TABLE 5.1

Preferences for Renting and Owning of Potential Filtering and Starting
Households in the Netherlands, 1977, 1981, 1985, and 1989

	Filterers				*Starters*			
Year	*1977*	*1981*	*1985*	*1989*	*1977*	*1981*	*1985*	*1989*
Renting	60.7	72.0	61.5	56.3	72.5	83.0	79.5	76.8
Owning	39.3	28.0	38.5	43.7	27.5	17.0	20.5	23.2
Total Percentage	100.0	100.0	100.0	100.0	100.0	100.0	100.0	100.0
Number (x1000)	962	1076	1193	1346	398	509	600	637

Source: Dieleman and Everaers, 1994. Reprinted from *Housing Studies*, vol.
9, by permission of Carfax Publishing Company, Oxfordshire, England.

Economic Contexts

The choice of a new residence occurs in a temporal and spatial
context, and perhaps the most critical influence on the choice is
the national and local economic climate. The availability of financing, the amount of new construction, the prices of new homes, and
the volatility of mortgage rates, all influence the probability of making the move from renter to owner. Additionally, these measures
vary from year to year and by locality. Thus, it can be argued that,
in addition to measures of family status, age, and income, the economic climate will have an important influence on the pattern of
housing choice. And, among all the choices, that which relates to
the movement between renting and owning will be most affected
by fluctuations in the economy. Therefore, the argument in this
section of the chapter will focus on tenure choice and tenure outcomes in economic contexts.

Context in the United States

To index the economic context and its potential for facilitating or constraining tenure change, one can use four simple variables—the price and amount of new construction, mortgage rates,

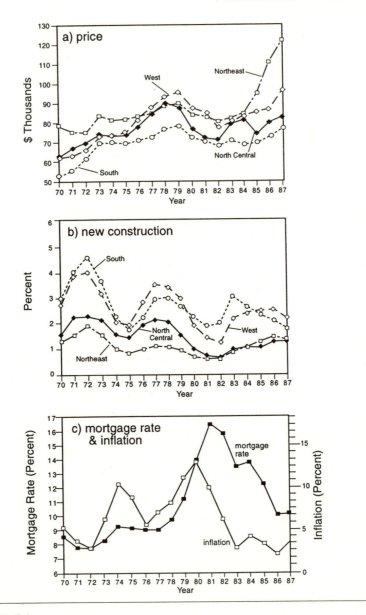

FIGURE 5.1
Economic context variables for the United States, 1970–1987: (a) price
of new single-family home, (b) new construction, number of private
units started as percent of total stock, (c) mortgage rates and inflation

Source: Clark et al., 1994. Redrawn from *Urban Studies*, vol. 31 by permission.

and inflation rates (fig. 5.1). The prices of single-family homes—
the most likely owner destination for tenure changes—have increased steadily, although not uniformly, during the last twenty
years in the United States. For example, the prices of new single-
family homes clearly declined in the early 1980s—a period of recession in the United States. The inflation rate has fluctuated dramatically during this period with peaks in 1974–1975 and 1980–1981
and troughs in 1971–1972, 1976–1977, and very low rates after
1983. Clearly, purchasing a home in 1980 involved different expectations than in 1986. Mortgage rates show a significant peak
during the early 1980s. Again, it is straightforward to suggest the
impact of these high rates in the house-buying behavior of households. Clearly, the individual economic variables are not independent, and simple correlation coefficients between these variables
over the years support this observation (table 5.2). For instance,
when inflation and mortgages are high, new construction is relatively low.

From the graphs one can identify the years 1970 to 1979 as a
relatively good period to buy a house. Mortgage rates were stable
and at moderate levels. Prices increased consistently, which meant
that buying a house was a good hedge against inflation. And, the
high level of new construction (with a trough in 1975) offered
ample opportunities for residential mobility. The years 1980 to
1982, by contrast, were a period in which it was more prudent to
wait, to remain in rental housing than to buy, as falling housing
prices were accompanied by very high mortgage rates. From 1983
to 1987, prices rose again, but price levels were unstable, and mortgage rates and rates of new construction fluctuated substantially.
Instability does not stimulate moves from the rental to the ownership sector; therefore, in general one would expect a dampening
in the propensity to change tenure in this period. The yearly percentage of moves of renters to ownership, graphed in figure 5.2,
roughly substantiates these expectations for families. In the period
1970–1979, a relatively high percentage of renters bought a house,
with a dip in 1975. For the period of 1980–1982, these percentages are much lower, followed by a moderate buying peak in 1983
and 1984 by families who had previously delayed the tenure
change. The level of shifts to ownership, however, remained relatively low when compared with the 1970s. For couples the picture

TABLE 5.2

Correlation Coefficients between the Time-Series for 1970–1987
of the Context Variables in the United States

	Amount of New Construction	Inflation	Mortgage
Inflation	−0.51		
Mortgage	−0.59	+0.24	
Price New Single-Family Homes (adjusted)	+0.14	+0.09	+0.21

Source: Clark et al., 1994. Reprinted from *Urban Studies*, vol. 31, by permission.

is somewhat different. In the early 1970s, only a small proportion of these households moved out of the renter market. These initial low levels and the much higher rates since 1975 may reflect the changing status of couples in society. Many couples, including cohabiting partners, are now two-earner households with ample financial resources—in many cases higher than those of families—and are now in a better position to purchase a house than fifteen years before.

The Dutch Context

There were equally important effects in the Dutch housing market but the actual economic changes were greater and, in turn, had a greater impact on the relative attractiveness of ownership. House prices for owner-occupied dwellings fluctuated dramatically in the Dutch housing market (fig. 5.3). The decade of the 1970s was a period of rapidly increasing house prices. Nominal prices tripled between 1970 and 1978. The average homeowner realized a substantial increase in housing assets. Between 1978 and 1982, prices decreased equally dramatically. An individual or household unfortunate enough to have bought a house at the average price of 166 thousand Dutch guilders in 1978 (about ninety thousand U.S. dollars) had lost more than one-third of the value of the house, in 1978 guilders, by 1982. And, prices have increased slowly since

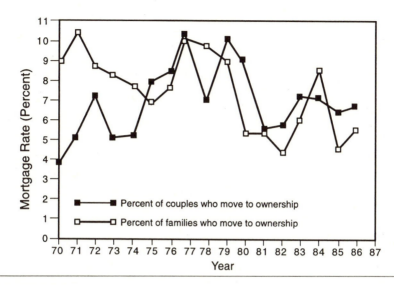

FIGURE 5.2

Renter to ownership moves by family type in the United States
1970–1986

Source: Clark et al., 1994. Redrawn from *Urban Studies* vol. 31, by permission.

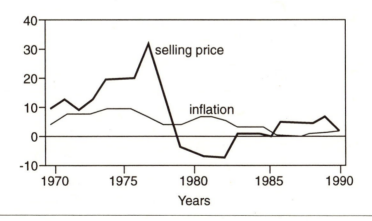

FIGURE 5.3

Average selling price of owner-occupied dwellings (percentage change
since previous year) and rate of inflation, 1970–1990, the Netherlands

Source: Dieleman and Everaers, 1994. Redrawn from *Housing Studies*, vol. 9,
by permission of Carfax Publishing Co., Oxfordshire, England.

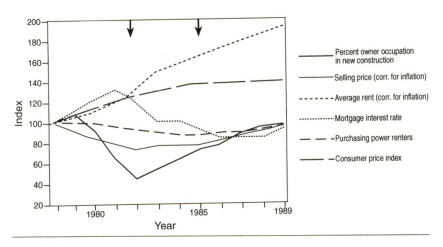

FIGURE 5.4

Average monthly rent, selling price, mortgage interest rate, consumer price index, purchasing power of renters, and proportion owner occupation in new construction, 1978–1989, the Netherlands

Source: Dieleman and Everaers, 1994. Redrawn from *Housing Studies*, vol. 9, by permission of Carfax Publishing Co., Oxfordshire, England.

the mid-1980s. The rate of inflation fluctuated at a relatively high level (by European standards)—between 5 percent and 10 percent until the mid-1980s—and was quite low in the second half of the decade. Mortgage rates peaked around 1981 or 1982 and have decreased consistently since that time. Low mortgage rates, along with low rates of inflation (fig. 5.4) and moderate wage increases, made the middle and later 1980s a period in which transitions from the renter to the owner market were much easier than during the 1970s. Declining or, at the very least, stable prices and rising wages worked to increase the buying power of renters and supported the propensity of those renters who planned to move anyway to become owners. A comparison of figures 5.4 and 5.5 suggests a parallel in the changes in the economic context and the changes in the propensity to move from rent to own. For renters in the age group twenty to fifty-nine, who are either couples or families and who have middle incomes or more, the propensity increased generally over the one and one-half decades from the late 1970s to 1989. However, there were two significant "dips" in the rate of

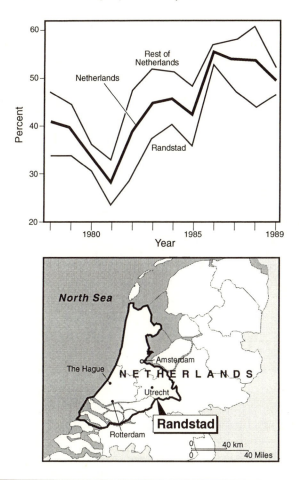

FIGURE 5.5
Moves to owner occupation, 1978–1989, the Netherlands

Source: Dieleman and Everaers, 1994. Redrawn from *Housing Studies*, vol. 9, by permission of Carfax Publishing Co., Oxfordshire, England.

transition. The actual rate varied from a low of near 30 percent to a high of over 50 percent after 1986. The patterns of transition reflect the changes in the economic context. Prices were high in the late 1970s and transitions to ownership were decreasing. Mortgage rates were higher, and so was inflation. It is possible to suggest a three-part structure to the economic contexts (arrows on fig. 5.4) that mirror the three-part structure of the moves to own-ership. The period 1978–1982 was not at all favorable for buying a house, as prices dropped rapidly. The period 1982–1985 was one in which owner-occupier dwellings were reasonably priced, but it was also a period in which the economic downturn discouraged risk taking and house purchasing. After 1986, a different structure with moderate mortgage interest rates, moderately rising incomes, and slowly rising prices induced shifts from the rental to the own-ership sector.

Modeling the Effects of Context

At this point, the economic variables can be added to the mea-sures of housing and household characteristics to evaluate their relative contribution to the likelihood of moving from renting to owning. The contextual variables actually help in understanding the likelihood of moving to homeownership (tables 5.3 and 5.4). New construction appears to play an important facilitating role and increases the likelihood of changing from rent to own. In years of substantial additions to the housing stock, the propensity increases considerably for renters to move to the ownership sector. Higher prices reduce the propensity to move to ownership, though the co-efficient is actually not significant in the model. Inflation stimu-lates the propensity to move to ownership, as one would expect. When inflation is high, house ownership is a hedge against infla-tion, as the value of the house will increase (keep pace) with in-flation. One would expect the mortgage rate to be negatively related to the propensity to move to ownership, but the sign is positive, though not significant. It is certainly possible that the actual ef-fect is confounded because of the interaction with the other eco-nomic variables.

In the case of the Netherlands, a simple set of correlation co-efficients and regression models confirms the visual relationship between shifts from rent to own and the prevailing economic con-text (table 5.5). The economic indicators, as expected, are highly intercorrelated. The mortgage rate closely follows the inflation rate. Both indicators are negatively related to the change in average rent level. The buying power of both renters and owners is negatively

TABLE 5.3

Proportional-Hazards Regression Model for Move-to-Own for Couple
Episodes in the United States, 1970–1987

Variable	Coefficient	Risk Change per Unit of Variable (Percentage)
Age at Start of Episode (Years)	–0.013	–1.3
Race (Black vs. Non-Black)	1.357*	288.5
Household Income ($1,000, adjusted)[a]	0.019*	2.0
Employment Status Head (no/yes)[a]	0.116	12.3
Number of Earners (0,1,2)[a]	0.477*	61.1
Rent of Last Unit ($100, adjusted)	0.013*	1.3
Number of Rooms of Last Rental Unit	–0.157	–14.6
New Construction (millions)[a]	0.641*	89.8
Price New Single-Family Homes ($1,000, adjusted)[a]	–0.010	–1.0
Mortgage (%)[a]	0.057	5.9
Inflation(%)[a]	0.065*	6.7
–2 log L		
Model	2429.5	
Without covariates	2713.2	

[a] Time varying
* Significant at the 0.01 level

Source: Clark et al., 1994. Reprinted from *Urban Studies*, vol. 31, by permission.

related to the trends in the inflation and mortgage rates. The co-efficients make intuitive sense apart from the negative relationship with new construction. To the extent, however, that new construction is almost totally controlled by government policy and is virtually stable from year to year, the relationship is probably not readily interpretable in the same sense as new construction in the United States.

The regression model excludes inflation (almost identical with mortgage rate) and new construction (for the reasons outlined above). Clearly, the price of dwellings, the buying power of renters, and the proportion of new construction for owners have

TABLE 5.4

Proportional-Hazards Regression Model for Move-to-Own
for Family Episodes in the United States, 1970–1987

Variable	Coefficient	Risk Change per Unit of Variable (percentage)
Age at Start of Episode (years)	–0.000	0.0
Race (black vs non-black)	0.778*	177.7
Household Income ($1,000, adjusted)[a]	0.017*	1.7
Employment Status Head (no/yes)[a]	0.934*	154.4
Number of Earners (0,1,2)[a]	0.067	6.9
Rent of Last Unit ($100, adjusted)	0.005*	0.5
Number of Rooms of Last Rental Unit	–0.241*	–21.4
New Construction (millions)[a]	0.817*	126.4
Price New Single-Family Homes ($1,000, adjusted)[a]	–0.031*	–3.0
Mortgage (%)[a]	–0.002	–0.2
Inflation(%)[a]	0.059*	6.0

–2 log L	
Model	4543.7
Without covariates	4944.2

[a] Time varying
* Significant at the 0.01 level

Source: Clark et al., 1994. Reprinted from *Urban Studies*, vol. 31, by permission.

important effects on the rate of transition (table 5.6). As rent level increases, the likelihood of purchasing a house rises. As income increases, the likelihood of purchasing a house increases. And, in sum, when there is a positive income change (increased buying power), when prices are moderate, and when mortgage rates are reasonable, large numbers of renters make the rent-to-own transition.

TABLE 5.5

Correlation Coefficients between the Indicators of General
Circumstances Influencing Renters to Stay in Rent
or to Buy a House, the Netherlands, 1978–1989

Renting to Owning (Percentage of Movers)	*0*	*1*	*2*	*3*	*4*
1. Price Owner Occupation	0.25				
2. Average Rent Level	0.81				
3. Mortgage Interest Rate	–0.95		–0.76		
4. Inflation	–0.96		–0.84	0.97	
5. Change Buying Power Renters	0.53	0.80		–0.62	
6. Owner Occupation in New Construction %	0.20				
7. New Constuction as Percentage of Stock	–0.58		–0.50	0.66	0.69

Note: All coefficients for rent-to-own, only coefficients of at least 0.50 for the indicators.

Source: Dieleman and Everaers, 1994. Reprinted from *Housing Studies*, vol. 9, by permission of Carfax Publishing Company, Oxfordshire, England.

TABLE 5.6

The Regression Coefficients of Five Indicators of Economic
and Housing Market Circumstances on the Propensity
to Move to Owner Occupation, the Netherlands, 1978–1989

Dependent Variable: Renting to Owning (Percentage of Movers)
Independent Variables

1. Price Owner Occupation	–0.30
2. Average Rent Level	0.54
3. Mortgage Interest Rate	–0.20
4. Change Buying Power Renters	0.63
5. Owner Occupation in New Construction	0.30
R square	0.94

Source: Dieleman and Everaers, 1994. Reprinted from *Housing Studies*, vol. 9, by permission of Carfax Publishing Company, Oxfordshire, England.

Effects for Subgroups

How do economic contexts affect different groups in the housing market? Are economic effects compounded for some groups and irrelevant for others? Aggregate effects may be felt quite differently by various groups in the housing market. This idea can be examined for the United States by focusing on four groups of households—those with above and below median incomes, and two-earner couples versus one-earner families.

When one graphs the groups with above and below median incomes, and the couples with two earners and families with one earner, there are extremely clear distinctions (fig. 5.6). Essentially, lower incomes are increasingly excluded from the owner-occupation market, beginning in the early 1970s, with a slight improvement around 1977, when new construction was rapid and mortgage rates were relatively stable and low. The high price levels and the high mortgage rates in the 1980s effectively restricted, or at least limited, entry into the ownership market for low-income groups. Higher income groups previously renting a house, however, moved into owner occupation in relatively high proportions in the late 1970s. They were much less affected in their access to owner-occupied housing by the economic circumstances during the 1980s.

It is not unrelated that families with one earner were also increasingly limited in their ability to enter the ownership sector. During the late 1970s, in the inflationary spiral that affected much of the U.S. housing market, there was a rush to enter the market. The escalating housing prices buoyed up those who entered the market and increased their equity substantially. Renters were often willing to make "sacrifices" to enter the ownership market. With the recession of the early 1980s and increasing unemployment, when house prices simultaneously remained high, there was a significant reduction in the number of those willing and able to enter the ownership market. The rent-own decision for two-earner couples seems to be the least influenced by economic circumstances.

Once again, a likelihood model provides formal estimates of the graphical presentations (table 5.7). For the subgroups that have difficulty entering the homeowner market—low-income households and one-earner families—the period effects are large, significant,

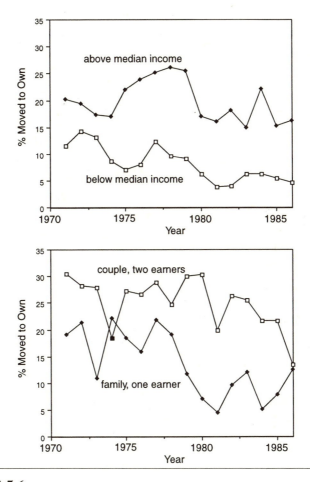

FIGURE 5.6
Propensity to move to ownership for (a) those above and those below
median income and (b) for couples with two earners versus families
with one earner in the United States, 1970–1985

Source: Deurloo et al., 1994. Redrawn from *Environment and Planning A*, vol.
26, by permission.

and negative. For these subgroups location is much less important
than the economic context that decreases their access to owner
occupation. Economic circumstances override the regional variations in price and levels of new construction for these groups.

For those household episodes with incomes above the median

TABLE 5.7

Hazards Model for Move to Own for Subgroups of Household Episodes
while at Risk, the United States, 1970–1987

Variable	Annual Income below Median	Annual Income above Median	Two-earner Couple	One-Earner Family	Two-Earner Family
Age	−0.00	0.00	0.01	0.02	0.05*
Race	0.74*	0.86*	1.22*	0.80*	0.54*
Income	−0.01	0.01*	0.02*	0.01*	0.01*
Employment status of head	0.73*	0.91*			
Number of earners	−0.04	0.07			
Household type	0.02	0.07			
Rent	−0.00	0.01*	0.01*	0.01	0.01
Size of rental house	−0.03	−0.12*	−0.06	−0.10	−0.01
Period 1974–79	−0.26	0.24	0.01	0.13	−0.25
Period 1980–83	−0.69*	−0.04	0.01	−0.56	−1.02*
Period 1984–87	−0.86*	−0.37	−0.45	−1.93*	−1.20*
Total number	2122	1014	767	636	583

*Significant at the 0.05 level

Note: This is only part of the full table relevant for the argument in this part
of the text.

Source: Deurloo et al., 1994. Reprinted from *Environment and Planning A*,
vol. 26, by permission.

the model shows that temporal effects are less important. The years
1974 to 1979 witnessed relatively high levels of rent-to-own transitions as the positive, though not significant, coefficient shows.
For this group, however, location is much more important. Households in the Midwest, South, and even in the more expensive housing market in the western United States are able to make the transition to ownership more easily than in the Northeast. These
regions also had high levels of new housing construction. The two-
earner couples are least affected by regional and time-period effects. They become owners whatever the time period or the re-

gion. They seem to delay that move only when circumstances are truly unfavorable, as in the very early 1980s.

This section clearly demonstrates how the fluctuation of economic circumstances is exhibited in the patterns of tenure choice. Microlevel circumstances of households and changes therein interact with macrolevel economic influences to create the process of matching household to housing as it evolves over time. But it is not *only* the "invisible hand" of the market that expresses itself in the choice processes; the influence of housing policy is also present in the data for the Netherlands.

The Context of Policy

As Harloe (1995) argues, the provision of housing in Europe is not like some other services, such as education and health care, and nowhere is it completely "socialized." There is always a sector of the housing market that is under the direct influence of market forces (usually the owner-occupier sector) and a sector that is regulated (usually the rental sector). Therefore, the influence of government regulation of housing can have various faces and effects that are difficult to understand and categorize because the various European countries have their own systems of control and regulation (Power 1993). Lundqvist (1992) has tried to explain these varying interventions by distinguishing regulations that mostly related to households and their ability to rent or purchase housing, and measures directed at housing provision and housing pricing (fig. 5.7).

The matching of households and housing is most directly influenced by housing allowances, taxation measures, and access rules (who can seek which type of housing). In the Netherlands, nearly one million households—approximately one-third of all renters—receive a housing allowance that permits them to live in more expensive housing than they could otherwise afford. And all homeowners can deduct fully the mortgage interest payments from their taxes. This naturally makes it particularly attractive for households with higher incomes to live in the ownership sector of the housing market. Such policy measures clearly influence choice patterns as described in chapter 4, where income and price factors

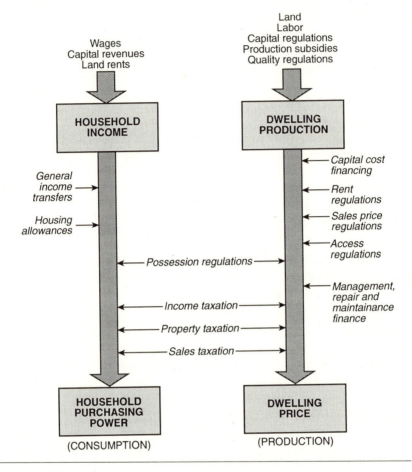

FIGURE 5.7
The structure of possible state interventions in the housing sector

Source: Lundqvist, 1992. Redrawn by permission of Delft University Press.

turned out to be just the critical factors in the choice process. Access rules for large parts of the housing stock—for example in cities such as Amsterdam and Rotterdam where public rent makes up more than 50 percent of the entire stock—also directly favor certain households. Households that meet local authority criteria are advantaged, while others are excluded or have to queue on a waiting list, sometimes for several years. The effects of these rules

TABLE 5.8

Registration Criteria
(a) and Urgency of Need of Housing
(b) Criteria for Public Rental Housing in the Netherlands;
the Percentage of All Housing Corporations Using the Criteria in 1990

a.	Age	59
	Resident of Municipality	53
	Economic Ties to Municipality	53
	Social Ties to Municipality	49
	Income	37
	Filterer	33
	Time in Need of Housing	27
	Crowding in Present Dwelling	25
	Cost of Present Dwelling	23
b.	Medical Indication	68
	Social Indication	60
	Time on Waiting List	52
	Commuting Distance	51
	Economic Ties to Municipality	50
	Filtering	46
	Number of Rooms/Person New Dwelling	46
	Urban Renewal	44
	Resident of Municipality	42
	Social Ties to Municipality	40
	Economic Indication	37
	Income/Cost New Dwelling	35
	Age	34
	Family Reunion (immigrants)	33
	Financial Indication	32
	Income	13

Source: Netherlands Ministry of Housing, Physical Planning, and the Environment (MVROM), 1992.

are hard to measure because they vary by municipality and housing officials have a certain amount of discretion in applying them in specific situations (table 5.8). The pervasiveness of such rules is well-illustrated for Amsterdam, whose local government is particularly active in directing choices.

The influence of government policy on the production of housing in Western Europe is probably most evident in the tenure

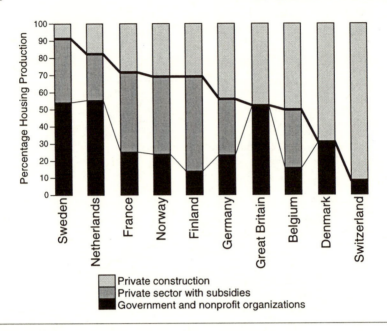

FIGURE 5.8
The structure of direct financial intervention in the housing market,
1950–1985, in selected European countries

Source: Feddes, 1995. Redrawn by permission of the Royal Netherlands Geographical Society.

structure of the housing stock. Substantial parts of the housing
stock are in the social or public rental sector. Large subsidies have
been supplied to create this stock and then maintain and repair it
(fig. 5.8). It is possible to show that household preferences become
adapted to the composition of the stock. For example, expressed
preferences in the three major housing markets in the Netherlands
are quite different (table 5.9). As the preparation of public rental
dwellings and the type of housing that constitutes the stock vary,
stated preferences vary (table 5.9). Fewer households express a
desire for ownership and for single-family housing in Rotterdam,
where this type of housing is relatively scarce, than in Bergwald, a
rural area where it is quite abundant.

More indirectly, government intervenes in the housing market by manipulating the market circumstances themselves. In the
Netherlands and, to a lesser extent, in other European countries,

TABLE 5.9

Stated Preferences for New Dwellings of Families Living in a City, a
Town, and a Rural Region in the Netherlands, 1993

Preference for	*City* (%)	*Town* (%)	*Rural* (%)
Single Family	81	90	94
Multi-Family	13	4	*
Other	6	6	*
Rent	33	18	8
Own	57	79	90
Indifferent	10	*	*

Source: Van Kempen et al., 1994. Reprinted by permission of the Faculty of
Geographical Sciences, University of Utrecht, Netherlands.

the most common approach is to regulate the price of housing services in the rental sector. After World War II, most Western European countries introduced rent controls in response to the acute
shortage of dwellings which threatened to drive up rents to what
were perceived to be unreasonable levels. Of course, these countries then removed the incentives for private investors to enter the
market to supply housing under very favorable economic conditions. In the Netherlands, rent controls and subsidies persist to this
day and, of course, influence consumer decisions in the housing
market. The previous section already noted the Dutch government
policy to raise rents annually above the rate of inflation and income growth. The proportion of ownership units in the new construction was also increased, which, in turn, stimulated the impetus of renters to shift to the ownership sector.

This brief discussion of policy contexts thus far clearly documents that government regulation of the housing market can have
an influence on the composition of the stock and, thereby, on the
opportunities for housing choice. It follows that policy has an effect on the matching of households and housing. At the same time,
if one examines the housing career as a whole one can ask whether
the "outcomes" for individual households are markedly different
in government-controlled situations and "relatively" free-market
contexts.

TABLE 5.10

Coefficients for Choices of (Previous) Owners in the United States
and the Netherlands (ANOTA analysis)

United States		Income (×1,000)			Value of Previous Dwelling (×1,000)		Size of Household	
		<$19	$20–29	>$30	<$50	>$50	1 Person	≥2 Persons
Rent		21.9	–6.9	–20.7	–8.4	–0.3	20.6	–6.4
Own	<$75	–7.3	14.0	0.5	21.1	–11.2	–8.2	2.6
Own	>$75	–14.6	–7.0	20.2	–12.7	11.4	–12.4	3.9

The Netherlands		Income (×1,000)			Value of Previous Dwelling (×1,000)		Size of Household	
		<g30	g30–42	>g42	<g150	>g150	1 Person	≥2 Persons
Rent		19.5	–3.9	–12.0	0.7	–7.4	22.3	–2.3
Own	<g 150	3.6	12.9	–2.5	8.8	–13.6	1.9	–0.2
Own	>g 150	–23.1	–9.0	14.5	–9.4	21.0	–24.1	2.5

g = guilders

Source: Dieleman et al., 1989. Reprinted from *Urban Studies,* vol. 26, by permission.

This section of the discussion of contextual effects on housing choice considers the specific issue of whether those countries and housing markets that are closely controlled by government policy exhibit different behavior patterns than occur in markets that are driven primarily by consumers. A working hypothesis of this conceptualization is that dwelling choices in the United States will be more clearly dominated by economic factors than in the Netherlands. In the latter, government policy has tried to make housing less dependent on income and the free forces of the housing market. Recall that the Netherlands has created a large public rental stock that is now 42 percent of the total stock. To reiterate, access to this sector is strictly regulated.

To make a comparison across housing market contexts, the set of dwelling choices was grouped into three very broad catego-

TABLE 5.11

Coefficients for Choices of (Previous) Renters in the United States
and the Netherlands (ANOTA analysis)

United States	Income (×1,000)			Size of household		
	<$15	$15–30	>$30	1 person	2 persons	3 or more
Rent, 5 or More Units or Multi-Family	6.4	–3.2	–12.6	20.1	1.7	–12.4
Rent, 1–4 Units or Single-Family	6.8	–1.9	–16.6	–16.4	–1.6	10.3
Own	–13.3	5.1	28.8	–3.8	–0.1	2.2

The Netherlands	Income (×1,000)			Size of household		
	<g30	g30–42	>g42	1 person	2 persons	3 or more
Rent, 5 or More Units or Multi-Family	12.3	–6.2	–15.8	24.5	8.2	–9.6
Rent, 1–4 Units or Single-Family	7.9	1.4	–17.7	–22.3	–5.5	7.7
Own	–20.2	4.8	33.6	–2.2	–2.7	1.9

g = guilders

Source: Dieleman et al., 1989. Reprinted from *Urban Studies*, vol. 26, by permission.

ries (tables 5.10 and 5.11). For owners, the choices were either to rent or to own a less or more expensive dwelling; for renters, the choices were dwellings in large multifamily rental structures, dwellings in small and single-family rental units, and ownership.

It is a notable finding that even with all the differences between American and Dutch societies and their housing markets, the models for owners generated for the Dutch sample and the U.S. sample are very similar. In both cases, income, value of the previous dwelling, and size of household are the three most important predictors of choice and enter the models in that order in both contexts (table 5.10; fig. 5.9). The relative contributions of the variables and the way they influence patterns of choice in the United

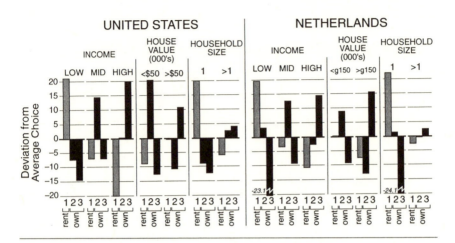

FIGURE 5.9
The effects of income, house value, and household size for owners in less controlled and more controlled housing markets (Classes 1, 2, 3 from Table 5.10)

Source: Constructed from data in Dieleman et al., 1989.

States and the Netherlands are likewise remarkably similar. In the United States, more households move from own to rent than in the Netherlands, but if one graphs the choice patterns, then the similarities are striking. Just as a reminder, the ANOTA coefficients are corrected for interactions between the explanatory variables and, therefore, represent "pure" effects that can be interpreted as partial regression coefficients. Of course, the "size" of the effects does vary across the housing market.

Income clearly determines and constrains choice in both countries; lower-income households that move have a strong propensity to choose a rental dwelling, and middle incomes have a relatively high probability of buying an inexpensive house (note that they have a positive value in the first category of ownership). The highest-income groups buy in the more expensive sectors of the housing market. At the same time, there are subtle differences. For example, the low-income U.S. households do not get into ownership (the bar is negative in the owner categories) but Dutch households do enter ownership at the low end. Here we see the effects of income/housing subsidies. The amount of capital accumulated

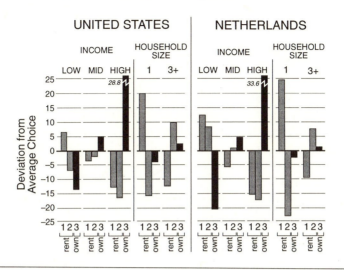

FIGURE 5.10

Measuring the effects of income and household size for renters in less controlled and more controlled housing markets (Classes 1, 2, 3 from Table 5.11)

Source: Constructed from data in Dieleman et al., 1989.

in the value of the previously owned dwelling also acts as a determining factor for the choice of less or more expensive owner-occupation. In both countries, one-person households have a relatively strong tendency to move to the rental sector just as income and accumulated wealth dominate choice patterns in a similar manner, and one-person households make different choices from two-or-more-person households.

Even for renters, the two countries show remarkable similarities (table 5.11; fig. 5.10). However, while two variables are quite comparable, there are differences in a third variable. For the United States, the rent of the previous dwelling plays a role, and, in the Netherlands, there is an effect of being in the Randstad or the rest of the country. This study has emphasized the similarities, but the fuller analysis is in Dieleman and associates (1989). Income is again the crucial and controlling variable. The structure of the bars is virtually identical for middle- and high-income households. Only low-income households are more likely to choose rent than U.S. households, which are really limited to the low end of the rental market. High-income households simply do not choose to rent or stay in the rental market. The highest income group in the United States has a probability of moving to the owner-occupier sector that is 0.29 percent higher than the average, and in the Netherlands this figure is 0.34. Again, as has been demonstrated throughout this analysis of the research findings, the lowest income groups basically do not buy houses. In both countries, one-person households have a high propensity to move to multifamily rental housing, while three-or-more-person households show greater preference for lower-density housing.

Again, as in the owner-occupier sector, there are remarkable similarities in the influence of income and household size on dwelling choice in both countries. Even for the rental sector, we have to conclude that choice patterns in both the United States and the Netherlands are dominated by income and price elements. At the same time, the differences in choice between the income categories seem rather larger in the Netherlands than in the United States. The only area in which the effects of a controlled housing market seem to play a role is in the household size variable. For renter choices, the roles of income and size of the household are equally dominant. In the Dutch case, the size of the household probably reflects the impact of policy controls on the access to the large public housing sector in the Netherlands. Size of household is an important criterion for access to this sector and also influences the type and size of the dwelling that households can obtain.

The presentation of the results of the comparability analysis emphasizes the real similarity of the variables and their impacts on the tenure choices in the two markets. The greatest difference is in the magnitudes, rather than the patterns, of effects. For example, low-income owners in the Netherlands are much less likely to find their way to more expensive ownership. And, single-person households almost never enter expensive ownership. Larger households in the United States, however, are more likely to rent than in the Netherlands. Thus, even with the caveats about household size for renters, the policy of a tightly controlled market has much less of an impact on the general pattern of the choice process than might be expected.

Geographical Context Effects

Geographical effects are focused on the spatial patterns of choice, where households move and where they, thus, select housing. The study will examine place effects in two forms—first, the way in which households take into account the constraining or enabling effects of particular residential environments; second, the way in which macroeconomic effects vary regionally and, thus, influence the choices that households make.

It is clear that the spatial structure of the city affects household choices. It was Michelson (1977) who first noted that families do not view home environments as black boxes or as passive contexts, but rather as environments which fulfill needs. Households sometimes choose residential environments which they believe will fulfill their *expectations.* At other times, they choose environments which they believe will fit their already established patterns of behavior. What we do know is that households purchase both a house and an environment, and that they pay attention to their environmental choices. Some have viewed the environmental choice as a cost constraint (Porell 1982). Here, however, the emphasis is on the role of the "preferred" residential environment as part of the bundle of choices that households make when they choose particular locations. It seems reasonable to argue that there are spatial or neighborhood effects beyond the effects of the house itself, and at least one study has already provided preliminary evidence of the role of residential environmental effects on residential choices. Boots and Kanaroglou (1988) have shown that measures of spatial structure are significant factors influencing choice.

Choices among Housing Markets

It is a well-established finding that the overwhelming majority of residential moves occur within specific housing markets. In the Netherlands, 60 percent to 80 percent of the choices are made within the housing market of origin. But even within an urban region such as the Randstad, the majority of moves are within housing markets segmented by urban size and then occur within the housing stock available in a fairly small area (table 5.12). The high

TABLE 5.12

Households That Moved in Randstad, Holland, in the Period 1981–1985 by Destination and by Original Residential Environment (%)

Origin	Destination					
	1	2	3	4	5	6
Large Cities						
1 Renting, Multi-Family	60.4	9.6	9.8	1.7	0.5	1.7
2 Renting, Single-Family	42.4	22.7	15.0	4.8	0.8	0.8
3 Owning	30.6	2.4	37.3	1.1	0.7	5.3
Medium-Sized Cities						
4 Renting, Multi-Family	1.4	0.3	0.7	39.5	25.3	17.7
5 Renting, Single-Family	2.1	—	—	27.0	33.4	18.8
6 Owning	2.2	—	2.5	20.6	7.6	37.5
Growth Centers						
7 Renting, Multi-Family	7.9	—	2.0	0.5	—	0.4
8 Renting, Single-Family	8.6	0.9	—	3.5	—	1.7
9 Owning	—	—	1.2	—	—	2.6
Suburb						
10 Renting, Multi-Family	4.5	0.3	2.2	2.5	1.0	1.1
11 Renting, Single-Family	2.1	3.5	0.4	1.6	1.0	1.9
12 Owning	2.7	1.2	2.7	—	1.1	2.7

proportion of those who choose dwellings in the multifamily sector in the large cities of the Randstad (Amsterdam, Rotterdam, The Hague, and Utrecht) illustrates the constraints of the housing stock on household choices. Because the majority of households move only relatively short distances when they make their housing changes, they are, in effect, selecting *within* the same housing type. Households that can and do change residential environments and move away from the large central cities select suburban owner occupation—an expected and replicated finding across national contexts. At the same time, there is a fairly significant flow from the new growth centers (new towns) and suburbs to multifamily housing in the large metropolitan areas. There is also an expected and replicable finding that younger renters leave home and move

TABLE 5.12 (continued)

Households That Moved in Randstad, Holland, in the Period 1981–1985
by Destination and by Original Residential Environment (%)

	Destination					
Origin	*7*	*8*	*9*	*10*	*11*	*12*
Large Cities						
1 Renting, Multi-Family	2.1	3.1	1.1	3.5	2.4	4.1
2 Renting, Single-Family	1.3	1.6	2.8	0.9	1.3	5.7
3 Owning	2.1	1.4	5.0	—	2.5	11.6
Medium-Sized cities						
4 Renting, Multi-Family	0.3	1.9	1.4	1.3	4.1	6.1
5 Renting, Single-Family	—	1.8	3.3	4.2	2.2	7.2
6 Owning	—	2.3	2.1	1.9	4.5	18.8
Growth Centers						
7 Renting, Multi-Family	19.2	33.1	21.6	4.2	1.0	10.1
8 Renting, Single-Family	11.0	22.2	31.6	3.9	7.1	9.5
9 Owning	12.0	16.3	34.8	4.7	2.3	25.9
Suburb						
10 Renting, Multi-Family	0.9	2.0	1.5	27.6	30.4	26.0
11 Renting, Single-Family	0.7	2.1	0.4	17.4	31.7	37.2
12 Owning	1.3	1.3	2.5	13.8	12.2	58.6

Source: Deurloo et al., 1990. Reprinted from *Urban Studies*, vol. 27, by permission.

to large cities to begin their housing career (Jobse and Musterd 1989). To reiterate, the large majority of moves occur within the residential environment of origin, as the large percentages on the diagonal of table 5.12 indicate.

The combined effects of the original residential environment and the effects of income and household composition (the choice variables from chapter 4) can be demonstrated with another ANOTA analysis (table 5.13). The previously seen choice emerges again. Low-income and single persons move to rental housing, while high-income households and families are more likely to move to single-family homes and into the owner-occupation sector. In

TABLE 5.13

Coefficients for Choices of (Previous) Renters,
Randstad, Holland (ANOTA analysis)

Choice	Average	Income (thousand guilders)			
		<21	21–29	30–47	>47
Renting, Multi-Family	47.8	19.3	8.7	–3.6	–14.4
Renting, Single-Family	27.0	–2.2	1.9	1.7	–8.5
Owning	25.2	–17.2	–10.5	2.0	22.9

Choice	Average	Composition of households			
		Single	Two-person	Family	One-parent
Renting, Multi-Family	47.8	16.7	4.1	–11.7	–5.6
Renting, Single-Family	27.0	–11.3	–2.1	6.3	9.9
Owning	25.2	–5.3	–2.0	5.3	–4.3

Choice	Average	Original residential environment			
		Large Cities	Medium Cities	Growth Centers	Suburbs
Renting, Multi-Family	47.8	14.2	–5.9	–13.4	–13.1
Renting, Single-Family	27.0	–9.4	6.6	4.0	8.6
Owning	25.2	–4.8	–0.7	9.4	4.5

Source: Deurloo et al., 1990. Reprinted from Urban Studies, vol. 27, by permission.

addition to these effects, which were seen in previous chapters, there is also a clear effect of the residential environment. In large cities, the likelihood of choosing a multifamily dwelling is high, even after income and family composition are considered. In the suburban and new towns (the cities built to relieve residential growth), the likelihood of moving into the ownership sector is higher for *all* households than in the large and medium-sized cities.

In figure 5.11, some of the coefficients from table 5.13 have been used to portray the "additional" explanation that is owing to

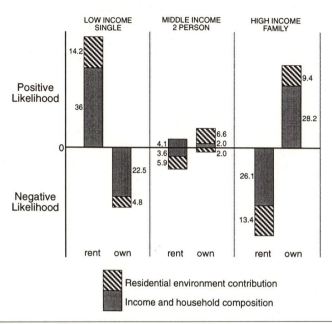

FIGURE 5.11

The additional effect of residential environment on housing choice by income category in the Netherlands

Source: Deurloo et al., 1994.

the effect of residential environment on choices. Low-income single persons are unlikely to move into ownership but are quite likely to choose multifamily rental housing wherever they are in the Randstad. If they live in cities before the move, however, this pattern is exacerbated. The most distinctive choices are by high-income families who reverse the process for low-income households. If the high-income families already live in one of the new towns, then the environmental origin adds to the contrasts in choice patterns. For middle-income households, the environmental effects are not as large but they are, in relative terms, an important effect on the choices of this group of households.

The fact that the current residential environment before the move influences the succeeding housing choice does not mean that the usual pattern of redistribution of population that occurs between central cities, suburbs, and nonmetropolitan areas is absent in the Randstad. This is a somewhat different view of the role of residential environment in the choice process. Since older and rental housing exists primarily in the inner areas of metropolitan regions and newer and owner-occupied housing is located predominantly in more suburban parts (see chapter 1), movements of households from the center outward predominate, as households make the hierarchical steps in their housing career.

During the 1970s the suburban expansion of population in the Netherlands replicated the 1950s and 1960s expansion in the United States. Large numbers of families in the Randstad left the central cities, and even the Randstad (Rotterdam, Amsterdam, The Hague, and Utrecht) as a whole, in search of single-family housing and owner occupation rather than rental housing (fig. 5.12). This population loss in the central cities was only partly offset by the effect of the expanding baby-boom population migrating to the central cities and by the influx of immigrants from outside the country. Although this pattern could be observed in many other cities and regions of the world, in the Netherlands, it was not without government influences and intervention (Jobse and Musterd 1992). New housing construction, almost completely under government control, took place in new towns and designated growth centers. New construction and rehabilitation of old housing in the cities was a much lower priority. When the effects of this policy—the rapid population outflow—became apparent, it was quickly reversed. New construction close to the central cities and in the old industrial sites within the central cities became the priority. At the same time, the government committed large sums of money to the renewal of the urban cores. The effects of this reversal of the physical planning policy (the housing agency of the government) are clearly visible in 1985 in the migration patterns between the cities, suburbs, and nonmetropolitan areas. Families are still suburbanizing but at a lower rate—a process that is greatly offset by young single persons moving into the cities of the Randstad from the suburbs and other parts of the country.

The patterns described for the Netherlands, with cities losing families and gaining young singles, is similar to what occurred in the United States, although the suburbs also absorb many migrants

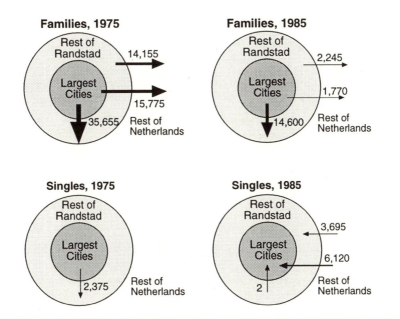

FIGURE 5.12
Migration between the largest central cities, the rest of the Randstad, and the rest of the Netherlands

Source: Jobse and Musterd, 1989. Redrawn by permission of Stedelijke Netwerken, Utrecht, the Netherlands.

from nonmetropolitan areas. During the 1960s and 1970s, there was a rapid deconcentration from central cities to suburbs and from both central cities and suburbs to nonmetropolitan areas (fig. 5.13). In 1975–1976 and 1982–1983, there were substantial net outflows from suburbs to surrounding nonmetropolitan rings but by the early 1980s this pattern had changed. Deconcentration within metropolitan areas continues the long process of urbanization. In 1983–1984, the net outflow was almost two million persons from central cities to suburbs and an additional very small flow to the nonmetropolitan ring (fig. 5.13). Of course, these net flows are derived from substantial gross flows that generated a gain of about 2.1 million suburban residents.

The central issue underlying the flows from central cities to suburbs is the difference in owner/renter ratios in the two markets.

(a) Gross flows

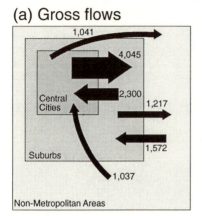

(b) Net flows

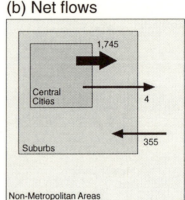

FIGURE 5.13

Gross and net flows between central cities and suburbs and non-metropolitan areas, 1983–1984, in the United States (width of arrows is proportional to net flows in thousands)

Source: U.S. Bureau of the Census, *Current Population Reports,* Series P. 20, No. 407.

The central city is predominantly renter, and there is a net flow of owners out and renters in. Interestingly, however, the suburbs are no longer owner enclaves. Substantial numbers of renters have been moving to the suburbs from both the central city and from other metropolitan areas (fig. 5.14)

The maps of the flows between cities and suburbs for a sample of cities pinpoint the importance of local effects on owner/renter mobility and tenure choices (fig. 5.15). The maps are designed to reflect the relative size of the city and suburban populations and the size of the flows—hence, the choices between central city and suburban environments. Because the interest of this study is principally in choice, it is unnecessary to comment at length on the differences between the much lower levels of interchange between the city and suburbs in Philadelphia and Detroit and the greater interaction in "newer" cities such as Phoenix and San Diego. There are clear contrasts between the dynamism of Phoenix and the lower mobility rates of Detroit and Philadelphia. Naturally, this reflects, in turn, the choice set for residents in these older inner-city com-

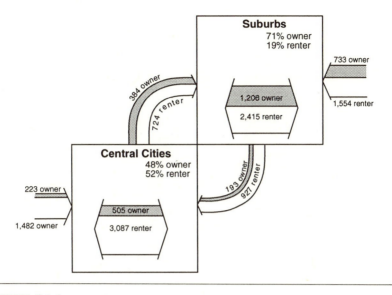

FIGURE 5.14
Household flows (000s) between central cities and suburbs by tenure,
1989–1990, in the United States

Source: U.S. Bureau of the Census, *American Housing Survey*, 1991.

munities. Such strong differences emphasize the separateness of
metropolitan housing markets. In all the cities, owners choose suburban locations if they are new to the metropolitan area, and when
moving within the city. In San Diego, a classically expanding and
growing city, the central city still attracts large numbers of owners. It is important, however, to reiterate the link between ownership, changes to ownership, and suburban markets. The spatial context is an important element of the selection process and has an
important differentiating effect on household location in the metropolitan area. Central cities, as will be seen later, are increasingly
dominated by renters over time, as suburban localities become the
preserve of owners.

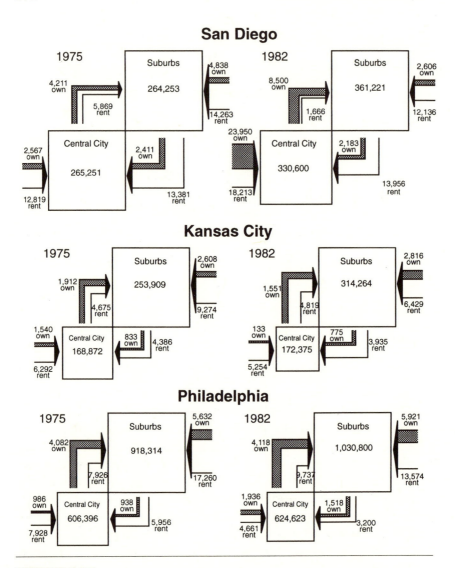

FIGURE 5.15
The structure of owner and renter flows across example metropolitan
areas

Source: U.S. Bureau of the Census, *American Housing Survey*, Metropolitan
Reports, 1991.

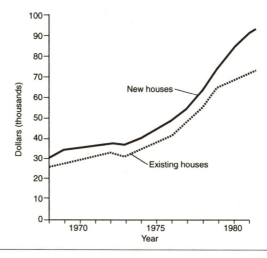

FIGURE 5.16
Median sales prices of new and existing homes in the United States

Source: U.S. Federal Home Loan Bank Board.

Regional Variations in Economic Impacts

The ability to move to ownership is also affected by the inter-section of the time in which the household wishes to move as well as by the regional or metropolitan housing market in which the household finds itself. During the mid-1970s, it was easier by far to purchase a house in the eastern cities of the United States than in California. Then, the housing market in the northeastern states "caught up" with the earlier rise in prices in California. At certain times, there are significant shifts in the prices for new and exist-ing homes. Beginning in the early 1970s, and continuing during the late 1970s, a significant upward spiral in house prices could be observed in the United States, notably for new houses (fig. 5.16). In some years, the average annual increase in prices was between 11 percent and 13 percent. In specific metropolitan areas, the price inflation was considerably greater than these averages. In Chicago during 1974–1976, the price increase was about 7 percent. A year later, in 1976–1977, it was 19 percent for new homes (Grebler and Mittlebach 1979). The patterns are locally variable with obvious consequences especially for first-time buyers. Indeed, first-time home buyers emerge as the main group that is disadvantaged by such rapid localized price increases. These rapid shifts increase the gap between house prices and the typical income of first-time purchasers.

To illustrate the impact of broad housing market contexts on the timing of the move from renting to owning a dwelling, this study used the time-series data already shown in figure 5.1 for each of the four regions (Northeast, North Central, West, and South) used by the U.S. Bureau of the Census. There are marked regional differences and even some "crossovers" in the regional patterns of price increases. It is clearly easier to move to ownership in the lower-priced North Central region and in the South compared with the Northeast. In the West and Northeast, house prices soared between 1984 and 1987, which made the decision to purchase more difficult for an increasing number of households.

The percentage of new construction shows large regional differences, with high rates of additions to the housing stock in the southern and the western United States, and a low rate in the Northeast. The combination of relatively low levels of new construction and high prices in the Northeast depressed the probability of a move to ownership. There was a dip in new construction in both 1975 and during the period 1980 to 1982 in all regions.

The inclusion of regional effects in the likelihood model highlights the housing market effects in the Northeast, which had much less favorable conditions for moving to homeownership during the late 1970s and the 1980s (table 5.14). The level of new construction was low, thus depressing the opportunities for movement, and prices were high. Living in the North Central region, the South, and even the expensive West considerably increased the likelihood of moving to ownership.

Observations and Summary

The decision to move or not, and the choice of a house with particular characteristics, are driven by individual and household preferences. These preferences are influenced and constrained by parallel events in the life course such as family formation and job career. But housing market choices do not occur in a vacuum; they

TABLE 5.14

Regional Effects on the Probability of Moving from Rent-to-Own for Families and Couples in the United States, 1970–1987

Variable	Parameter	Risk ratio
Age (t)	−0.01	0.99
Race	0.76*	2.13
Income (t)	0.01*	1.01
Employment Status of Head (t)	0.67*	1.96
Number of Earners (t)	0.24*	1.27
Couple or Family Status (t)	−0.09	0.91
Change Couple to Family in Previous Year (t)	0.38*	1.46
Change 1 to 2 Earners in Previous Year (t)	−0.19	0.83
Positive Income Change in Previous Year (t)	0.18	1.20
Rent (t)	0.01*	1.01
Size of Rental House (t)	−0.10*	0.91
North Central Region vs. Northeast	0.46*	1.58
West Region vs. Northeast	0.02	1.03
South Region vs. Northeast	0.32*	1.37
Period 1974–79 vs. 1970–73	0.09	1.10
Period 1980–83 vs. 1970–73	−0.20	0.82
Period 1984–87 vs. 1970–73	−0.26	0.77

(t) Time varying
* Significant at the 0.01 level
−2log L: without covariates 5037.3; with covariates 4682.5
Model X^2 is 354.8 ($p = 0.0001$)

Source: Deurloo et al., 1994. Reprinted from *Environment and Planning A*, vol. 26, by permission.

are affected by an array of contextual circumstances, including changing economic circumstances, housing market circumstances as they differ between regions and countries, and government housing policy.

Economic circumstances, buying power, the interest on mortgages, relative cost of renting and owning, and the level of new construction of dwellings can fluctuate considerably over the course of time. These fluctuations directly affect tenure choice. When prices of owner-occupation are relatively moderate, and levels of new construction are high and interest rates are low, more people can afford ownership, and the choice to own is increasingly attractive to lower-income purchasers. At the same time, high rents push those who can afford it to buy a house even when the cost of housing is higher and interest rates are rising. Of course, households at different income levels are affected differently: two-earner couples particularly seem to be least susceptible to economic fluctuations in their tenure decision.

The composition of the housing stock in the local housing market in terms of tenure, single or multifamily dwelling, and so on, cannot change rapidly, because housing has a long life span. Consequently, the composition of the local housing stock constrains the choice possibilities of households and, particularly in the Netherlands, households with the same characteristics end up in different parts of the housing stock in differently structured housing markets.

An important geographical context in housing choice is the central city–suburbs contrast that exists almost everywhere in the Western world. There are great differences in quality and owner/renter ratios between these two residential environments in metropolitan areas; therefore, the central city–suburb element is an important aspect of housing choice. Relative sizes of these environments vary between cities and over time, and generate complicated patterns of aggregate flows of residential moves between these environments.

Finally, government influence on the operation of the housing market is quite extensive in Western Europe, and certainly in the Netherlands. Matching households and housing in controlled housing markets is most directly influenced by housing stock. Governments intervene indirectly by manipulating the housing market circumstances themselves. Rent controls, building subsidies, and residential zoning regulations greatly affect the tenure and type of new construction as well as relative pricing in various segments of the housing stock. Yet, the influence of housing policy on the general patterns of housing choices must not be overrated. In both the United States and the Netherlands, income, household size, and status still largely determine housing choice between the available alternatives, although the alternatives are certainly different in the two countries.

The interest in examining housing choice in controlled and uncontrolled housing markets becomes even more important given recent research suggesting that housing market control has not improved the optimal provision of housing. The empirical evidence provided in Nesslein (1988) suggests that market mechanisms can efficiently allocate housing, that housing markets do respond to the demands of consumers, and that rising real incomes will, in turn, create an increased supply of good housing (Nesslein 1988, 106). As a parallel to the research on the supply side of the housing market in controlled systems, the analysis reported here examines the demand side of the equation and demonstrates striking parallels between controlled and less-controlled housing markets. This consumption approach offers further documentation for the Nesslein arguments that activities in the housing market may be much less affected by policy than is commonly believed in Europe.

6

Outcomes of Housing Choices

Earlier chapters in this book established the ways in which mobility and housing choices are interlinked. Those chapters developed an explanation for the way in which individuals, with particular age and income characteristics, relocate within particular housing markets, and what influences their choices. The interplay of mobility and the development of the housing stock create the aggregate pattern of housing occupancy in a nation as a whole. Moreover, economic and social contexts also affect the form of the outcomes. The aim of this concluding chapter is to illustrate how the overall pattern of outcomes is the result of the aggregation of individual choices. It is also designed to demonstrate the similarities and differences in outcomes in our two "very different" housing nations—the United States and the Netherlands. This final chapter has been organized around three questions: who gets which housing; in terms of tenure and type, what does it cost; and where do households live? Thus, an attempt is made to parallel these themes, which were used as the organizing structure for chapter one. It is not the intention to cover all aspects of outcomes.

Tenure and Type of Housing

Throughout this book the emphasis has been on the critical role of tenure both in terms of the development of housing markets in general and in the choice process of individuals and households. Over the last two decades there has been a consistent shift toward more owner occupation throughout the Western world, and it reflects the change in consumer preferences, even in the Netherlands whose rental sector is well-developed and attractive to a broad section of households. Notwithstanding, not all households end up in the ownership sector; ultimately, this is related to household characteristics such as position in the life course, household stability, and job security. Renting or owning a house is also very directly related to the type of dwelling—whether it is multifamily or single family, detached or row housing—as well as to its quality. It is now time to consider the issue of how choices made at the individual level are translated into aggregate patterns of housing occupancy in the two countries.

In the United States, ownership increases with age; by their early thirties, over half of all heads of household in the United States are homeowners. The rate of increase in homeownership levels off in the age group forty to forty-four, but significant declines in ownership do not begin until household heads enter the retirement years (fig. 6.1[a]). Clearly, there are large numbers of older households still in housing that had been purchased in much earlier periods of the housing cycle with the attendant "overuse" of space, which was noted in the earlier chapters.

The rate of increase in ownership with increases in income is not as rapid as the increase with age (fig. 6.1[b]). Overall, households with more than fifty thousand dollars in annual income are 60 percent more likely to own than households earning less than fifteen thousand dollars. When both age and income are plotted on the same graph, the relative roles of age and income become clear (fig. 6.1[c]). The rate of increase in ownership is extremely steep for wealthy households. They reach an 80 percent ownership rate by age group thirty to thirty-four. Low-income households have a rate closer to 30 percent. Clearly, younger, wealthier households enter the homeowner market with relative ease. Age plays a greater role for low-income households which, in older years, reach almost 80 percent of the rate of ownership of the wealthiest households (the age sixty to sixty-four low-income group has a 0.72 ownership rate, while the same group earning over fifty thousand dollars has an ownership rate of 0.93). The dip in ownership rates for the wealthiest income groups in the twenty to twenty-four age group seems to be related to young households in "family-owned" units during college attendance. It is also affected by relatively small

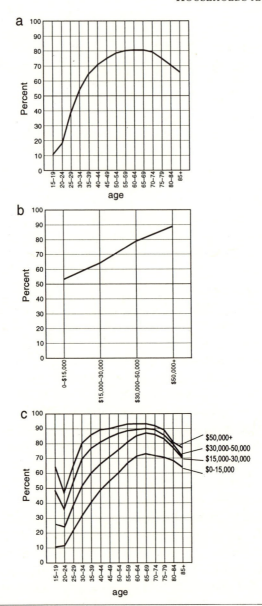

FIGURE 6.1

For the United States in 1990, proportion of all household heads who are (a) owners; (b) owners by income category; and (c) owners by age and income category

Source: U.S. Bureau of the Census, *Public Use Microdata Sample (PUMS)*, 1990.

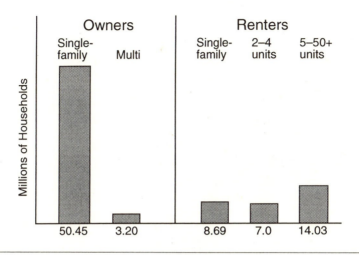

FIGURE 6.2

Distribution of tenure for U.S. households in 1990

Source: U.S. Census of Population and Housing, 1990.

numbers of households with very high incomes. The dip should not be given too much weight.

Although the majority of households are owners, there are almost thirty million renter households (fig. 6.2). Clearly, single-family owners dominate the housing structure and multifamily renter households are the second largest category, but it is the composition of the households in each of the sectors that reveals a great deal about the impacts of age and income on the likelihood of owning or renting.

The contrast between owners and renters, in both single-family units and multifamily units, is striking (fig. 6.3). Owners in single-family housing are disproportionately older in comparison with renters. More than 60 percent of all owners are over forty-five years old, and nearly 85 percent of multifamily renters are under thirty-five years of age. Although there is a division by income, it plays a greater role, as expected, for younger households. Households with heads between thirty-five and forty-four years of age who earn more than forty thousand dollars are more likely to be owners (fig. 6.3). The largest group of single-family renters are between twenty-five and thirty-four years of age and earn less than thirty thousand dol-

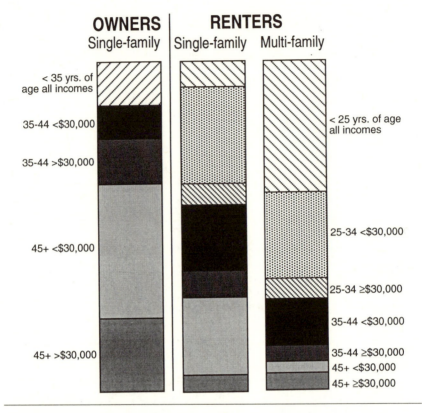

FIGURE 6.3
Composition of owner and renter tenures for U.S. households in 1990

Source: U.S. Census of Population and Housing, 1990.

lars. There is an almost equally large group of older renters (over forty-five years of age) with incomes under thirty thousand dollars. For multifamily renters the largest group is the older, lower-income heads. The second largest group is composed of those between thirty-five and forty-four years of age and earning under thirty thousand dollars. In sum, older, better-off households are not renters.

A comparison of the rates of ownership for 1980 and 1990 shows a slight dip in ownership, which reflects the increasing difficulty of achieving ownership in a more stringent economic climate. One way of examining the effects of changing conditions is

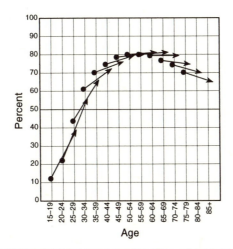

FIGURE 6.4
Cohort trajectories of ownership for 1980–1990 for all U.S. households

Source: U.S. Bureau of the Census, *Public Use Microdata Sample (PUMS)*, 1980 and 1990.

to plot the trajectories of cohorts over time. This demonstrates the nature of change over time and introduces the longitudinal dimension to our aggregate presentation of ownership trends. The cohort trajectories are plotted by drawing a line between the ownership rate in 1980 for a particular cohort to that cohort ten years older in 1990, linking the same cohort at two different points in time. For example, 13 percent of the cohort that was fifteen to nineteen years old in 1980 were owners. Ten years later, at age twenty-five to twenty-nine, 37 percent were owners. Cohorts increase their ownership as they age (fig. 6.4). Younger cohorts clearly increased their ownership but households in the middle age range had only modest increases in ownership over time. Notably, the older age groups showed significant declines in ownership.

Cohort trajectories were originally used by Pitkin and Masnick (1986) and Pitkin (1990). Masnick, Pitkin, and Brennan (1990) emphasized cohorts' distribution across housing types. Myers and Wolch (1995) used the technique in a study of housing polarization, and Myers (1992) applied it to cohorts segmented by race. For a discussion of the method see Pitkin and Myers (1994).

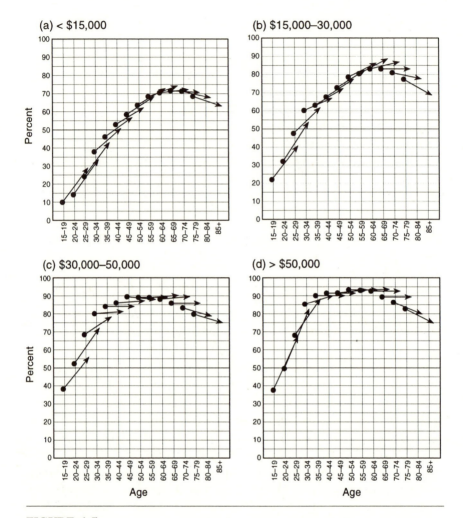

FIGURE 6.5
Cohort trajectories of ownership for 1980–1990 for U.S. households by
income class

Source: U.S. Bureau of the Census, *Public Use Microdata Sample (PUMS)*,
1980 and 1990.

The young-adult households show rapid movement into single-
family homeownership. The rate of movement into ownership is
far greater than at any other period in the housing–life cycle trajectory. However, after age forty-five, cohorts begin to reduce their

movement to ownership. In the past a slowing of the movement to ownership was tied to "trading down" by widows and couples in the empty nest syndrome. Now the slowing may be related to economic constraints on homeownership, and this is investigated by examining trajectories for four categories of income.

When the trajectories are plotted by income category, it becomes clear that lower-income groups are still moving into ownership (fig. 6.5). However, a critical interpretation of this process is to recognize that less wealthy households take longer to enter the homeowner market and never reach the average rate of ownership that is standard for wealthy households. It is the constraint of income that so clearly emerges in the models of tenure choice being played out in the aggregations of income categories. Comparing segment (a) incomes under fifteen thousand dollars of figure 6.5 with segment (d) for incomes over fifty thousand dollars, highlights the process of entry into ownership. Not only does the trajectory begin at a much lower level for low-income households than for higher-income groups, but there is little or no plateau that occurs for the high-income households. The latter group reaches the more than 80 percent ownership rate by a very early age and stays at that level of ownership almost through the entire life course. By comparison, the poorest households never reach that level of ownership and have a much narrower plateau in which they can enjoy the status of ownership.

In the Netherlands as in the United States, age, income, and family type are important determinants in the distribution of the housing stock among households. Young singles usually live in the multifamily stock, while couples and families are most visible in the detached and semidetached single-family homes (table 6.1). Older households (higher incomes in general) are most able to access the attractive detached housing. The row housing is occupied by a wide variety of households with a substantial range of ages and incomes. This housing seems to act as an equalizing factor in the Netherlands housing market. Indeed, it is often difficult to tell if the row houses are in owner occupation or in rent, and both tenures are frequently mixed in the new neighborhoods, which were built in the past twenty-five years. The influence of government policy on the composition of the stock is most evident in this sector. Because the government also subsidized the construction of

TABLE 6.1

Households by Type and Age as Distributed over the Housing Stock by
Type of Housing in the Netherlands, 1990 (percentage)

	Single Person		Couple without Children		Family		% of Stock
	<45	≥45	<45	≥45	<45	≥45	
Single Family							
– Detached	4	10	12	20	16	26	16
– Semi-Detached	3	6	11	11	14	13	10
– Row House	21	33	44	43	54	48	43
Multi-Family	72	52	32	26	17	12	31
Total (%)	100	100	100	100	100	100	100

Source: Netherlands Central Bureau of Statistics (CBS), 1992.

owner-occupation housing for median-income households, they
also show up in the higher owner-occupation rates of median-
income families.

In the Netherlands, ownership increases with income (table
6.2). The rate of ownership is about 0.2 for low-income households
and rises to just over 0.75 for the highest income category. In the
Netherlands, households with an income in the range that includes
the median (thirty-one thousand to forty-one thousand guilders,
about twenty-one thousand to twenty-six thousand dollars) are
evenly divided between renting and owning—approximately 10
percent in both cases (table 6.2). This suggests that, until recently,
there was no strong preference for owning over renting, as there
has been in the United States. For households in the income categories above the median, homeownership increases of course,
while toward the lower end of the income scale, ownership rates
fall off, but are not close to zero. Thus, there appears to be less
income polarization in tenure status than in the United States.

The low polarization by income between tenures also appears
to be true for the larger cities. The stock of the cities can be classified into five tenures. Municipal housing (equivalent to public
housing in the United States) and private rental housing owned by
small private landlords are usually of the lowest quality. The stock

TABLE 6.2

Net Household Income and Tenure Status, the Netherlands, 1990

Net Household Income (× 1,000 guilders)	% Own	*% of Total Stock in Use by Group*	
		Rent	Own
<15	21	8	2
15–<18	19	5	1
18–<21	28	5	2
21–<26	25	9	3
26–<31	36	8	5
31–<41	50	10	10
41–<51	63	5	9
≥ 51	76	4	13
Total	45	55	45

Source: Netherlands Ministry of Housing, Physical Planning, and the Environment (MVROM), 1992.

owned by the housing corporations holds the middle ground with respect to quality and price, while the private rental stock, in the hands of institutional investors, and the small stock of owner-occupied dwellings are at the top of the housing market in the cities. The households in the various income deciles are, of course, unevenly represented in these five tenures, with the higher incomes overrepresented in the higher quality stock. The differences are gradual over most of the tenures, but there is a major difference for owner-occupied housing (fig. 6.6).

As in other countries, ownership rates have been rising during the 1980s (table 6.3). For the lower-income groups, the picture is mixed. Ownership rates at first declined in the earlier part of the 1980s but increased later. The early 1980s was a period of low consumer confidence during a prolonged economic downturn. This certainly discouraged lower-income groups and starters from moving into ownership. Even for income categories of twenty-three thousand guilders (well below the median income), however, ownership rates were on the rise. The table suggests an increasing division between renting and owning for higher and lower income groups.

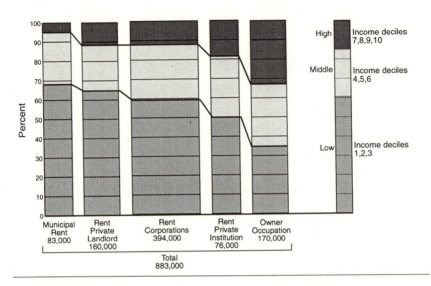

FIGURE 6.6
Households by tenure sectors and income deciles in the four largest
cities in the Netherlands, 1989

Source: Dieleman, 1994. Redrawn from *Urban Studies*, vol. 31, by permission.

TABLE 6.3

Households by Net Income and Percentage Owner Occupation, the
Netherlands, 1982, 1986, 1990

Income (1,000 guilders)	1982	1986	1990
< 15	24	20	27
15–<18	21	17	18
18–<21	28	24	28
21–<24	25	23	25
24–<29	28	30	33
29–<38	36	41	44
38–<47	45	52	57
≥ 47	62	67	72

Source: Netherlands Ministry of Housing, Physical Planning and the Environment (MVROM), 1992.

TABLE 6.4

Housing Costs as a Percentage of Total Household Expenditure,
Based on Current Prices, 1975–1987

	1975	1980	1985	1986	1987
Netherlands	13.9	15.9	19.4	19.0	18.0
Germany (West)	17.4	18.8	21.9	21.1	20.6
France	15.8	17.5	19.1	18.8	18.9
Belgium	15.4	16.4	18.7	17.5	17.1
United Kingdom	18.3	18.8	20.7	20.4	—
Denmark	22.8	27.0	25.4	25.2	26.6
Sweden	21.7	25.0	26.4	25.6	25.2

Source: Organisation of Economic Cooperation and Development (OECD), 1988.

Affordability

The cost of housing varies substantially among countries and regions, and across time (table 6.4). Comparisons of this nature are difficult to make because what is recorded as housing costs varies from country to country, and there are different ways of treating costs in the owner-occupier sector. Nonetheless, the variations are significantly different, even allowing for uncertainties, and cannot be explained on the basis of variations in wealth and quality of housing between countries alone. Traditions of how much one finds reasonable to spend on housing, as well as attitudes deriving from historical circumstances, are important factors in what households are prepared or expected to spend on shelter.

In the United States, for at least two decades after World War II, when the expansion of the stock of single-family housing was increasing rapidly, the cost of housing actually declined in real dollars. The U.S. building industry constructed large numbers of relatively modest, detached single-family houses. Despite the media commentary on the "sameness" of suburban America, this increase in the housing stock contributed significantly to the improvement of housing quality in the United States.

During the last decade, however, the research commentary has

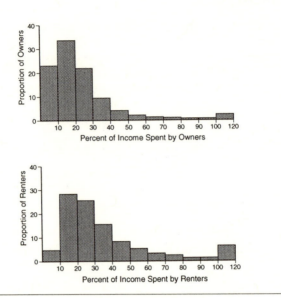

FIGURE 6.7
Housing affordability for U.S. owners and renters

Source: U.S. Bureau of the Census, *American Housing Survey,* 1989.

turned to the crisis of affordability and the difficulty of entry into ownership (Nelson 1994; Gyourko and Linneman 1993). This same commentary also emphasizes the differences between central cities and suburbs both in increasing income differentiation and in increasing differences between renters and owners. Currently, approximately 42 percent of owners and almost half of renters—47 percent—spend more than one-third of their income on housing. There are important differences between owners and renters (fig. 6.7). In general, the "affordability" histograms show that the peak proportion of income to housing, the most common expenditure on housing, is in the range of 10 percent to 20 percent for owners, but in the 20 percent to 30 percent range for renters. Of course, renters are younger and have lower incomes, and housing cost as a proportion of income is clearly more punitive for them than for owners.

A breakdown of housing costs for low- and high-income households shows even more dramatically the outcome of what it costs to own and rent for different subgroups of the population. Low-income households are disproportionately renters, of course. For both owner-occupation and for rental housing, however, low-income households spend a greater proportion of their resources on housing than do high-income households, notwithstanding that, in total, the latter groups spend more on their housing. As in the figure for ownership trajectories, there is a notable difference between housing costs for households under fifteen thousand dollars and households earning more than fifty thousand dollars (fig. 6.8). The bimodal structure for low-income owners reflects a large number of elderly low-income owners who purchased their houses early in the life course and, consequently, have low mortgage payments.

Although the housing policy in the Netherlands was very different, there was also the tradition of spending little on shelter and of a cheap housing stock as well. Until well into the 1970s, government policy kept rents low, partly to keep inflation under control and partly to moderate the demand for wage increases by the labor unions. The change in government policy during the 1980s to raise rents in accordance with market levels, even in the public rental sector, shows up in the increased housing costs for the Dutch population (fig. 6.9). This policy has also brought housing costs in the Netherlands to a level that is more prevalent in other parts of Western Europe.

Housing costs vary dramatically in the Netherlands as they do in the United States (table 6.5). Due to a threshold in the cost of dwellings below which housing is simply unavailable, low-income households must spend a much larger proportion of their income on shelter than people with a higher income. Even in the Netherlands, where a large stock of relatively cheap housing is available, those with an income below twenty-one thousand guilders (about thirteen thousand dollars) have to expend 20 percent to 30 percent of their earnings to be able to live independently in the rental sector. With increasing income, this percentage spent on housing declines to as little as about 1 percent, a far lower proportion than in the United States.

In the owner-occupier sector, the picture is more complicated because mortgages and interest paid on mortgages play an important role in the costs of housing (table 6.5). Housing costs for households with a mortgage on their house and for renters are not very

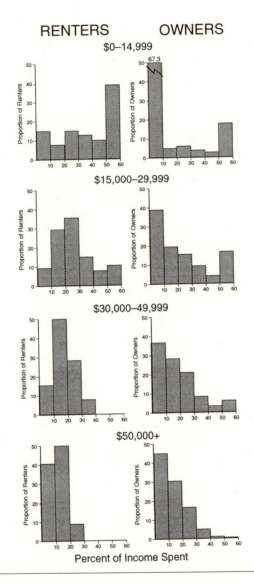

FIGURE 6.8

Housing affordability for U.S. owners and renters by income

Source: U.S. Bureau of the Census, *Public Use Microdata Sample (PUMS),* 1990.

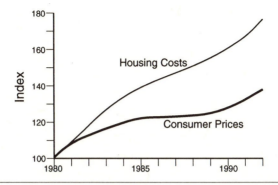

FIGURE 6.9

Index of consumer prices and housing costs, the Netherlands, 1980–1992

Source: Netherlands Ministry of Housing, Physical Planning and the Environment (MVROM).

TABLE 6.5

Households by Net Income and Percentage of Net Income Spent on Housing, the Netherlands, 1990

| Income (guilders in thousands) | *Percentage of Income Spent on Housing* | | | |
	Rent	Own	Own With Mortgage	(%) No Mortgage
< 15	27.7	9.7	32.9	81
15–<18	21.1	9.2	26.8	76
18–<21	19.9	6.4	20.7	80
21–<26	17.9	9.8	16.4	46
26–<31	17.1	12.3	16.1	28
31–<41	15.8	12.4	14.2	15
41–<51	13.5	11.9	13.0	11
≥ 51	11.3	10.9	11.7	8
Total	18.2	11.2	13.7	22

Source: Feddes, 1995. Reprinted by permission of Faculty of Geographical Sciences, University of Utrecht, the Netherlands.

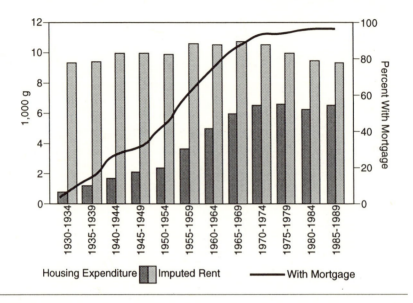

FIGURE 6.10
Net housing expenditure and gross imputed rent by date of initial
housing purchase, the Netherlands

Source: Everaers, 1990. Redrawn by permission of Netherlands Central Bureau of Statistics and Delft University Press.

different. As in the United States, low-income Dutch owner households spend a large portion of their income to attain this goal, although it is less than what their counterparts in the United States
must pay. Again, the percentage spent on housing decreases with
increasing income. The relationship of decreasing percentages of
income spent on housing as incomes rise, however, is counterbal-
anced by the fact that low-income householders are often elderly
and no longer have a mortgage on the house. Owner-occupiers of
long duration have very low housing costs (fig. 6.10). Mortgages
have been paid off, or, if there is still a mortgage, the amount is
small in 1990 guilders because of inflation. Nearly all recent buyers have a mortgage on the house. Those who have been in ownership over a long period are relatively "well-off" in the balance of
housing costs to housing assets. The imputed rent of older vintage
dwellings—an indication of their quality and value—is not much
below the average imputed rent of newer dwellings. Thus, these

TABLE 6.6

Households by Type and Tenure, and Percentage of Net Income
Spent on Housing, the Netherlands, 1981 and 1993

	Rent		*Own*	
	1981	1993	1981	1993
Single Person	19.5	24.9	14.0	13.1
Two Adults	13.8	17.2	14.0	13.1
Family with Children	14.2	18.9	18.2	15.1
Other	22.8	30.9	15.7	13.4

Source: Netherlands Ministry of Housing, Physical Planning, and the Environment (MVROM), 1994.

longtime owner households have property of considerable value at only minimal annual costs. Of course, it is this prospect, along with tax deductions of mortgage payments, that continues to motivate young households to move into homeownership.

The same pattern of decreasing housing expenditures with increasing occupancy duration is true for renters but to a much lesser extent. Those who moved into rental housing before 1960 in the Netherlands pay about 15 percent of their income for housing, while this percentage increases to levels of 20 percent to 25 percent for more recent movers.

The expenditure on housing also varies considerably with household status, especially for renters (table 6.6). Single-person and other types of households spend far more of their income on housing than do couples and families. This is partly a reflection of the lower average incomes of the first two categories of renters. In the owner-occupier sector, these differences are less pronounced. It is clear from the percentages in table 6.6 that the national policy of raising rents during the 1980s has affected mainly households in the rental sector. Owners have been much less affected by rising housing costs. These figures suggest that the effects of government policies can be just as unpredictable as market circumstances and do have major impacts on those who are least able to move out of the rental sector. At the same time, the Dutch government provides substantial housing support, mostly in the form of rent

subsidies and tax deductions on mortgage payments, for both renters and owners. These contributions average approximately 100
guilders (about sixty-five dollars) a month for the housing costs of
Dutch households, nearly one-fifth of their average expenditure on
shelter (EIB 1994).

Where Do Households Live?

Housing is obviously not distributed evenly within metropolitan
areas (cf. chapter 1). Older, and thus cheaper, housing is located
mostly in the centers of urban regions. The higher quality and more
expensive dwellings are concentrated in the suburbs in the United
States but to a lesser extent in European cities. This general pattern is naturally much more varied at the microscale of neighborhoods, but the overall pattern of separation exists at all scales. And,
although the process of gentrification in the United States, and extensive urban renewal schemes in the Netherlands, have modified
and diversified the simple central city versus suburban contrasts,
there is still marked housing separation between these two zones
of the city and neighborhoods within these zones. These contrasts
are important, as this section will illustrate.

The uneven spatial distribution of the housing stock, defined
in terms of quality, tenure, and price, also leads to a geographical
sorting of households by type, income, and race over the urban
mosaic. Residential choice and preference is expressed in neighborhoods with many inhabitants sharing the same ethnic background or country of origin. When these variations in race and origin interact with income differences and differences in labor market
participation, the results create significant differences in the quality
of life among neighborhoods. Landscapes of poverty and landscapes
of wealth develop despite government intervention and efforts to
ensure equal access to housing. Efforts to reduce the patterns of
extreme residential segregation, mostly by countries in Western
Europe, have not been very successful. For example, the provision
of nonprofit housing as a way of decreasing housing segregation
has sometimes created pockets of extreme poverty in the less-
attractive parts of the housing stock. As a result, governments have
become more reluctant to provide social housing (Power 1993).

TABLE 6.7

Distribution of Occupied Housing Units
(thousands) in U.S. Metropolitan Areas

	Central City	*Suburbs*
Owner	14,422	30,461
	49.1%	70.8%
Renter	15,422	12,575
	51.9%	19.2%

Source: U.S. Bureau of the Census, *American Housing Survey*, 1991.

Only the mass provision of public housing, as in Sweden and the Netherlands, has avoided or, more pessimistically, delayed the development of urban landscapes of poverty versus wealth in these countries. The model, however, of mass provision of social housing has already been modified. Both countries have cut back on available social housing under pressure to reduce government spending and return to market forces as a means of providing housing services.

The topics of residential segregation, neighborhood change, and urban poverty zones have become areas of extensive research with well-developed bodies of literature (Huttman et al. 1991; Armor and Clark 1995). As far as these topics provide a context for housing outcomes, they are relevant here. There will, however, be only brief comment on some illustrations from the United States and the Netherlands. The emphasis will be on central city-suburban contrasts and on patterns of residential segregation based on ethnic/country of origin measures. These two topics seem to be the most salient expressions of housing segregation.

Residential Patterns in the United States

Residential segregation, which occurs through the operation of the housing market, has a tendency to exacerbate central city-suburban differences (table 6.7) because concentrations of renters

TABLE 6.8

Mean Incomes for U. S. Central City and Suburban
Owners and Renters

	Central City	Suburbs
Owner	$35,464	$42,048
Renter	18,938	24,637

Source: U. S. Bureau of the Census, American Housing Survey, 1991.

and owners and of poor and rich households are reflected in the
quality of services such as retail stores, schools, sports facilities,
and the general appearance of neighborhoods. These differences
then influence the choices of mobile households and further
strengthen residential separation by income and tenure.

Renter incomes are lower than owner incomes, which reflects
the younger ages of renters in general, and both central city owners and renters have lower incomes than suburban owners and
renters (table 6.8). The distributions are far more skewed in the
rental than the ownership sector and for the central city versus
the suburbs (fig. 6.11). Although 84 percent of household renters
in the central city have incomes of less than forty thousand dollars, the corresponding percentage for renters in the suburbs is 77
percent. For owners in the central city, 55 percent have incomes
below forty thousand dollars, and of owners in the suburbs approximately 47 percent earn less than that amount. To put the income
figures into context, mean personal income in the United States
in 1990 was about thirty thousand dollars.

Maps of racial and ethnic groups reveal "separate" societies,
although there are some small steps toward integration in suburban communities (Clark 1996). The continuing separation of racial and ethnic groups is important for our discussion of housing
to the extent that it has created a polarized housing market. Central areas dominated by minorities are areas of rental housing, often with the greatest concentration of substandard housing. Ownership rates are lowest for blacks and Hispanics. In 1990, the black
homeownership rate for younger households was about one-half

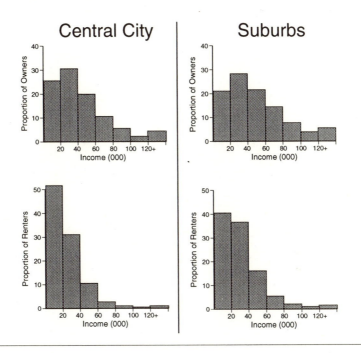

FIGURE 6.11
Household income for owners and renters by central city and suburbs in the United States

Source: U. S. Bureau of the Census, *American Housing Survey*, 1991.

that of non-Hispanic whites. And even for older groups, sixty-five to seventy-four, the ownership rate of black households was around 75 percent of non-Hispanic whites. The combination of lower income, smaller asset-to-income ratio, preference for similar race communities, and past private discrimination has created a spatially restricted housing market for minority groups, although primarily for low-income groups. The failure of minorities to enter the housing market in earlier decades now limits the chance of receiving asset increases from inherited housing bought at a time of rapidly rising housing prices. Again, one can see the effects of income on tenure opportunities, but this time they are modified by the polarizing effects of race and ethnicity.

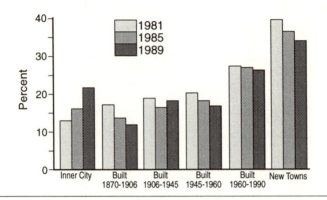

FIGURE 6.12
Percentage of households with incomes in the highest quartile by urban
zone in the major Dutch cities, 1981–1989

Source: Everaers et al., 1992. Redrawn by permission of Netherlands Central
Bureau of Statistics.

Residential Patterns in Dutch Urban Regions

Ethnic segregation in Dutch cities developed later and at less
intense levels than in the United States. Later and slower rates of
suburbanization and more recent ethnic in-migration created a
more diversified residential mix. Beginning in the early 1960s, both
suburbanization and ethnic in-migration changed the pattern of
residential racial/ethnic separation in the Netherlands.

Before the wave of suburbanization in the Netherlands, the
population profile of central cities did not differ much from the
surrounding suburban areas. Large numbers of families with children lived in inner-city areas, and in 1960, income levels in the
central cities were higher than those in the rest of the country.
Beginning in 1970, this situation changed dramatically. One- and
two-person households now dominate the household composition
in the central cities. Income levels are much lower in the central
cities than in the surrounding suburbs (fig. 6.12). In all zones of
the urban regions of Amsterdam, Rotterdam, and The Hague there
are numerous low-income households, while in the outer zones,
growth centers, and suburbs, higher incomes predominate. However, the inner city is recovering to some extent its socioeconomic

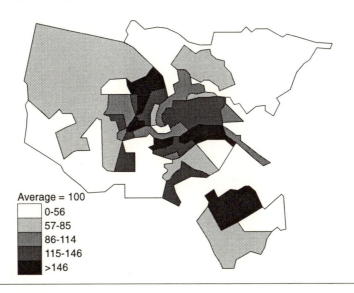

FIGURE 6.13
Variations in the number of persons on social security, by neighborhood
in Amsterdam, 1993

Source: Everaers et al., 1992. Redrawn by permission of Netherlands Ministry
of Housing, Physical Planning and the Environment.

position due to massive urban renewal sponsored by national government funding.

The contrast in income levels between central zones and outer zones of the urban regions is still much less than the more extreme contrasts for U.S. cities and even for some other cities in Europe (Musterd 1994). At a more detailed geographical grain, contrasts are more notable (fig. 6.13). Households on welfare payment schemes are clearly concentrated in the ring of neighborhoods surrounding the inner city in Amsterdam, principally because the older, smaller, and cheaper housing can be found in these areas.

These contrasts between central city and suburban population characteristics, such as age, rate of participation in the labor force, and income, clearly coincide with the quality, price, and tenure of the housing stock (table 6.9). The central parts of Dutch cities (developed before 1945) are predominantly rental stock, and rents are generally low. For the zone developed between 1945 and 1990,

TABLE 6.9

Households in Amsterdam, Rotterdam and The Hague,
by Zone of Residence and Tenure of the House, 1989
(percentage)

Zone	Rent	Own	Total
Urban before 1945	81	19	100
Urban 1945–1990	85	15	100
Suburban/Growth Centers	58	42	100

Source: Everaers et al., 1992. Reprinted by permission of Netherlands Central Bureau of Statistics.

rents are also low because of the massive construction of public rental housing during this period. The suburbs and growth centers have higher percentages of owner-occupied housing, but they also have substantial proportions of rental housing. Thus, the outer zone of the urban regions has not developed as an exclusively owner-occupied sector.

At the same time that the suburbanization wave occurred in the Netherlands, the country became a destination for immigrants (Dieleman 1993). Guest workers were actively recruited in Morocco and Turkey, and large numbers of inhabitants of Surinam arrived during the 1970s and 1980s. Following a fairly standard pattern, many of the immigrants settled in the major cities. Forty-four percent of these now live in the largest urban centers—Amsterdam, Rotterdam, The Hague, and Utrecht. Twenty-three percent of the population of these cities is now of foreign descent. Twenty years earlier, in 1970, the presence of an immigrant population in the cities was virtually undetectable. Figure 6.14 shows the pattern of dominance of a young immigrant population in the younger age cohorts.

The large public rental sector in the cities continues to play an important role in the development of patterns of housing for the immigrant population. Public housing was initially closed to immigrants, because they did not have the necessary "period of residence" or the necessary family structure (Dieleman 1993). When the rules were changed during the late 1970s to accommo-

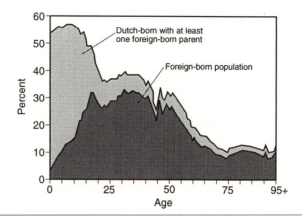

FIGURE 6.14
Foreign-born and Dutch-born population with at least one foreign-born parent per 100 persons, by age, in the four largest cities, January 1992

Source: Statistics Netherlands, *Monthly Bulletin of Population Statistics* 41, 1993–1997. Redrawn by permission of Netherlands Central Bureau of Statistics.

date immigrants, many of them moved into public housing. This process dispersed the immigrant population across the urban area. For a brief period, the government pursued a policy of relatively even geographical distribution of immigrants over public housing, but this is now illegal.

Various neighborhoods in the three largest cities are now home to a majority of the immigrant population, although few neighborhoods are exclusively dominated by one ethnic group or immigrants from a single country. With an immigrant population of 79 percent, Bijlmer-Centrum in Amsterdam contains the highest concentration of foreigners in the Netherlands. Of these only 39 percent are Surinamese, which is the largest immigrant group in any neighborhood in Amsterdam and the country (van Eijk 1995). The general picture of immigrant housing in Dutch cities is one of mixed rather than of segregated neighborhoods. Typically 10 percent to 20 percent of the population in ethnic neighborhoods are of Surinamese, Turkish, Moroccan, and various other nationalities. The allocation of housing in the social rented sector plays a vital role in this blending of immigrants from various countries since origin may not be used as a criterion in the allocation system.

Concluding Observations

The outcomes just discussed are the result of individual decisions in the housing market. As various individuals of different ages and incomes select housing, they slowly but surely influence the residential fabric. Thus, the outcomes of housing choice create the housing market. At the same time, however, the market constrains and guides the choices. Thus, throughout this study, an effort was made to provide a simple but complete interpretation of how choices are made in the housing market, and how these choices further the understanding of the structure of the housing market as it exists at a particular time. This study has made a strong argument for the concept of the life course as a way of approaching decision making in the housing market and the mobility and tenure choices of individuals. The use of the life course is central to this conceptualization of a choice process that is linked with other choices individuals and households make as they pass from household formation to household dissolution. The event of selecting a house does not occur in a vacuum, it occurs in combination with other events in the life course of the household. These events relate to changes in the household itself. Marriage, the birth of children, and changes in household composition are effects that are, in turn, linked to household relocation and changes in tenure. In addition, however, events in other domains of life have a direct influence on behavior in the housing market. Factors such as stable employment, two earners in the household, and increase in income level have a direct bearing on the patterns of housing and tenure choice.

Use of the life course approach emphasizes the dynamic nature of the housing choice process. As noted previously, households do not make a single decision to move and change tenure status. Rather, they evaluate their situation in relation to other changes in their personal affairs and to changes in the local and national economy. Thus, the intervals between moves, and of renting and owning vary across households and by the socioeconomic status of households. As was emphasized from the outset, decisions in the housing market are not only intimately related to other events in the life course, but they are also guided by circumstances and structure of the local housing market and the state of the economy at the time a move is considered. Therefore, the context shapes the eventual housing decision and, at the same time, at the aggregate level, the sum of all individual choices determines how general patterns of occupancy of housing evolve over time.

Equally important, therefore, is the comparative focus on countries at both ends of the tenure structure scale and on the scale of government regulation of the housing market. Indeed, the comparison of the Dutch and U.S. housing markets is central to the arguments advanced in this book. Comparing a European market with the housing market in the United States is a way of highlighting both differences and similarities. It is apparent that from these very disparate examples, one can emphasize the generality of the housing tenure process and the role of both household circumstances and the microlevel and macroeconomic variations in limiting and enhancing the ability to make tenure choices. The comparative approach demonstrates convincingly that the same critical variables affect the choices households make in both housing markets, and that, at the general level, the housing choice process shows remarkably clear and stable patterns across national circumstances and over time. That households in the Netherlands, even in the government-subsidized sector, are acutely aware of the limits that income places on tenure change is demonstrated in the pattern of outcomes across household types and by household socioeconomic status. The study indicates that households in both markets are driven in their choices by identical forces.

Emphasizing the similarities and commonalities in the process of housing choice, however, should not obscure some clear differences in consumer preferences and aggregate patterns of housing occupancy that have developed in the two individual contexts. There are a few observations on the intersection of choices, outcomes, and policy and planning that can be made without involving an extended discussion of the merits of either of the two housing systems.

It is apparent from chapter 1 that the housing markets are different. The U.S. market is actually heavily weighted toward owner occupation (64 percent of the units at a national level), while the Dutch market is almost the mirror image in which 57 percent of the units are rentals. In addition, although a minuscule fraction of all units in the United States are subsidized or in the public sector, that same proportion is nearly two-thirds of all housing units in the Dutch housing market. This is directly reflected in consumer preferences in the two countries.

Even now, in a changed and less favorable economic situation, there is no doubt that purchasing and owning a house is still the tenure of choice in the United States, Canada, Britain, Australia, and New Zealand. Even the rise in prices in Britain and North America during the mid 1970s, and again the early 1980s, did little to deflect the desire and expectation of homeownership. In a survey of the desirability and expectation of purchasing among a sample of renters in Los Angeles, during and after the price inflation of the late 1970s and early 1980s, the results reiterated, in one of the most difficult home-buying markets, both the desire and the expectation of home purchase. Over 90 percent of those under the age of forty wanted to buy a house. Almost 70 percent of those between forty and sixty wanted to buy a house, and the latter group expressed the greatest concern about being able to afford a house (Heskin 1983, 184-185). Not only was there a strong, inherent preference for ownership, many renters were certain that they would be able to fulfill their expectation. Two-thirds of those who wanted to buy a home believed that they would be able to achieve their aim, and 75 percent of those under forty expected to fulfill their "dream" of homeownership. Women and individuals with lower incomes, however, had lesser expectations for achieving homeownership (Heskin 1983, 186).

In contrast, surveys in the Netherlands show that renting remains the most preferred tenure for those already in the housing market, and even more so for those first entering the housing market, the so-called "starters" (Dieleman and Everaers 1994). Among the last group, three-quarters still wanted to rent in 1989, even after a decade of steep rent hikes induced by government policy and continuing low prices for owner-occupation. These differences between the two countries show how deeply housing patterns are embedded in the more general drift of social, economic, and political development of countries in this century (Harloe 1995; Power 1993). Even if patterns of individual housing choices are quite comparable across differently organized societies, aggregate outcomes may vary appreciably. The aggregate differences are related to the development of housing patterns that are only partly driven by choices of individual households. Clearly, the supply side of the housing equation and the economic and political contexts have important impacts.

The findings suggest that the rental sector in the Dutch housing market is more attractive than in the United States. As this study has maintained, a good deal of moderately priced row housing of reasonably good quality can be found in both the rental and in the owner-occupied sectors, and median incomes had a real choice between the two tenures, until government policy induced recent rent hikes.

If one examines the distribution of housing costs across the different income strata of the population, the patterns for the two countries do not differ greatly. Low-income households are faced with much higher costs in terms of the proportion of income expended on shelter than higher-income households. The single advantage of the large (public) rental sector in the Netherlands, however, may be that income and ethnic polarization between the two tenures is less evident. Clearly, Dutch policy of supporting mass production of assisted housing has provided some attractive alternatives to relying solely on the private housing industry. The assisted housing sector accommodates a wide range of households from low-income minorities to median- to high-income Dutch households; therefore, the residential mosaic across the metropolitan space is far more varied than in the United States. And, undoubtedly, the lower socioeconomic strata of the population are relatively well-housed in the Netherlands, where the size of the homeless population is insignificant. The model of mass provision of good public housing, however, is difficult to maintain in an era of lower economic growth and the government's retreat from being deeply involved in all spheres of society. This situation has already led to significant rent hikes during the late 1980s, resulting in high housing costs for the households that chose to remain in the rental sector in contrast to those who became homeowners. There has been an unmistakable trend toward greater tenure segregation by income—a trend that will continue in light of the decreased financial support for public rental housing and the tax advantages of owner occupation.

Because of the continuing globalization of the world economy, patterns of international migration are likely to continue to swell the foreign-born populations of large metropolitan areas in the United States and in the Netherlands and, indeed, of all "global cities." This influx is likely to continue to affect the housing markets of these large metropolitan areas. Thus, the housing markets in these cities are likely to be increasingly divided between the low-end housing, dominated by immigrant workers who are employed in the expanding service sector of these global cities, and high-end housing, serving highly skilled and well-paid professional workers. Just how the immigrant workers will fit into existing housing markets is unclear, but it is apparent that the impact of continuing international migration on the housing markets of the developed economies cannot be ignored.

APPENDIX

Statistical Techniques

Introduction

Much of the data that is used in studies of residential mobility and housing and tenure choice is categorical or, at best, ordinal in nature and requires specific categorical techniques to tease out the complex relationships among the variables. Data from surveys, such as the American Housing Survey (AHS) and the Dutch National Housing Survey (WBO), usually provide information on variable categories such as ownership (yes/no), housing type (single-family/multifamily), and so forth. Even when the original variable is on a higher measurement scale (for example, age of householder), the data are frequently classified into age categories.

Because the survey data is in categorical form, one is actually analyzing the relationships in large contingency tables in which each variable is one dimension of the table. One appropriate method of analyzing the relationships between categorical variables is logit analysis. Direct application of logit analysis to a cross-classification of, say, six variables with two to five categories each, is problematic, however, because such a table has a very large number of cells. This can be illustrated from table A.1, which will be used as an example in the first part of this appendix. A cross-classification of all the variables in table A.1 would yield 61,440 cells,

---

The material in this appendix is drawn from Clark et al., 1988 and is reprinted here by permission. Copyright 1988 by Ohio State University Press. All rights reserved.

TABLE A.1

Housing Choice and Eight Variables
Related to Choice in the Netherlands

Variable	Categories	Number of Cases
Housing Choice	1. multi-family rent	914
	2. single-family rent	1,076
	3. owner occupation	933
Household Characteristics		
Income (Guilders in thousands)	1. < 20	445
	2. 20–30	878
	3. 31–42	938
	4. > 42	662
Age of Head of Household (Years)	1. <34	1,397
	2. 35–44	622
	3. 45–54	306
	4. 55–74	598
Size of Household (No. of Persons)	1. 1	375
	2. 2	861
	3. 3 or 4	1,391
	4. 5 or more	296

most of which would be empty because the sample size is 2,923. Parametric modeling of such sparse tables is meaningless. Thus, it is necessary to search for the strongest relationships between the variables and then, on this basis, reduce the number of variables and numbers of categories on these variables. PRU (Proportional Reduction of Uncertainty) and CHAID (Chi-Squared Automatic Interaction Detection) are useful tools for this task. Because illustrations in this book frequently refer to these techniques, we will give a brief explanation of the way they can be applied. This modeling strategy is discussed in detail in Clark and associates (1988), on which the first part of this appendix is largely based.

Essentially PRU is a preprocessing technique, and CHAID can also be useful as a preprocessing technique. These techniques re-

TABLE A.1 (continued)

Housing Choice and Eight Variables
Related to Choice in the Netherlands

Variable	Categories	Number of Cases
Characteristics of Previous House		
Previous Tenure	1. public rental	1,934
	2. private rental	989
Number of Rooms	1. 1 or 2 rooms	406
Previous Dwelling	2. 3 rooms	625
	3. 4 rooms	1,346
	4. 5 or more rooms	546
Type Previous Dwelling	1. single-family	1,098
	2. multi-family	1,825
Rent Previous Dwelling (Guilders)	1. < 150/month	428
	2. 150–349/month	1,324
	3. 350–449/month	513
	4. 450–549/month	325
	5. ≥ 550/month	333
Type Housing Market	1. periphery	502
	2. south	672
	3. middle	727
	4. Randstad	1,022

Source: Clark et al., 1988. Reprinted from *Geographical Analysis*, vol. 20, by permission.

duce the size of the tables that can then be analyzed with ANOTA (Analysis of Tables) techniques. ANOTA has been developed because logit models of (dependent) variables with more than two categories lead to many parameters, and because the logit transformation hampers the interpretation of the linear parameters. This makes research outcomes using logit modeling difficult to understand even for those familiar with logit techniques. ANOTA results,

however, are easy to interpret and have, therefore, been used frequently as illustrations in this book. A brief explanation in this appendix will also use table A.1 as an example.

The final technique that is important in this book is event history analysis and the proportional hazards model. Data from surveys like AHS and WBO are cross-sectional because respondents
are contacted only once at one point in time. In panel surveys,
respondents are contacted repeatedly—usually once a year though
occasionally more often. The data from such surveys such as the
Panel Study of Income Dynamics are, therefore, longitudinal. It is
for panel data that hazards models are appropriate. The definition
of episodes as units of analysis is a useful way to analyze such data,
and hazards models are the main tool for parametric modeling of
the relationships. Both will be described briefly here, again because
many illustrations in the book are drawn from our longitudinal research.

Proportional Reduction of Uncertainty (PRU)

Table A.1 illustrates a situation one often encounters in the analysis of mobility and housing choice from existing surveys. There is
a choice set that one wants to relate to a set of variables that have
been shown in the literature to be related to choice. As we have
argued, direct analysis of such a table is meaningless, but PRU can
be used to produce a reduced table highlighting the major relationships among the variables.

The PRU technique is based on an asymmetric measure of the
relationship between a categorical dependent variable and one or
more independent variables, and measures the explanatory power
of the set of independent predictor variables. PRU uses a stepwise
procedure to accomplish the reduction. At each step, the next most
effective variable is added to the tabulation of the dependent variable—housing choice—and the previously selected explanatory
variables. This new dimension is examined for its effect on association between the dependent variable and the set of independent
variables in the tabulation as categories are aggregated. This often
reduces the detail of the categorization dramatically without a no-
ticeable effect on the level of association. In the earliest reference

we know of (McGill and Quastler 1955), the PRU measure is called the "coefficient of constraint." Hays (1980) calls it "the relative reduction in uncertainty" and Nie and associates (1975) refer to it as the "uncertainty coefficient." There is a strong analogy between the PRU for discrete variables and the coefficient of determination (the square of Pearson's correlation coefficient) for continuous variables.

The PRU is also generally related to the likelihood ratio test statistic G2 (see Clark et al. 1986). But G2 can be used to determine only whether significant differences exist. This statistic is used in the present analysis but only in a secondary manner and only after the PRU measure. We believe that PRU provides better insight into the *level* of association between the dependent variable and independent variable(s) and, thus, of the relevancy rather than the significance of the relationships. Lammerts Van Bueren (1982) discusses the measure and its usefulness in detail. In our opinion (see Clark et al. 1986), the PRU has some advantages over other preprocessing approaches, such as those of Higgens and Koch (1977) and Conant (1980). Computationally, the PRU technique is available in the Statistical Package for the Social Sciences (SPSS).

The selection of variables and the reduction of the number of categories follow a simple forward-step procedure. In the first step, the PRU is calculated for the two-way cross-tabulation of housing choice and each of the independent variables (table A.2). Income is by far the most important predictor of housing choice, and is, therefore, chosen as the first step in the construction of meaningful cross-tabulation.

In step 1B, the four categories of income are examined to see whether any simplification can be effected. Collapsing categories one and two would be most appropriate. Indeed, the decrease in PRU is smallest in that case, indicating the lowest reduction in explained variation of choice. But even then, the reduction in PRU is fairly large. The substantial decrease in G2 between the original table and the smaller table also indicates this (710.4 – 658.8 = 51.6). With two fewer degrees of freedom, one would combine only categories one and two at the 1 percent significance level, if the decrease in G2 were less than 9.2. Therefore, on the basis of PRU and G2, income should retain its original four categories.

In step 2A, the two-way table resulting from the first step is

TABLE A.2

Steps in the Analysis with the PRU Criterion

Independent Variables	Number of Categories	PRU	G^2
Step 1A: selection of the first variable			
Income	4	0.111	710.4
Age of head of household	4	0.064	409.5
Size household	4	0.052	330.8
Rent previous dwelling	5	0.039	248.8
Type housing market	4	0.035	222.5
No. of rooms previous dwelling	4	0.024	156.2
Type previous dwelling	2	0.015	93.7
Tenure previous dwelling	2	0.007	43.0
Step 1B: income category simplification			
1+2,3,4		0.103	658.8
1,2+3,4		0.088	561.0
1,2,3+4		0.091	581.9
Step 2A: selection of the second variable			
Housing market		0.155	995.1
Size household		0.150	963.5
Age of head of household		0.145	927.6
No. of rooms previous dwelling		0.141	903.6
Type previous dwelling		0.135	836.0
Rent previous dwelling		0.134	859.5
Tenure previous dwelling		0.120	767.6
Step 2B: housing market category simplification			
1,2,3,4		0.155	995.1
1+2,3,4		0.155	991.2
1+3,2,4		0.154	984.4
1+4,2,3		0.131	841.3
1,2+3,4		0.153	978.3
1,2+4,3		0.124	797.1
1,2,3+4		0.137	877.5
1+2,3,4		0.152	973.2
1+2,4,3		0.114	730.2

TABLE A.2 (continued)

Independent Variables	PRU	G^2
Step 3A: selection of the third variable		
Size household	0.203	1301.3
Age of head of household	0.190	1215.1
Rent previous dwelling	0.181	1159.9
No. of rooms previous dwelling	0.180	1152.2
Type previous dwelling	0.166	1065.6
Tenure previous dwelling	0.161	1031.2
Step 3B: size household category simplification		
1,2,3,4	0.203	1301.3
1+2,3,4	0.189	1209.5
1,2+3,4	0.185	1187.2
1,2,3+4	0.199	1277.7
1,2+3+4	0.185	1185.9
1,2+3+4	0.179	1148.1
Step 4A: simplification of income in the four-dimensional table		
1,2,3,4	0.199	1277.7
1+2, 3,4	0.192	1230.5
1,2 +3,4	0.174	1117.0
1,2, 3+4	0.175	1121.1

Step 4B: Further simplification
Categories:

Income	Market	Size	PRU	G^2
1+2,3,4	1+2+3,4	1,2,3+4	0.192	1230.5
1+2+3,4	1+2+3,4	1,2,3+4	0.156	1000.6
1+2,3+4	1+2+3,4	1,2,3+4	0.168	1073.8
1+2,3,4	1+2+3,4	1+2,3+4	0.180	1154.8
1+2,3,4	1+2+3,4	1,2+3+4	0.172	1101.9

Source: Clark et al., 1988. Reprinted by permission of *Geographical Analysis*, vol. 20, and Ohio State University Press.

expanded to a three-way table with the addition of a new dimension. The variable housing-market type increases the PRU substantially and by more than any other potential explanatory variable (table A.2). The increase is also significant at the 1 percent level (the increase of G2 is 284.7 with 24 df). In step 2B, categories one and two of housing-market type are added without real loss in PRU, and category three also can be combined with these categories. It is clear that housing choice in the Randstad (choice four) is very different from what it is elsewhere in the Netherlands. Whenever category four (Randstad) is collapsed with another category, the PRU decreases drastically. The PRU after simplification of housing-market type (0.152) is still higher than the second variable that had a high PRU in step 2 (size of household, 0.150), so we can proceed to the next step.

In step 3A, size of household is added to the three-way cross-tabulation and increases the PRU significantly. Categories three and four of this variable can be collapsed (step 3B).

In the next step of the analysis, a critical point is reached in the PRU procedure. The addition of yet another variable (either rent of previous dwelling or age of head of household are the candidates) increases the PRU significantly, but, at the same time, many empty cells occur, and even some row and column marginals now have zero cases. We are, thus, well beyond the limit for meaningful addition of variables to the table and no further variables are added after step 3. After the final step in the forward selection procedure of variables and categories with PRU is completed, it is sometimes useful to perform a backward simplification procedure. The categorization of variables in the earlier steps of the forward selection procedure may be simplified further at this point, because other variables have been added to the table. In our analysis, further simplification is considered in steps 4A and 4B. In step 4A, only the categorization of income has to be reconsidered, because the housing-market variable is already simplified to two categories, and size of household has just been considered in step 3B. Collapsing categories one and two of income decreases the PRU slightly, although the loss of information is significant at the 1 percent level. As has been suggested above, we attribute more value to the *absolute* level of the PRU for the selection of the model than to considerations of significance. The simplification of income to three categories decreases the cross-tabulation to eighteen cells, with only a slight loss in the PRU value. Further combination of cells leads to a much larger decrease in PRU (as step 4B illustrates) and, thus, the process of combining categories was terminated with three categories of income.

TABLE A.3

Housing Choice of Movers Previously in the Rental Sector by Income, Type of Housing Market, and Household Size; Result of PRU Analysis (Table A.2)

Income (Guilders ×1,000)	Housing Market	Size	Housing Choice			
			Multi-Family Rent (%)	Single-Family Rent (%)	Own (%)	No.
< 30	Rest of Netherlands	1 person	65	28	7	173
		2 persons	47	44	9	228
		3 or more	18	64	18	487
	Randstad	1 person	84	10	6	126
		2 persons	69	24	7	126
		3 or more	60	32	9	183
30–42	Rest of Netherlands	1 person	24	30	46	33
		2 persons	29	35	36	122
		3 or more	7	48	45	456
	Randstad	1 person	38	5	57	21
		2 persons	54	30	16	50
		3 or more	34	40	27	256
> 42	Rest of Netherlands	1 person	—	—	—	8
		2 persons	11	16	73	211
		3 or more	4	19	77	183
	Randstad	1 person	—	—	—	14
		2 persons	32	15	53	124
		3 or more	23	29	48	122
Total			31	37	32	2,923

Source: Clark et al., 1988. Reprinted by permission of *Geographical Analysis*, vol. 20, and Ohio State University Press.

The PRU measure helps to select the most relevant variables from a larger set, but simplifying the categorization of the variables is equally important. The original categorization of income, housing market, and size of household would lead to a table of 192 cells, while after the combination of categories, there are only 54 cells. The PRU values for these tables are 0.219 and 0.192, respectively.

Therefore, the number of cells in the table is reduced to 88 percent of the original PRU. Table A.3 is the result of the PRU procedure. To reiterate, PRU analysis can be performed with the Statistical Package for the Social Sciences (SPSS).

Chi-Squared Automatic Interaction Detection (CHAID)

CHAID, like PRU, is a method with which to detect the most important relationships in a large multidimensional cross-classification. The original automatic interaction detection (AID) procedure, developed by Sonquist and Morgan (1964), has its origins in the analysis of variance. It assumes an interval-level dependent variable and qualitative (or categorized) independent variables and is a stepwise procedure, providing at each step an optimal split of the data into two subsets. The between-subset sum-of-squares is maximized at each bisection. The technique was extended to the case where the dependent variable was qualitative, and one of these extensions is known as Chi-Square AID (CHAID) (Kass 1980). This technique provides optimal splits, not necessarily bisections, by maximizing the significance of the chi-square statistic at each step. In this way, it is possible to achieve a parsimonious description of the data by partitioning it into mutually exclusive, exhaustive, subsets that best describe the dependent variable. The subsets are constructed by using small groups of predictors, and the procedure provides for special predictors that can be used in handling missing information.

First, the CHAID procedure begins by searching for the best partition for each predictor. This is achieved by finding the contingency table of Y and the predictor with the highest significance level of the chi-square test. In this process, the type of predictor defines the allowable number of categories. Secondly, the results of individual predictors are compared and the best prediction is chosen. The data are then split according to this chosen predictor. Next, each of these subgroups is analyzed further using the same procedure. Therefore, the standard problem of CHAID is to reduce a given RxCj cross-table ($r \geq 2$ categories of the dependent variable, $Cj \geq 2$ categories of a predictor) to the most significant RxDj table ($1 \leq Dj \leq Cj$).

In practical situations, when there are many predictors, it is unrealistic to explore all possible reductions. Therefore, CHAID uses an alternative method that gives satisfactory results but does not guarantee the optimal solution. This method is derived from the one used in stepwise regression analysis for judging whether a variable should be included or excluded. It operates in the following manner. Find the two categories of the predictor for which the Rx2 subtable has the lowest significance. If this significance is below a certain user-defined threshold value, the two categories are merged. This process is repeated until no further merging can be achieved. In the next step, each resulting category composed of three or more of the original categories is checked; if the most significant of the compound categories rises above a certain chosen threshold value, the split is carried out, and the previous step is repeated (this extra step ensures a better approximation of the optimal solution). Both steps are repeated until no further improvement is obtained. This procedure is executed for each predictor. For each predictor optimally merged in this way, the significance is calculated, and the most significant one is selected. If this significance is higher than a criterion value, the data are divided according to the (merged) categories of the chosen predictor. The method is applied to each subgroup, until the number of objects left over within the subgroup becomes too small. This simplifying method has an accounting effort of order c for monotonic predictors and of order c2 for free predictors.

It is not straightforward to establish the significance of an optimal merged predictor, because the algorithm ensures that the reduced table is the best one possible for its size. The normal X2 test can be applied only if the original contingency table has not been recombined as a method of reducing large contingency tables as a prelude to more refined analysis (Langeheine 1984; Magidson 1982; Perreault and Barksdale 1980).

In this appendix, we again use table A.1 as an example. The results of applying CHAID to this table are given in figure A.1. As in the PRU, independent variables are selected in a "forward" fashion. Categories of an independent variable chosen by the method are merged, if they show a comparable pattern of choices (and, in our analysis, if they are adjacent, except for the categories of housing market, which are allowed to combine in any order). For each of the categories of the independent variables selected in previous

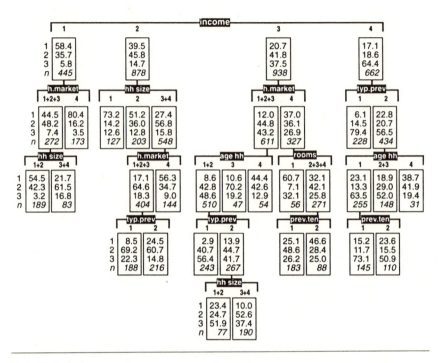

FIGURE A.1

CHAID dendogram for renters; table values are the percentage moving to each destination category

Source: Redrawn from Clark et al., 1988, by permission of *Geographical Analysis,* vol. 20, and Ohio State University Press.

steps, the technique considers the most important predictor in the next step. Therefore, the results of the analysis are "nested" and can be presented in the form of an inverted tree; some predictors occur only at specific levels of other independent variables. Thus, a very detailed picture of choice patterns of the different types of households emerges (fig. A.1). In this sense, CHAID places more emphasis on specific *groups of households*, while the procedure using the PRU criterion is geared more toward finding a set of good *predictors* for the entire sample of households. Figure A.1 shows the results of an analysis of renter choices.

For the CHAID analysis, no program known to the researchers is included in any of the usual statistical computer packages such as SPSS, BMPD, and so forth. However, Kass (1980) developed a special program for CHAID written in PL/I. A Fortran V translation of his program can also be obtained by contacting Dr. M.C. Deurloo, Department of Geography, University of Amsterdam, Nieuwe Prinsengracht 130, 1018 VZ Amsterdam, The Netherlands.

Analysis of Tables (ANOTA)

This study uses the ANOTA technique as an alternative to logit analysis primarily because it is a relatively simple way of handling several categories of a dependent variable. In addition, the technique provides coefficients that can easily be interpreted as percentages, and they can be summed to provide a cumulative interpretation of the contribution of several independent variables. ANOTA provides a number of simplifications, when the restriction is dropped that the estimated coefficients must be in the 0 – 1 range. Then, the coefficients can be estimated with ordinary least squares methods.

It is true that the ANOTA model does not guarantee a good fit, but even for fully specified logit models, good fit can be guaranteed only for the saturated model and the saturated model is not an end in itself, but only a starting point for a process of reduction to a parsimonious form. It is also true that the interaction effects of independent variables on the dependent variables are ignored. Given that PRU and CHAID have filtered out the strongest interaction effects, ANOTA provides a table that is readily interpretable. Table A.3 is used to illustrate the technique. A more extended discussion of Multivariate Nominal Scale Analysis (MNA) and its reformulation as ANOTA can be found in several works (Andrews and Messenger 1973; Keller et al. 1984; and Clark et al. 1988).

The core of the ANOTA model is formed from the estimated coefficients that show the "effect" of membership in the particular (nominal) category of the independent variable on the likelihood of membership in each (nominal) category of the dependent variable (table A.4). The coefficients are corrected for possible interactions between the explanatory variables, and therefore represent "pure" effects, which can be interpreted as partial regres-

TABLE A.4

Coefficients for Housing Choices from the ANOTA Analysis

	Coefficients for								
	Income (000s guilders)			Housing Market		Size Household			
Housing Choice	Average	< 30	30–40	>40	Rest Neth.	Rand-stad	1p	2p	3 or more
Multi-Family Rent	31.3	12.3	–6.2	–15.8	–9.2	17.1	24.5	8.2	–9.6
Single-Family Rent	36.8	7.9	1.4	–17.7	4.6	–8.6	–22.3	–5.5	7.7
Owner Occupation	31.9	–20.2	4.8	33.6	4.5	–8.4	–2.2	–2.7	1.9

Source: Clark et al., 1988. Reprinted by permission of *Geographical Analysis*, vol. 20, and Ohio State University Press.

sion coefficients. Thus, these coefficients can be added together (literally) across the several independent variables to predict the household's score on the dependent variable (the expected probability for any household is obtained by summing the base likelihood and the coefficients that pertain to that household and dividing by 100).

For example, in table A.4, the expected probability of a one-person household moving from the rental sector, with an income below thirty thousand guilders, living in the Randstad, and choosing a multifamily rental dwelling, is 0.313 (the base likelihood or average) plus 0.123 (income effect) plus 0.171 (Randstad effect) plus 0.245 (size of household effect), a total of 0.852. Thus, the expected probability of making a particular choice, given the categories of the independent variables of a moving household, can be determined in a simple and straightforward manner. It is also possible to focus on a particular column of coefficients in table A.4. The coefficients associated with any category of any predictor sum to zero across the categories of the dependent variable, and so can be interpreted as deviations from the average.

The coefficients in table A.4 show the relationship of the predictors with housing choice more clearly than the percentages in table A.3, because the coefficients are "pure" effects as a result of the assumption of independent influences of the independent variables. If the assumptions of the model are severely violated, the ANOTA parameters will be misleading. But this does not seem to be the case here, as inspection of the bivariate tables for independent variables indicates. Income, in particular, affects the choice between owning and renting. Keeping size of household and housing-market type constant in the lowest income category, the likelihood of buying a house for households that were originally in the rental sector is low ($0.319 - 0.202 = 0.117$), while it is high in the highest income category ($0.319 + 0.336 = 0.655$). In the case of housing-market type, it affects the decision to select multifamily rental housing. In the Randstad the expected probability of choosing a multifamily dwelling is nearly 0.50, while in the rest of the Netherlands the probability is below 0.25, again keeping household income and size constant. Choice patterns vary widely between one- and two-or-more-person households. For example, the expected probability of a single person (controlling income and housing market type) moving into multifamily housing is 0.558, against 0.145 for moving into a single-family rental house. For ANOTA an elegant computer program that runs on a microcomputer can be obtained by contacting J.G. Bethlehem, Central Bureau of Statistics, Department for Statistical Methods, P.O. Box 959, 2270 AZ Voorburg, The Netherlands.

Panel Data and Hazard Models

In panel surveys, respondents are interviewed repeatedly. The advantage of panel data is that changes in the circumstances of individuals and households can be followed over time, and events, such as birth of a child, change of job, and moves from one house to another, which occur at various points in time, can be observed and linked. Such data are, of course, valuable for the analysis of residential mobility, because this mobility is often related to other changes in the life of persons and families, as has been demonstrated in this study. For this reason, we have frequently used results from our own research with the Panel Study of Income

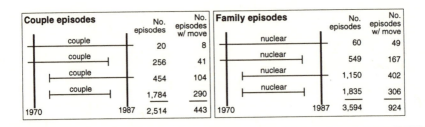

FIGURE A.2
Couple and family episodes started in rental dwelling, 1970–1987, in the
United States

Source: Clark et al., 1994. Reprinted from *Urban Studies*, vol. 31, by
permission.

Dynamics (PSID), which is a large panel survey for the United
States, initiated in 1968 (Hills 1992).

Panel surveys are not easy to analyze especially if the household is the unit of observation, as it usually is in studies of migration and residential mobility. The unit of observation is prone to
change frequently because households change as children are born,
people marry and divorce, and children leave the family. Consequently, episodes are used in this study as the unit of observation.
An episode is the time period for which a household exists in a
particular situation. In the example taken from Clark and associates (1994), an episode was defined as being in a certain family
type (single, couple, single-parent, family, other) over a certain time
period. An episode was initiated when the individual was a head
of one of these family types at the time of the interview. Subsequent years were added to the episode as long as the family type
remained the same. Another criterion used in the example was that
the individual was a renter, because moves from renting to owning were analyzed for couple and family episodes (fig. A.2). The
episode was ended as soon as the household type changed. In the
case of a move to own, the episode was flagged for that event in
that year.

As can. be observed in figure A.2, not all episodes are of the
same character. Some episodes already existed before the survey
started (1970) and are still in the survey in the last year used
(1987). Therefore, the start-year and end-year of these episodes

is unknown. For other episodes, either the start-year or end-year is unknown ("left or right censored" in terms of panel surveys). For most episodes, both years are known. In the example, the interval from the start of the episode as a renter until the eventual move to own is the length of a spell. This is the dependent variable in the hazards models used in this example. Not all episodes can be used for such analyses, because for some episodes the start-year is unknown; therefore, the length of the spell is unknown (left censored episodes).

An appropriate way of analyzing such episodes is the use of event-history models. Such models can be used to evaluate the role of explanatory variables in understanding the way in which household composition changes and economic and regional context variables might influence the lengths of duration in the renter status or the likelihood or hazard of making a move to owning. The evolution of event history analysis has favored Cox's proportional hazards model. Proportional hazard models are a large class of models, including Cox's model, which use partial likelihood estimation and parametric models. The use of partial likelihood, and consequently leaving out the specification of the baseline hazard, is the special character of the Cox model, which can be written as:

$$\log h_i(t) = h_0(t) + ßZ_i$$

where,

$h_i(t)$ = the hazard function of the survival time of each household,

$h_0(t)$ = any function of time (baseline hazard),

Z_i = a vector of measured explanatory variables for the ith household,

and, ß = the vector of unknown regression parameters associated with the explanatory variables (Z).

The principal advantage of the proportional hazards model over parametric event history models is that the ß-parameters can be interpreted as constant proportional effects (independent of duration) generated by the explanatory variables on the conditional probability of completing a spell. This is the analog, in a hazard

TABLE A.5

Proportional Hazards Regression Model for Move to Own for Couple
Episodes in the United States, 1970–1987

Variable	Coefficient	Risk Change per Unit of Variable (%)
Age at start of episode (years)	–0.013	–1.3
Race (black vs. non-black)	1.357*	288.5
Hh. income ($1,000, adj.) (t)	0.019*	2.0
Empl. status head (no/yes) (t)	0.116	12.3
No. of earners (0,1,2) (t)	0.477*	61.1
Rent of last unit ($100, adj.)	0.013*	1.3
No. of rooms of last rental unit	–0.157*	–14.6
Region North Central (vs. Northeast)	0.700*	101.3
Region West (vs. Northeast)	0.479*	61.4
Region South (vs. Northeast)	0.714*	104.3
New construction (millions)[a]	0.641*	89.8
Price new single-family homes ($1,000, adjusted)[a]	–0.010	–1.0
Mortgage (%)[a]	0.057	5.9
Inflation (%)[a]	0.065*	6.7

[a] time varying
* significant at the 0.01 level

Source: Clark et al., 1994. Reprinted from *Urban Studies*, vol. 31, by permission.

function framework, of the interpretation of an unstandardized regression coefficient in a linear regression model framework. Moreover, in Cox's partial-likelihood approach to the proportional hazards model, the ß's can be estimated without specifying the form of the baseline hazard function. The advantage of this is that there is no risk of misspecification of $h_0(t)$ and consequent misspecification of ß. A thorough discussion of this model can be found in Kiefer (1988) and Yamaguchi (1991).

In the example taken from Clark and associates (1994), the actual calculation of the parameters was performed with the SAS procedure PHREG (table A.5). Although there are many statistical computer packages that can run proportional hazard models, in our experience this relatively new SAS program is one of the most powerful and flexible. The hazard $h_i(t)$ is the rate at which spells as a renter household will be completed at duration t by a move to owning, given that the renter situation lasted until t. Cox's model is simple to interpret. The hazard itself corresponds to the notions of risk. If two households have hazards of 0.5 and 1.5, it is possible to say that the second household's risk of an event is three times greater, or that the expected length of time until the event occurs will be one-third of the first household's length of time. The effect of the regressors is to multiply the log of the hazard function itself by a scale factor such that the baseline hazard is multiplied by a factor that does not depend on duration. The coefficients can be interpreted analogously to unstandardized regression coefficients in the linear regression model.

An alternative, somewhat more intuitive, interpretation of the coefficients involves taking the antilog and then interpreting this as the multiplication factor of the hazard. An addition of one unit in an independent variable reduces (if a negative coefficient), or increases (if a positive coefficient), the log of the hazard by the value of the regression parameter, controlling for the effects of other variables and time. The (conditional) risk change for each unit of the variable measured in its original form is also added to ease the interpretation. To indicate which factors are more important than others, we report the significance of the Wald statistic for the .01 level, which indicates important and less important variables.

Bibliography

Allison, P.D. 1982. Discrete-time methods for the analysis of event histories. In S. Leinhardt, ed. *Sociological methodology*. San Francisco, CA: Jossey-Bass.

Allison, P.D. 1984. *Event history analysis: regression for longitudinal event data*. Beverly Hills, CA: Sage.

Ambrose, P. 1992. The performance of national housing systems—a three-nation comparison. *Housing Studies* 7, 163–176.

Andrews, F.M. and Messenger, R.C. 1973. *Multivariate nominal scale analysis*. Ann Arbor, MI: University of Michigan, Institute for Social Research.

Armor, D., and Clark, W.A.V. 1995. Housing segregation and school desegregation. In D. Armor, ed. *Forced justice: school desegregation and the law*. New York: Oxford, 117–153.

Arnott, R. 1987. Economic theory and housing. In E.S. Mills, ed. *Handbook of regional urban economics*. Vol. 2, Urban Economics. Amsterdam: Elsevier Science Publishers B.V., 959–988.

Badcock, B. 1989. Home ownership and the accumulation of real wealth. *Environment and Planning D* 7, 69–91.

Blossfeld, H., Hamerle, A., and Mayer, K. 1989. *Event history analysis*. Hillsdale, NJ: Lawrence Erlbaum.

Boehm, T.P. 1981. Tenure choice and expected mobility: a synthesis. *Journal of Urban Economics* 10, 375–389.

Boelhouwer, P., and Van Der Heijden, H.M.H. 1992. Housing systems in Europe: part I, a comparative study of housing policy. *Housing and Urban Policy Studies 1*. Delft, Netherlands: Delft University Press.

Boelhouwer, P.J., Van Der Heijden, H.M.H., and Papa, O.A. 1991. *Nederlands volkshuisvestingsbeleid in Europees perspectief*. Delft, Netherlands: Delft University Press.

Boots, N.B., and Kanaroglou, P.S. 1988. Incorporating the effects of spatial structure in discrete choice models of migration. *Journal of Regional Science* 28, 495–507.

Bourne, L.S. 1981. *Geography of housing*. London: Winston.

Brown, C.C. 1975. On the use of indicator variables for studying the time dependence of parameters in a response-time model. *Biometrics* 31, 863–872.

Brown, L.A., and Moore, E.G. 1970. The intra-urban migration process: a perspective. *Geografiska Annaler* 52, 1–13.

Chevan, A. 1989. The growth of home ownership: 1940–1980. *Demography* 26, 249–266.

Clark W.A.V. 1986. *Human migration*. Beverly Hills, CA: Sage.

Clark W.A.V. 1992. Comparing cross-sectional and longitudinal analyses of residential mobility and migration. *Environment and Planning A* 24, 1291–1302.

Clark, W.A.V. 1996. Residential patterns: avoidance, assimilation, and succession. In R. Waldinger and M. Bozorgmehr, eds., *Ethnic Los Angeles*. New York: Russell Sage.

Clark, W.A.V., Deurloo, M.C., and Dieleman, F.M. 1986. Residential mobility in Dutch housing markets. *Environment and Planning A* 18, 763–788.

Clark W.A.V., Deurloo, M.C., and Dieleman, F.M. 1988. Modeling strategies for categorical data: examples from housing and tenure choice. *Geographical Analysis* 20, 196–219.

Clark W.A.V., Deurloo, M.C., and Dieleman, F.M. 1990. Household characteristics and tenure choice in the U.S. housing market. *The Netherlands Journal of Housing and Environmental Research* 5, 251–270.

Clark, W.A.V., Deurloo, M.C., and Dieleman, F.M. 1991. Modeling categorical data with chi square automatic interaction detection and correspondence analysis. *Geographical Analysis* 23, 332–345.

Clark W.A.V., Deurloo, M.C., and Dieleman, F.M. 1994. Tenure changes in the context of micro-level family and macro-level economic shifts. *Urban Studies* 31, 137–154.

Clark, W.A.V., Dieleman, F.M., and De Klerk, L. 1992. School segregation: managed integration or free choice. *Environment and Planning C: Government and Policy* 10, 91–103.

Clark, W.A.V., Dieleman, F.M., and Deurloo, M.C. 1984. Housing consumption and residential mobility. *Annals, Association of American Geographers* 74, 29–43.

Clark, W.A.V., and Huff, J. 1977. Some empirical tests of duration of stay effects in intraurban migration. *Environment and Planning A* 9, 1357–1374.

Clark, W.A.V., and Onaka, J. 1983. Life cycle and housing adjustments as explanations of residential mobility. *Urban Studies* 20, 47–57.

Clark, W.A.V., and Onaka, J. 1985. An empirical test of a joint model of residential mobility and housing choice. *Environment and Planning A* 17, 915–930.

Conant, T.R. 1980. Structural modeling using a simple information measure. *International Journal of Systems Science* 11, 721–730.

Cox, D.R. 1970. *The analysis of binary data*. London: Methuen.

Cox, D.R. 1972. Regression models and life-tables (with discussion). *Journal of the Royal Statistical Society B* 34, 187–220.

Crouchley, R., ed. 1987. *Longitudinal data analysis: survey conference on sociological theory and method 4*. Aldershot, Hampshire: Avebury, Ashgate Publishing.

Davies, R.B., and Crouchley, R. 1985. Control for omitted variables in the analysis of panel and other longitudinal data. *Geographical Analysis* 17, 1–15.

Davies, R.B., and Pickles, A.R. 1983. The estimate of duration of residence effects: a stochastic modelling approach. *Geographical Analysis* 15, 305–317.

Davies, R.B., and Pickles, A.R. 1985. Longitudinal versus cross- sectional methods for behavioral research: a first-round knockout. *Environment and Planning A* 17, 1315–1329.

Davies, R.B., and Pickles, A.R. 1991. An analysis of housing careers in the Dutch housing market. *Environment and Planning A* 23, 629–650.

Deurloo, M.C. 1987. *A multivariate analysis of residential mobility*. Amsterdam: Instituut voor Sociale Geografie, Universiteit van Amsterdam.

Deurloo, M.C., Clark, W.A.V., and Dieleman, F.M. 1990. Choice of residential environment in the Randstad. *Urban Studies* 27, 335–351.

Deurloo, M.C., Clark, W.A.V., and Dieleman, F.M. 1994. The move to housing ownership in temporal and regional contexts. *Environment and Planning A* 26, 1659–1670.

Deurloo, M.C., Dieleman, F.M., and Clark, W.A.V. 1987. Tenure choice in the Dutch housing market. *Environment and Planning A* 19, 763–781.

Deurloo, M.C., Dieleman, F.M., and Clark, W.A.V. 1988. Generalized log-linear models of housing choice. *Environment and Planning A* 10, 55–69.

Deurloo, M.C., Dieleman, F.M., and Hooimeijer, P. 1986. Regionale verschillen in de woningmarkt; een typologie van woningmarkten. *Stedebouw en volkshuisvesting* 67, 237–245.

Dickens, P., Duncan, S., Goodwin, M., and Gray, F. 1985. *Housing states and localities* London: Methuen.

Dieleman, F.M. 1993. Multicultural Holland, myth or reality? In R.J. King, ed. *Mass migration in Europe*. London: Belhaven Press.

Dieleman, F.M. 1994. Social rented housing: valuable asset or unsustainable burden? *Urban Studies* 31, 447–463.

Dieleman, F.M., Clark, W.A.V., and Deurloo, M.C. 1989. A comparative view of housing choices in controlled and uncontrolled housing markets. *Urban Studies* 26, 457–468.

Dieleman, F.M., Clark, W.A.V., and Deurloo, M.C. 1995. Falling out of the home owner market. *Housing Studies* 10, 3–15.

Dieleman, F.M., and Everaers, P.C.J. 1994. From renting to owning: life course and housing market circumstances. *Housing Studies* 9, 11–25.

Dieleman, F.M., and Musterd, S. 1992. *The Randstad: a research and policy laboratory*. Dordrecht, Netherlands: Kluwer Academic Publishers.

Dieleman, F.M., and Schouw, R.J. 1989. Divorce, mobility, and housing demand. *European Journal of Population* 5, 235–252.

Dieleman, F.M., and Van Kempen, R. 1994. The mismatch of housing and income in Dutch housing. *Netherlands Journal of Housing and the Built Environment* 9, 159–171.

Dynarski, M. 1985. Housing demand and disequilibrium. *Journal of Urban Economics* 17, 42–57.

Dynarski, M. 1986. Residential attachment and housing demand. *Urban Studies* 23, 11–20.

Efron, B. 1977. The efficiency of Cox's likelihood function for censored data. *Journal of the American Statistical Association* 72, 557–565.

EIB. 1994. *Woonuitgaven en financiele stromen van het rijk*. Amsterdam: Economisch Instituut voor de Bouwnijverheid.

Eijk, D. van 1995. Atlas van het ongenoegen—waar liggen de potentiële getto's van Nederland? *NRC Handelsblad* 18 maart, 1995.

Elsinga, M.G. 1995. *Een eigen huis voor een smalle beurs: Het ideaal voor bewoner en overheid?* Delft: Delft University Press.

Everaers, P.C. 1990. Residential mobility in the Netherlands: a descriptive analysis based on the Housing Demand Survey 1985/86. *Supplement bij de sociaal-economische maandstatistiek*, 28–45.

Everaers, P.C. 1991. Verhuizen in Nederland: een beschrijvende analyse gebaseerd op het woningbehoeftenonderzoek 1985/1986.

Everaers, P.C., and Davies, S. 1993. Verhuizen in Nederland in de jaren tachtig. *Maandstatistieken Bouw* CBS 93/12, 5–26.

Everaers, P.C., and Dieleman, F.M. 1992. Van huur naar koop: levensloop en omstandigheden op de woningmarkt. *Supplement bij de sociaal-economische maandstatistiek*, 46–54.

Everaers, P.C., Jobse, R.B., and Musterd, S. 1992. Population change in subareas of the urban regions of Amsterdam, Rotterdam, and The Hague, 1981–1989. *Supplement bij de sociaal-economische maandstatistiek*.

Feddes, A. 1995. *Woningmarkt, regulering en inflatie. Het naoorlogse volkshuisvestingsbeleid van tien Noordwest-Europese landen vergeleken*. Utrecht: Faculty of Geographical Sciences, Utrecht University.

Filius, F. 1993. Huishoudensopheffing en woningverlating in een vergrijzende samenleving. *Nederlandse Geografische Studies* (Netherlands Geographical Studies).

Forest, R., and Murie, A. 1989. Differential accumulation: wealth, inheritance, and housing policy reconsidered. *Policy and Politics* 17, 25–39.

Glennon, D. 1989. Estimating the income, price, and interest elasticities of housing demand. *Journal of Urban Economics* 25, 219–229.

Glick, P. 1957. *American families*. New York: John Wiley.

Gober, P. 1986. How and why Phoenix households changed: 1970–1980. *Annals of the Association of American Geographers* 76, 536–549.

Goldscheider, F., and Le Bourdais, C. 1986. The decline in age at leaving home 1920–1979. *Sociology and Social Research* 72, 143–145.

Goldscheider, F., and Da Vanzo, J. 1985. Living arrangements and the transition to adulthood. *Demography* 22, 545–563.

Goldscheider, F., and Da Vanzo, J. 1989. Pathways to independent living in early adulthood: marriage, semiautonomy, and premarital residential independence. *Demography* 26, 597–614.

Goldscheider, F., Thornton, A., and Young-DeMarco, L. 1993. A portrait of the nest-leaving process in early adulthood. *Demography* 30, 683–699.

Gray, F. 1976. Selection and allocation in council housing. *Transactions Institute of British Geographers* 1, 34–46.

Grebler, L., and Mittlebach, F. 1979. *The inflation of house prices*. Lexington, MA: D.C. Heath.

Grigsby, W. 1978. Response to John Quigley. In L.S. Bourne and J. Hitchcock, eds. *Urban housing markets: recent directions in research and policy*. Toronto: University of Toronto Press, 45–49.

Gyourko, J., and Linneman, P. 1993. The affordability of the American dream: an examination of the last 30 years. *Journal of Housing Research* 4, 139–172.

Hamnett, C. 1992. The geography of housing wealth and inheritance in Britain. *The Geographical Journal* 158, 307–321.

Hamnett, C. 1994. Socio-economic change in London: professionalization not polarization. *Built Environment* 20, 192–203.

Hanushek, E.A., and Quigley, T.M. 1978. An explicit model of intra-metropolitan mobility. *Land Economics* 54, 411–429.

Harloe, M. 1995. *The people's home? Social rented housing in Europe and America.* Oxford: Basil Blackwell.

Haurin, D.R., and Gill, H.L. 1987. Effects of income variability on the demand for owner-occupied housing. *Journal of Urban Economics* 22, 136–150.

Hays W.L. 1980. *Statistics for the social sciences.* 2d ed. Chichester, Sussex: Holt, Rinehart, and Winston.

Heckman, J.J., and Singer, B. 1985. *Longitudinal analysis of labor market data.* Econometric Society Monograph No. 10. Cambridge: Cambridge University Press.

Henderson, J.V., and Ioannides, Y.M. 1983. A model of housing tenure choice. *The American Economic Review* 73, 98–113.

Henderson, J.V. and Ioannides, Y.M. 1985. Tenure choice and the demand for housing. *Economica* 53, 231–246.

Henderson, J.V., and Ioannides, Y.M. 1987. Owner occupancy: investment vs. consumption demand. *Journal of Urban Economics* 21, 228–241.

Henderson, J.V., and Ioannides, Y.M. 1989. Dynamic aspects of consumer decisions in housing markets. *Journal of Urban Economics* 26, 212–230.

Heskin, A. 1983. *Tenants and the American dream.* New York: Praeger.

Higgens, J.W., and Koch, G.Y. 1977. Variable selection and generalized chi-square analysis of categorical data applied to a large cross-sectional occupational health survey. *International Statistical Review* 45, 51–62.

Hills, M.S. 1992. *The panel study of income dynamics: a user's guide.* Newbury Park, CA: Sage Publications.

Hoekveld, G.A., Jobse, R.B., and Dieleman, F.M. 1984. *Atlas van Nederland in 20 delen, Deel 5–Wonen.* The Hague: Staatsuitgeverij.

Hoogvliet, A. 1992. *Wijken in beweging-bevolkingsdynamiek en wooncarrières in vroeg-20ste-eeuwse woongebieden.* Utrecht: Stedelijke Netwerken.

Hooimeijer, P., Clark, W.A.V., and Dieleman, F.M. 1986. Households in the reduction stage: implications for the Netherlands' housing market. *Housing Studies* 1, 195–209.

Hooimeijer, P., Dieleman, F.M., and Kuijpers-Linde, M. 1993. Is elderly migration absent in the Netherlands? *Espace Populations Societ-ies* 3, 465–476.

Hooimeijer, P., Dieleman, F.M., and Van Dam, J. 1988. Residential mobility of households in the reduction stage in the Netherlands. *Tijdschrift voor Economische en Sociale Geografie* 79, 306–319.

Hooimeijer, P., and Linde, M. 1988. *Vergrijzing, individualisering en de woningmarkt, het wodyn-simulatiemodel*. Utrecht: Faculty of Geographical Sciences, Utrecht University.

Hsiao, C. 1986. *Analysing Panel Data*. Econometric Society Monographs No. f11. Cambridge: Cambridge University Press.

Huttman, E.D., Blauw, W., and Saltman, J., eds. 1991. *Urban housing segregation of minorities in Western Europe and the United States*. London: Duke University Press.

Jobse, R.B., Kruythoff, H.M., and Musterd, S. 1990. Stadsgewesten in beweging migratie naar en uit de vier grote steden. *Stedelijke Netwerken werkstukken* 20. Utrecht: Utrecht University.

Jobse, R.B., and Musterd, S. 1989. Dynamiek in de Randstad-een analyse van de woningbouw—en migratiestatistieken in de periode 1970–1985. *Stedelijke Netwerken Werkstukken* 10, Utrecht University.

Jobse, R.B., and Musterd, S. 1992. Changes in the residential function of the big cities. In F. M. Dieleman and S. Musterd, eds. *The Randstad: a research and policy laboratory*. Dordrecht: Kluwer Academic Publishers, 39–64.

Kass, G.V. 1980. An exploratory technique for investigating large quantities of categorical data. *Applied Statistics* 19, 129–217.

Keller, W.J., Verbeek, A., and Bethlehem, J.G. 1984. *Analysis of tables*. Voorburg: Central Bureau of Statistics.

Kempen, R. van, Floor, H., and Dieleman, F.M. 1994. *Wonen op Maat*. Utrecht: University of Utrecht, Faculty of Geographical Sciences.

Kendig, H.L. 1984. Housing careers, life cycle, and residential mobility: implications for the housing market. *Urban Studies* 4, 271–283.

Kendig, H.L. 1990. A life course perspective on housing attainment. In D. Myers, ed. *Housing Demography*. Madison, WI: University of Wisconsin Press, 133–156.

Kiefer, N.M. 1988. Economic duration data and hazard functions. *Journal of Economic Literature* 26, 646–679.

Kleinman, M. 1995. Meeting housing needs through the market: an assessment of housing policies and the supply/demand balance in France and Great Britain. *Housing Studies* 10, 17–38.

Lammerts Van Bueren, W.M. 1982. *Measuring association in nominal data*. Dissertation, Department of Economics, Erasmus University of Rotterdam.

Langeheine, R. 1984. Exploratieve Technieken or Identifikation von Strukturen in Grossen Kontingenztabellen. *Zeitschrift fur Sozial-Psychologie* 15, 254–268.

Lansing, J., and Morgan, J. 1955. Consumer finances over the life cycle. In L. Clark., ed. *Consumer Behavior*. Vol. 2. New York: New York University Press.

Latten, J., and Cuypers, P. 1994. Alleenwonen en samenwonen bij jongeren: individualisering en binding sluiten elkaar niet uit. *Nederlands Interdisciplinair Demografisch Instituut* (DEMOS) 10, 72–75.

Lelievre, E., and Bonvalet, C. 1994. A compared cohort history of residential mobility, social change and home-ownership in Paris and the rest of France. *Urban Studies* 10, 1647–1665.

Linde, M.A.J., Dieleman, F.M., and Clark, W.A.V. 1986. Starters in the Dutch housing market. *Tijdschrift voor Economische en Sociale Geografie* 77, 243–250.

Linde, M.A.J., Van Schie, L., and Dieleman, F.M. 1986. De omloopsnelheid van woningen in de bestaande woningvoorraad. *Planologische diskussiebijdragen*. 1986 deel II, Delftse Uitgevers Maatschappij B.V.

Long, L. 1991. Residential mobility differences among developed countries. *International Regional Science Review* 14, 133–147.

Long, L. 1992a. Changing residence: comparative perspectives on its relationship to age, sex, and marital status. *Population Studies* 46, 141–158.

Long, L. 1992b. International perspectives on the residential mobility of America's children. *Journal of Marriage and the Family* 54, 861–869.

Long, L., Tucker, C.J., and Urton, W.L. 1988. Migration distances: an international comparison. *Demography* 25, 633–640.

Lundqvist, L.J. 1992. Dislodging the welfare state? Housing and privatization in four European nations. In *Housing and Urban Policy Studies* 3. Delft: Delft University Press.

MacLennan, D., Munro, M. and Wood, G. 1987. Housing choices and the structure of housing markets. In B. Turner, J. Kemeny, and L.J. Lundqvist, eds. *Between state and market: housing in the post industrial era*. Stockholm: Alinquist and Wiksell International.

Magidson, J. 1982. Some common pitfalls in causal analysis of categorical data. *Journal of Marketing Research* 19, 461–471.

Masnick, G., Pitkin, J., and Brennan, J. 1990. Cohort housing trend in a local housing market: the case of Southern California. In D. Myers, ed. *Housing demography: linking demographic structure and housing markets*. Madison, WI: University of Wisconsin Press.

Mayer, K., and Tuma, N. 1990. *Event history analysis in life course research*. Madison, WI: University of Wisconsin Press.

Mayo, S.K. 1981. Theory and estimation in the economics of housing demand. *Journal of Urban Economics* 10, 95–116.

McCarthy, P., and Simpson, B. 1991. *Issues in post-divorce housing*. Aldershot, Hampshire: Avebury.

McGill, W.J., and Quastler, H. 1955. Standard nomenclature, an attempt. In H. Quastler, ed. *Information theory in psychology*. New York: Free Press, 83–92.

McHugh, K., Gober, P., and Reid, N. 1990. Determinants of short- and long-term mobility expectations for homeowners and renters. *Demography* 27, 81–95.

Michelson, W. 1977. *Environmental choice, human behaviour and residential satisfaction*. New York: Oxford University Press.

Moore, E.G., and Clark, W.A.V. 1990. Housing and households in American cities: structure and change in population mobility, 1974–1982. In D. Myers, ed. *Housing Demography*. Madison, WI: University of Wisconsin Press, 203–231.

Morrow-Jones, H.A. 1988. The housing life-cycle and the transition from renting to owning a home in the United States: a multi-state analysis. *Environment and Planning A* 20, 1165–1184.

Mulder, C.H. 1993. *Migration dynamics: a life course approach*. Amsterdam: Thesis Publishers.

Mulder, C.H., and Manting, D. 1994. Strategies of nest-leavers: 'settling down' versus flexibility. *European Sociological Review* 10, 155–172.

Mulder, C.H., and Hooimeijer, P. 1995. Alleen of met een partner uit huis: de dynamiek in twee processen. *Stepro werkdokument*. Utrecht: Utrecht University, Faculty of Geographical Sciences.

Murie, A., Dieleman, F.M., and Hooimeijer, P. 1991. Housing asset values and the mobility of elderly homeowners. Housing research and policy issues. *The Netherlands Journal of Housing and the Built Environment* 1, 21–35.

Musterd, S. 1994. A rising European underclass? *Built Environment* 20, 185–191.

Mutchler, J.E., and Krivo, L.J. 1989. Availability and affordability: household adaptation to a housing squeeze. *Social Forces* 68(1), 241–261.

Muus, J.P., and Kuyer, A. 1994. *Migration, immigrants, and policy in the Netherlands*. Report for the continuous reporting system on migration of the OECD, 1993. Amsterdam: University of Amsterdam, Department of Human Geography.

MVROM. 1989. *Nederlandse huishoudens in de periode 1960–1985*. Zoetermeer: Ministry of Housing, Physical Planning and the Environment.

MVROM. 1992. *Volkshuisvesting in cijfers, 1991*. The Hague: Ministry of Housing, Physical Planning and the Environment.

MVROM. 1994. *Volkshuisvesting in cijfers, 1993*. The Hague: Ministry of Housing, Physical Planning and the Environment.

Myers, D. 1983. Upward mobility and the filtering process. *Journal of Planning Education and Research* 2, 101–112.

Myers, D. 1985. Wives' earnings and rising costs of home ownership. *Social Science Quarterly* 66, 319–329.

Myers, D. 1992. *Analysis with local census data: portraits of change*. New York: Academic Press.

Myers, D., and Wolch, J. 1995. The polarization of housing status. In R. Farley, ed. *State of the union: America in the 1990s*. Vol. 1. New York: Russell Sage.

Nelson, K. 1994. Whose shortage of affordable housing? *Housing Policy Debate* 5, 401–442.

Nesslein, T.S. 1988. Housing: the market versus the welfare state model revisited. *Urban Studies* 25, 95–108.

Netherlands Central Bureau of Statistics. *Housing Demand Survey*, 1985/1986, 1989/1990.

Netherlands Central Bureau of Statistics. 1992. Gerealiseerde en gewenste verhuizingen van huishoudens. *Sociaal economische maandstatistieken* CBS 92/7.

Netherlands Central Bureau of Statistics. 1993. Statistics on housing and construction in the Netherlands. *Netherlands Journal of Housing and the Built Environment* 8, 131–141.

Netherlands Central Bureau of Statistics. 1993. Statistics on housing and construction in the Netherlands, residential mobility. *Netherlands Journal of Housing and the Built Environment* 8, 347–356.

Netherlands Central Bureau of Statistics. 1993. Statistics on housing and construction in the Netherlands, increases and decreases in the dwelling stock since 1970. *Netherlands Journal of Housing and the Built Environment* 8, 237–245.

Netherlands Central Bureau of Statistics. 1994. Statistics on housing and construction in the Netherlands, residential mobility. *Netherlands Journal of Housing and the Built Environment* 9, 311–324.

Nie, H., Hull, C.H., Jenkins, H.G., Steinbrenner, K., and Bent, D.H. 1975. *Statistical package for the social sciences*. New York: McGraw-Hill.

OECD. 1988. *Urban housing finance*. Paris: Organisation for Economic Cooperation and Development.

Odland, J., and Shumway, J.M. 1993. Interdependencies in the timing of migration and mobility events. *Papers in Regional Science, The Journal of the RSAI* 72, 221–237.

Olson, E.O. 1987. The demand and supply of housing service: a critical survey of the empirical literature. In E. S. Mills, ed. *Handbook of regional urban economics.* Vol. 2, Urban Economics. Amsterdam: Elsevier Science Publishers B.V., 989–1022.

Pahl, R. 1975. *Whose city?* London: Penguin.

Perreault, W.D., Jr., and Barksdale, H.C. 1980. A model-free approach for analysis of complex contingency data in survey research. *Journal of Marketing Research* 27, 503–515.

Pitkin, J. 1990. Housing consumption of the elderly: a cohort economic model. In D. Myers, ed. *Housing demography: linking demographic structure and housing markets.* Madison, WI: University of Wisconsin Press.

Pitkin, J., and Masnick, G. 1986. Households and housing consumption in the United States, 1985 to 2000, projections by a cohort method. *Report to the U.S. Department of Housing and Urban Development.* Cambridge, MA: Joint Center for Housing Studies of MIT and Harvard.

Pitkin, J., and Myers, D. 1994. The specification of demographic effects on housing demand: avoiding the age-cohort fallacy. *Journal of Housing Economics* 3, 240–250.

Plaut, S.E. 1987. The timing of housing tenure transition. *Journal of Urban Economics* 21, 312–322.

Porell, F.W.C. 1982. *Models of intraurban residential relocation.* The Hague: Kluwer Nijhoff Publishing.

Post, H.E., and Grootenboer, A.J. 1994. *Woonuitgaven en financiële stromen van het rijk.* Amsterdam: Economisch Instituut voor de Bouwnijverheid (in opdracht van VROM).

Power, A. 1993. *Hovels to highrise, state housing in Europe since 1850.* London: Routledge.

Priemus, H. 1995. How to abolish social housing? The Dutch case. *The International Journal of Urban and Regional Research* 19, 145–155.

Quigley, J. 1983. Estimates of a more general model of consumer choice in the housing market. In R. Greisan, ed. *The urban economy of housing.* Lexington, MA.: Lexington Books, 125–140.

Quigley, J. 1987. Housing market information and the benefits of housing programs. In B. Turner, J. Kemeny, and L.J. Lundqvist, eds. *Between state and market: housing in the postindustrial era.* Stockholm: Alinquist and Wiksell International, 53–70.

Quigley, J., and Weinberg, D. 1977. Intra-urban residential mobility: a review and synthesis. *International Regional Science Review* 2, 41–66.

Relou W., and Keilman, N.W. 1991. Ontwikkelingen in de huishoudens-en huisvestingssituatie van ouderen. In N. Nimwegen and H. Solinge, eds. *Bevolkingsvraagstukken in Nederland anno 1991: demografische ontwikkelingen in maatschappelijk perspectief.* s'Gravenhage: Netherlands Interdisciplinary Demographic Institute (NIDI), 51–59.

Richards, T., White, M., and Tsui, A. 1987. Changing living arrangements: a hazard model of transitions among household types. *Demography* 24, 77–97.

Roseman, C. 1971. Migration as a spatial and temporal process. *Annals of the Association of American Geographers* 61, 589– 598.

Rossi, P.H. 1955. *Why families move.* New York: Macmillan.

Rouwendal, J. 1992. The hedonic price function as an envelope of bid functions: An exercise in applied economic theory. *Netherlands Journal of Housing and the Built Environment* 7, 59–80.

Rudel, T.K. 1987. Housing price inflation, family growth, and the move from rented to owner-occupied housing. *Urban Studies* 24, 258–267.

SAS Institute, Inc. 1991. *SAS Technical Report P-217* SAS/STAT Software: The PHREG Procedure, Version 6, Cary, NC, USA.

Saunders, P. 1990. *A nation of homeowners.* London: Unwin Hyman Ltd.

Smith, L., Rosen, K.T., Markandya, A., and Ullmo, P. 1986. The demand for housing, household headship rates, and household formation. *Urban Studies* 21, 407–414.

Sonquist, J.A. and Morgan, J.N. 1964. *The detection of interaction effects.* Ann Arbor, MI: University of Michigan, Institute for Social Research.

Sorokin, P., Zimmerman, C.C., and Galpin, C.J. 1931. *A systematic source book in rural sociology.* Vol. 2. Minneapolis, MN: University of Minnesota Press.

Stapleton, C. 1980. Reformulation of the family life-cycle concept: implications for residential mobility. *Environment and Planning A* 12, 1103–1118.

Sternlieb, G., and Hughes, J.W. 1980. *America's housing: prospects and problems.* New Brunswick, NJ: Center for Urban Policy Research.

Sternlieb G., and Hughes, J.W. 1986. Demographics and housing. *Population Bulletin* 4–1. Washington, DC: Population Reference Bureau.

Tuma, N.B., and Hannan, M.T. 1979. Approaches to the censoring problem in analysis of event histories. In K.F. Schuessler, ed. *Sociological methodology.* San Francisco, CA: Jossey-Bass, 209–240.

Tuma, N.B., and Hannan, M.T. 1984. *Social dynamics: models and methods.* New York: Academic Press.

U.S. Bureau of the Census. Various years. *American Housing Survey. General housing characteristics.* Washington, D.C.: U.S. Government Printing Office.

Warnes, A.M. 1993. Residential mobility and housing strategies in later life. *Aging and Society* 13, 97–105.

Wassenberg, F.A.G., Kruythoff, H.M, Leliveld, T.A.L., and Heijde, J.E.H. 1994. *Wonen op niveau-de markt—raag voor VINEX-locaties in de Randstad gepeild*. The Hague: Ministry of Housing, Physical Planning and the Environment.

Weesep, J. van. 1995. Housing the "guestworkers." In C. Hadjimichalis and D. Sadler, eds. *Europe at the margins: new mosaics of inequality*. Chichester, Sussex: Wiley, 167–194.

Wolpert, J. 1965. Behavioral aspects of the decision to migrate. *Papers of the Regional Science Association* 15, 159–169.

Yamaguchi, K. 1987. Event history analysis: its contribution to modeling and causal inference. *Sociological Theory and Methods* 2, 61–82.

Yamaguchi, K. 1991. *Event history analysis*. London: Sage.

Index

Note: Italicized page numbers refer to tables and figures.